FIFTY YEARS
OF
TROPHY HUNTING

Gary Joll

DEDICATION

This book is for my wife Susan.
The woman who forsook city life
To join me in the remote High Country.

From the outset you understood there were
Two passions in my life,
My love for you, my love of hunting,

Thank you darling for your acceptance
And loving understanding
Over these so many years.

Gary

Gary and Sue

FIFTY YEARS
OF
TROPHY HUNTING

Gary Joll

The
Halcyon
Press

Published by

The Halcyon Press

A division of

Halcyon Publishing Ltd

P.O. Box 360, Shortland St, Auckland, 1140, New Zealand

Printed through
Prolong Press Ltd
China

ISBN 978-1-877566-69-1
Copyright © 2014 Gary Joll
First Published 2014
All Rights Reserved
Cover Photograph by
Gordon Roberts
Cover Design (based on an original concept) by
Blockstart Design
www.halcyonpublishing.co.nz

TABLE OF CONTENTS

A Few Words To Begin With   8

SECTION ONE   -   New Zealand   9

SECTION TWO   -   Australia   65

SECTION THREE - New Caledonia   89

SECTION FOUR   - Alaska   97

SECTION FIVE   -   USA (Lower Forty-eight)   133

SECTION SIX   -   South Africa   167

SECTION SEVEN - Zimbabwe   217

SECTION EIGHT - 'Bucket List'   225

A Few Words To Begin With

As you progress through the following chapters you'll discover that wherever possible I have included measurements of both horn and antler length plus scores, whether they be Douglas, Boone and Crockett, or SCI, plus (at times) the placing of the trophy in one record book or another.

Let me make it patently clear that this information is not included to enhance me or my hunting skills in any way, for it is a simple truth that I personally had nothing what-so-ever to do with the growth or length of horn or antler. I cannot legitimately make any claim at all in that regard.

No, I include measurements and scores solely to better inform you, the reader, as to the size of a trophy.

Over the years I've been involved with the hunting fraternity I've had many dozens of hunters tell me they've shot a BIG something or other. Now BIG is different to all of us, relative to our experience, our past successes, past trophies. I lost count years ago of hunters who made contact with me to report they'd shot a VERY BIG bull Tahr, (or some other species), only to discover that the tape measure has told us all that with an SCI Score (or Douglas Score) of 40 the Tahr trophy is very good but not BIG in Top Shelf Tahr terms.

If I provide a horn or antler measurement with the information that the trophy is an SCI Gold Medal then you immediately comprehend the trophy to be in the top one-third of all trophies for that species listed in the Safari Club International Record Book. If a trophy is a SCI Silver Medal then it is placing in the middle third of all trophies listed for that species, with Bronze occupying the lowest third.

As the Boone & Crockett Book of Records is somewhat unfamiliar to Kiwi hunters I have, where possible, provided the placing of a given trophy in the book, solely to give you that additional snippet of information to provide a better understanding of size and quality. Me, I am simply the lucky hunter who happened to be in the right place at the right time, (guided or otherwise), and when the chips were down managed to place a shot where it needed to be.

I make no bones about the fact that I am a Trophy Hunter. After thirty-odd years of guiding my clients for trophies the concept finally rubbed off on me, and with my advancing years I became more and more selective as to what I would and wouldn't shoot.

You are about to join me on many hunts, spanning fifty years, most successful, some unsuccessful.

Gary Joll

SECTION ONE

– New Zealand

First Trophy
Hunting Trophy Tahr
A Long Day
Deer By The Dozens
Porridge & Pipis
Zis Von Ve 'Ave
Forty Year Trophy
Another First
Trials & Challengers for a Professional
Hunting Guide

First Trophy

Roger and I were beginning to regret having Dorothy along on the hunt.

We were only halfway to our destination, largely due to Dorothy's slow plodding pace.

Arriving at the motor shed on the Macaulay River a little before 8am, we shouldered our packs and after crossing the river had trudged across the Macaulay Flats to the homestead at Lilybank Station. Our destination was Red Stag Hut some thirty kilometres up the Godley Valley. With the help of Alan Dick, the runholder at Lilybank Station, members of the South Canterbury Branch of NZDA had located the hut near the mouth of Lucifer Stream in August 1958. It was now early January 1959 and we would be the first hunting party to use the newly located hut. My team leader was my brother-in-law Roger Eade, who'd been a member of the party that had set up the hut.

Roger had arranged our hunt as a summer excursion knowing that we'd not have ice and snow and bitter conditions to deal with. My very first trophy Tahr hunt was to take place when alpine conditions were at their most benign.

Despite it being early January the conditions were still a challenge, for along with a lashing sandblasting nor'west gale, the Godley River was in high summer thaw flood. We'd not taken a great deal of notice of the river until we'd reached the Weka Fan where we discovered the entire volume of the river in one roiling channel, eroding the face of the fan. Never in my short life had I seen such a river. The water was the colour of opaque glass, and due to the suspended glacial flour seemed to be the viscosity of light oil. I remember a cold chill running up my back at the thought of having to wade across such a threatening turbulence. We didn't, we sidled the mountain face until we could once more drop down to the riverbed.

Roger had estimated that from Lilybank homestead to Red Stag Hut would be about a four hour trek, but here we were

The author's guide for his very first Tahr hunt was brother-in-law Roger Eade. They were the first party to use the recently located (August 1958) Red Stag Hut, January 1959.

at the Weka, roughly the halfway point and already we had four hours under our belts. We were beginning to regret we'd included Dorothy in our party for she seemed to have just the one speed, dead slow…..!

The section of that boulder-strewn riverbed between the Weka and the beginning of Lucifer Flats was known to be about a forty-five minute gut-busting straight-line slog over ankle twisting rocks of every size. The wind and Dorothy had us finally at the Lucifer Flats an hour and a half after departing the Weka. It was becoming an inordinately long day.

Finally, after seven and a half hours, we arrived at Red Stag, which in earlier life had been a single man's hut at Tekapo during the building of the hydro dam. Once we'd dumped our heavy packs on the hut doorstep we pointed Dorothy south and with a solid slap on her rump headed her for her home. Yes, Dorothy was a Lilybank Station packhorse Alan Dick had kindly offered us to carry our packs. We were most grateful for his offer and his packhorse, despite her having been stuck in "crawler gear" for the duration.

Water? All day we'd had little to drink so a couple of brews were our first priority, even ahead of unpacking gear. Each with a bucket in hand we searched an ever widening circle for a source of drinking water and found none? In final desperation we headed west, out onto the Godley until we were able to each fill our buckets, but only with the milky glacial flour laden water from the Godley itself.

Roger was somewhat concerned at our drinking this water; so back at the hut he filled an Agee jar, with the opinion that we should wait for an hour or more for the sediment to settle. It

did. Amazing as it may sound about the lower eighth of the jar showed a thickening of colour while the upper seven-eighths started to clear. Over the next couple of hours we had two or three brews, skimming water carefully from the top of each bucket, knowing the sediment would also be settling.

The nor-west gale screamed and whistled around the hut all night and into the following day, so we spent our time sorting and organising gear, R&R after our long trek of the previous day. We did brave the gale to each collect another bucket of Godley River water. With the setting of the sun the gale slowly abated and we had an undisturbed night's sleep that is until Roger's alarm woke us at 3am…

At 4am we were out the hut door and immediately tackling the high very steep face overlooking the hut. It was one hell of a gut-buster for a lad from the North Island who'd never before climbed in the Alps. Progress was slow, very slow. Roger wanted us to be as high on the mountain as possible before the sun touched the peaks above. It must have been about three hours after departing the hut that we heard a short sharp whistle from about? I had no idea what animal or bird had made this sound, but Roger did.

Whispering and pointing to a ragged outcrop of grey rock about one hundred metres above us Roger finally had me locating a solitary nanny Tahr looking down at us from between two large rocks. As I watched she stamped her foot and once again whistled.

"There'll be more with her," whispered Roger.

Quickening our pace we climbed to the rocks where we'd seen the nanny disappear over a skyline. Slowly we eased between some large rocks until the ground fell away sharply below us and… before us was the head of a wide grey gravel shingle slide which started at the skyline ridge and continued, uninterrupted, to the Lucifer Creek far, far below.

But it wasn't this enormous area of gravel that caused me to catch my breath. Scattered across the gravel, slowly moving away from us, was a mob of fifty, sixty, maybe more, female Tahr with young at foot. I think I gave them a one second fleeting sweeping glance, for the lowest, and largest, of all the Tahr in this large mob was, without doubt, a trophy bull.

In nervous haste I shook off my pikau to place it on a convenient boulder. Settling I worked the bolt of my .303 and soon had the crosshairs centred between the shoulders of the bull. With the echoes of the shot the nanny group raced across the width of the gravel slide, the bull slumped, but his head was still up.

"Put another one in," from Roger.

I did. The bull reacted to this shot by going into what had to be a death-throe, then as we watched he started to roll, faster and faster, to finally come to rest maybe one hundred and fifty metres below. I remember how silent it was after the echoes ceased, how the dust from the fleeing nanny group slowly drifted downhill with the night-time thermal, how there wasn't a Tahr in sight.

Typical Godley Valley Tahr country. Take care to avoid the Spaniard Grass (foreground) for the needles on the end of each are exceptionally sharp and nasty to encounter.

Opposite: The author aged 21 with his very first trophy a 13⅞ inch bull Tahr with a Douglas score of 44¼. Rifle a P14 modified by Parker Hale in .303.

That's when the discussion began. Roger was of the opinion that the bull wasn't really large enough to be classed as a trophy, while I was determined that as it was my very first bull Tahr I wasn't going to leave it down there on the gravel slide for I may not get a chance at another bull. I'd come all the way from Hamilton to seek a trophy and wasn't about to leave a possible trophy to rot on the mountain.

Unwillingly Roger agreed to lose all the height we'd gained early in the day, climbing in the cool early morning shadows. My first impression upon finally reaching the bull was just how large they were. Roger expressed the opinion that the horns were no better than ten or eleven inches. After a few photos Roger cut off the head of the bull, we stuffed it into my pikau and began the struggle up the gravel slide to regain the height we'd lost.

Eventually we reached the ridgeline between McKinnon Stream and Lucifer Creek, providing us with panoramic views into both watersheds. We spent the balance of our day slowly working along the ridge, seeing multitudes of female Tahr, but not a single bull. This ridge is very narrow, so when we reached a very large flat rock about fifteen or twenty metres square and (say) two metres deep, we had no choice but to climb up onto the rock for we couldn't sidle under it on either side. I was the first to step onto the rock and that is when it tipped about a third of a metre under my weight. For a heart-stopping instant I feared I was about to be tipped into the McKinnon to die.

We finally arrived back at the hut sixteen hours after our 4am departure. First priority was a brew, or two, or three. The glacial flour in our drink water had settled out nicely during our long day. It wasn't until after we'd had an evening meal and tidied

camp that Roger pulled his tape measure from an outside pocket of his pack and suggested we measure my trophy. His surprise was even greater than mine for the tape told us I had a 13⅞ inch trophy bull Tahr.

Next morning we didn't hasten to get up for we'd had a long strenuous day the day before. We had a good "binder" of a breakfast, made sure camp was "ship-shape" and cleaned our rifles. My rifle, my very first centre-fire, was in .303 calibre, a P14 modified military firearm. Parker Hale had milled off the robust rear sight and had drilled and taped the receiver for scope mounts. This invited me to fit a telescopic sight. I bought a Nickel 4 x 81 and this served me for many years until I discovered separation in the front lens. The military-style stock wasn't at all suited to having a scope mounted on the rifle, so after managing to get a couple of pieces of fine walnut timber, we cut the stock and after gluing the new walnut above and below I spent a long Sunday afternoon, with file and spoke-shave, forming a high Monte Carlo comb above and below a comfortable pistol grip. The adding of a very good quality rubber butt pad completed this "modification".

Over the following days we searched for more bull Tahr and had a number of encounters with flighty groups of Chamois, never once successfully getting close enough to mobs of fifteen to twenty for a shot. Our trek back down the Godley took us a smidgen over four hours, for we were fit now and the ever-present nor'west gale was providing wind assistance.

POSTSCRIPT TWO – It would be fourteen years before Gary bettered his 13⅞ inch trophy – SCI Score – 44⅜, with a 14 ⅞ inch bull shot in a tributary of the Macaulay River – SCI Score – 47½.

Originally a single man's hut in Tekapo during the building of the Tekapo power station the hut was bought by South Canterbury Branch of the NZDA for ten pounds and aided by run holder Alan Dick transported up the Godley to be located close to Lucifer Creek.

POSTSCRIPT - Upon arriving at the junction of the Lilybank Road and Highway 8 we were stopped by military personnel, for in the middle of the Highway was a caravan being rapidly consumed in flames. It seems that a family had hired the caravan in Christchurch and set the kerosene-fired refrigerator going before departing for their holiday. Somehow kerosene had spilled; the caravan was ablaze from end to end.
Roger and I were dressed in lightweight khaki shirts and long trousers, looking very much like the soldiers doing their best to quell the fire. Before we were aware of his presence a rather stuffy officer sidled up to us and asked, in an imperious tone, if we were under his command. "No", Roger informed him, "we're under our own command."
At this response the officer strutted off mumbling - "Scruffy looking pair…."

Hunting Trophy Tahr

During the twenty-two years we operated our "Lilybank Safari Lodge" trophy hunting operation at the head of Lake Tekapo I lost count of the numbers of times recreational hunting parties, upon return from the Upper Godley late Sunday afternoon, would drop in to inform us they'd be back the following weekend. Their motivation, they'd sighted a bull Tahr on a skyline – jet black from head to tail. He had to be a real trophy.

Not wishing to burst their bubble of anticipation I never did tell them that without me seeing the bull their description of jet black from head to tail told me immediately that such a bull would be about a three-to-four-year-old and his horns would likely be about ten inches long. Definitely not a trophy to be harvested for he was far too young.

Put a man on the hill, month after month hunting Tahr, and if he has any powers of observation he must begin to learn a few valuable lessons about the species he is hunting. When a guide has a largely unfit client, who is going to really struggle to get within range of a trophy bull Tahr, the guide needs to do his best to make the climbing of a mountain for a bull Tahr a one-off experience, thus negating a need to climb again another day.

From the valley floor we were largely able to decide whether or not to climb to a bull simply by assessing him from a distance, by means of a good spotting scope, for features of his body and coat, plus the attitude of other bulls around him, would signal whether to climb the mountain or not. The old true adage of "…you'll learn more sitting on your arse…" holds dramatically true when seeking a top shelf trophy bull Tahr.

With a prospective trophy bull in your spotting scope half close your eyes. Is the mane on the bull a minimum of half his body length? If the mane is only a quarter or one-third the body length of the bull forget this bull, find another for this bull will have disappointingly small horns. If, on the other hand, the mane is closer to threequarters of the body length of the bull, lace up your boots and start climbing for there is every chance that bull is in the 13 inch+ class.

Pre-rut the bulls are to be found in bachelor groups. This is an excellent time for trophy hunting for the group can be compared, one against the other, and after careful study with a good quality spotting scope the finest set of horns will be discovered.

But wait, there are other "signals" for you before starting to climb and stalk. Take time to look for the following "signals" of trophy. Are the cream stripes on either side of the dark dorsal strip wide and clearly visible, (the older the bull the wider these stripes.) Can you clearly see that the back of the hock is also a deep cream in colour? (Immature bulls have no cream hock colouring).

Don't hasten to start your climb just yet, be patient and take time to watch the attitude of other bulls in the mob to the bull you are interested in. If he is indeed the Master Bull of this section of mountain the lesser bulls in the group will tell you for sure that he is. They'll appear to be pretending that he isn't present. It is almost comical to study a mob of Tahr and note the body language of the young immature non-breeding bulls as they studiously avoid acknowledging The Master is at hand.

So, you're carefully watching a mob of Tahr, for an hour or more, with three or four bulls in the group and they all seem to be happy with the company of their peers. What does that tell you?

It tells me the Master Bull on that section of mountain is not present in this mob. It is now a well known fact that a Master Bull Tahr does not stay with a single group of females, he instead has a circuit he travels regularly visiting a number of nanny + young groups. It is fascinating to actually be watching a group of Tahr when the Master Bull arrives, for by their body language the immature non-breeding bulls will tell you instantly the Master has arrived, your potential once-in-a-lifetime trophy bull Tahr is in your spotting scope. Time now to climb the mountain.

Be extra careful while climbing to your target for there is yet

Undoubtedly a Top Shelf trophy bull. Note the very wide light coloured dorsal stripe and mane half of body length.

another trap so many inexperienced Tahr hunters fall in to. I guess it is because we all have a sort of Red deer hunting mind-set, that the biggest and best stag on a mountain will be holding the largest number of hinds in his harem during the rut. I've heard many a recreational Tahr hunter tell of being out hunting for the weekend and seeing one bull holding one nanny in some secluded location. He'd not given this bull a second thought for he knew a Master Bull would be holding more than one nanny. MISTAKE…

When a Master Bull locates a female fully in oestrous, and ready to be mated, he will usher her away from the herd and for the next day or two will consort with her in private in a location some distance from the mob. So, if you are ever climbing in Tahr country, during the rut, and you are lucky enough to ambush one large bull with one female, this bull's horns are worthy of close study before you settle the crosshairs on his chest.

In assessing horns, ask yourself these questions:-

1. If I imagine two equal sized squares drawn side-by-side on the base of the horns do these two squares cover the horn bases before the horn taper begins? (see drawing.) If a pair of such squares does fit then you are guaranteed a 13 inch+ bull trophy. If only one square appears to fit, due to horns tapering, (see drawing) then the horns are likely to be from 10 to 11 inches, no more.

A set of 13⅜ inch tahr horns with a 10⅝ inch set. The author strongly recommends getting above and looking down onto the horns where the inward curving sweep of an aged bull's horn will be immediately obvious, as in this photo.

2. Do the horns appear to stand high above the head or do they seem to sweep backwards almost immediately from the bases? Don't shoot for here again is a non-trophy bull.

3. It is honestly acknowledged that assessing horn length on a bull Tahr, when he has his mane erect and in full display, is perhaps one of the most difficult tasks for guide or recreational hunting, but if you can be very patient and position yourself where you can look down on the bull from above you will immediately see that tell-tale inward sweep of the tips of the horns, a positive signal that before you is a bull with horns in the 13 inch+ to 14 inch class. (see photos)

As our years at Lilybank progressed through the 1970s to the 1990s a myth slowly developed that on Lilybank was a Super Herd of Tahr, a herd that produced consistently better trophy

The inward curve on the horns of this 14⅞ inch set of horns screams TROPHY in capital letters. Yes?

18

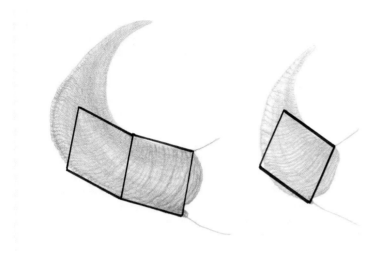

The author has a simple rule for determining if a set of horns on a bull are trophy or not, when viewed from the side. If you can visualise two equal sided squares over the base of the horns you are looking at a 13 inch plus set of horns. If you can visualise just the one square, then the horn tapers rapidly, leave the bull to get some more age on his shoulders.

horns than all the Tahr elsewhere on the South Island. Members of the recreational hunting fraternity got hold of various record books and the information within these publications clearly cemented that the myth was fact. Not so.

The Tahr on Lilybank were/are no different to all the Tahr elsewhere, they'd come from the original release at Mt. Cook, they had the exact same genes. So why did Lilybank produce so many of the very best trophy bull Tahr ever shot in New Zealand? Simple, we let the young bulls get plenty of age on their shoulders, bulls were not taken as trophies until we were sure

the bull in the rifle scope was in the "aged" class.

How many times has one of your hunting mates told you about getting on to a mob of Tahr and after "bombing them up" discovering that not one of the six or eight bulls dead on the gravel slide had trophy horns? "We killed every bull in the mob, not one was worth carrying out…." Like me you've heard the same comment…? This same group of hunters will be the first to complain that there are no trophy bulls left. Two things we can draw from this ever repeated carnage. One – the Master Bull wasn't in the group. Two – had all these young and immature bulls been left to become ten to twelve years old every one of them would have been a 12 to 13 inch trophy. Please, please, please take note of the helpful information I am offering you. If all Tahr hunters exercise the same mature constraints everyone who hunts Tahr will eventually secure a trophy the same as and perhaps even better than the Super Bulls we guided our clients to.

In almost thirty years of guiding on Lilybank – operating as "Lilybank Safari Lodge" – the best three Tahr trophies were – 15 inch with an SCI Score of - 48¼, 14⅞ SCI Score - 47½

14¾ SCI Score – 46½.

Such bulls could have been found everywhere else in Tahr country, if only they were allowed to get very old and not killed before reaching their horn length potential.

In a sense we practised a most simple form of game management, let them get old. Not rocket science, not requiring an expensive computer program. When we finally sold our operation in 1992 the most recent Safari Club International Record Book was Edition VI, Volume 2. Turning to the Section listing Tahr trophies we discover "Lilybank" trophies occupy the following placings:-

Top Ten – 8/10 including #1, #3, #4, #5, #6, #7, #8, #10.
Top Twenty – 15/20
Top Fifty – 35/50

The #50 trophy Tahr listed has a horn length of 12¼ inches and an SCI Score of 41. Yes, we made every effort to not kill any bulls where it was possible the horns would be less than twelve inches. If everyone hunting Tahr in the future, was to practise the same simple rule, we'd re-write the Record Book in the coming decade… How about it?

If you've been lucky – like me – to live with Tahr season after season, year after year, you'll know that come October the bulls depart the nanny and young groups, where they've spent all winter, to trek to their summer country. My family and I have, on more than one occasion, witnessed this trek, so slowly garnered enough information to know where we'd find bulls, gathered in aged groups, over the summer months, to remain there until early May when the seasonal trek to join the nanny + young groups takes place once more.

Do you live on the North Island, are you somewhat intimidated by the prospect of hunting Tahr in snow, in the depth of winter in the Southern Alps? If your answer is a timid 'Yes' then why not hunt for a trophy bull in the summer? Summer hunting for Tahr in the Alps offers long days, freedom (usually) from risk of snow, the opportunity to camp safely at high altitude, and the chance of finding a group of Grand Daddy Master Bulls all in

Joyce Stratton with our second best bull. – Length 14⅝ inches SCI – 46⅛.

the one group.

Find a group of really old bull Tahr, sneak up on them and study them from a concealed vantage point and you'll discover that by comparing horn length to horn length you have every chance, with patience and careful assessment, of killing an outstanding trophy bull. I have no idea how many readers are

**Gilbert Diaz with the best bull ever shot by a client.
Length 15 inches SCI – 48⅜.**

aware that as summer progresses all bulls lose their long winter coats so by mid-January they have a short coat, no mane to obscure horns. Many a summer-coated bull has been mistaken for a big nanny by those who knew nothing of bulls losing their long winter coats.

The only disadvantage – aside from having to climb high – of summer hunting for trophy bulls is the fact that your time for productive hunting is limited to the very first hour of daylight in the morning, and the last hour of available shooting light at night. It is during the summer that all bulls are laying on a great deal of body fat reserves to carry them through the rigors of winter. With this accumulation of fat the bulls suffer from the searing heat of high altitude summer sun, so seek cool hiding places each morning as soon as the sun lightens the eastern horizon.

I have watched bulls settle for the day in a crevasse between a rock cliff and where an avalanche has melted away from the warm rocks. I have also seen bulls walk in to the ice tunnel created by a stream flowing under an avalanche, causing melt, and a cool daytime resting place for bull Tahr. Look for bulls in cool shady places such as on the south side of steep cliffs that offer cooling shade throughout the day. If you are lucky enough to locate a cool damp cave approach it with great care for twice in my guiding career I've found aged Master Bulls in such hiding places.

It is the laying on of body fat, and a wish to not overheat through the summer, that dictates the daily summer movements and habits of the bulls. Don't expect to have a successful summer hunt over a weekend for it takes much more time than a couple of days to climb the mountain and locate a mob of aged bulls. Remember you'll have only two hours in each day to sight your prospective target, so allow plenty of time to ensure success.

Finally, ask any taxidermist who is receiving Tahr trophies for mounting and he'll tell you that over the past few years

Twice during his hunting career the author saw bull Tahr seek to escape from the summer heat by hiding for the day in such an ice cave – a tunnel carved into avalanche debris by the slightly warmer waters of the stream.

NOTE – We sold Lilybank Safari Lodge at the end of 1992. At that time Lilybank held seven of the Top Ten Tahr trophies in the SCI Record book and sixteen of the Top Twenty, a clear documentation of how selective we were in taking only the Top Shelf trophies for our clients. If we could do it so could all others hunting trophy bulls.

the average quality of trophy has slowly diminished, and is continuing to do so. Twenty years ago there were few bulls with horns less than 12 inches deposited with a taxidermist for mounting. Next time you visit a taxidermist ask how many bulls under 12 inches they are mounting, how many over 13 inches they are mounting? I think you will be, like me, saddened and discouraged. The future quality of trophy bulls in this country is in your hands, four 10 inch bulls dead at your feet or one 13 inch+ bull mounted and on the wall of your den. Which do you want…?

A Long Day

The crosshairs of my scope were steady on the biggest of the three stags.
I was waiting for him to offer a better broadside shot.
Suddenly, an aircraft roared over us, before we knew it the stags were in alarmed flight. Stalk ruined.

Roger Eade, Bob Hart and myself were hunting on Mt Creighton Station, which is located on the east side towards the head of Lake Wakatipu. Those were the days when the road connecting Queenstown and Glenorchy didn't exist; so all access from Queenstown to Mt Creighton was by boat. A local Queenstown commercial launch operator had transported us to Mt Creighton where due to a nor'west gale churning the lake surface the launch operator couldn't tie up to the wharf. He was forced to nose in as close as possible to the wharf where with a nod at the appropriate instant we were required to toss all our gear up on to the wharf. He could hold his position only briefly so a number of passes were made before we, plus all our gear, was safely ashore. All three of us stood on the wharf somewhat queasy from the rough trip up the lake.

Upon arrival we'd checked in with Bob Key, settled into the shearers' quarters and then spent an hour with Bob sussing out where we should hunt for a trophy Red stag. He kindly reported

A view of Mt Creighton Station, looking north towards the Dart and Rees Valleys.

23

that he'd recently seen three stags in a basin to the north of the homestead and suggested that could be our best chance of success.

We had no wheels so it was a couple of hours before daylight that we set off on the formed road connecting Mt Creighton with Glenorchy. Bob Key had given us clear instructions, but it was still dark when we turned right and began climbing, following the banks of a modest stream flowing from the chosen basin. The only sound was the chuckles from the stream.

Sheep tracks gave us easy travel conditions, even through the gorge. So it was just as dawn was breaking that the vista of a vast alpine basin began to become clear to us. At the first possible spot where we were offered a good view we stopped and began glassing. The basin was like a giant bowl tipped on its side with us standing at the lowest point. The head of the basin consisted of jagged mountain peaks dark and in deep shadow against the lightening eastern sky. Those peaks were maybe a thousand metres above us. We were in big country.

Within five minutes we'd located the three stags. They were low in the basin, less than 500 metres from us and feeding slowly uphill. It was easy. All we had to do was drop into the bed of the creek, where the sound of the stream would cover any noise we made, and at a spot we had marked we'd ease out of the creekbed and hope for a shot. With the drawing of straws it was I who was to take the best stag.

We pulled off the perfect stalk. With my pikau as a rest I was prone and watching the stags through my scope. They had no idea we were there. The crosshairs of my scope were steady on the biggest of the three stags. I was waiting for him to offer me a

The author would see trophy Fallow bucks, such as this pair, on Mt Creighton Station, but over many attempts the bucks always outsmarted him, until he figured he was 'jinxed'.

broadside shot. Suddenly, an aircraft roared over us and before we knew it the stags were in alarmed flight. Stalk ruined.

The twin-engine Dragon Rapid bi-plane slowly circled the basin, obviously showing its passengers-tourists the fleeing Red stags. With each close pass the three stags increased their speed, heading for the distant head of the basin high above.

To start with I had dashed after the stags in the hope of maybe getting a shot, but quickly realised the distance between them and me was rapidly increasing. In my angry haste I'd not picked up my pikau, so stopped to figure my next move. Upon looking back I could see Bob had started climbing towards me and he was carrying my pikau. I waited for him to reach me and thanked him.

Bob reported that Roger had decided to not climb after the stags, but would spend his day at lower altitude in the hope of sighting a nice Fallow buck. Bob was happy to join me in the hope of us both re-locating the three stags and maybe each shooting a trophy?

And so began the climb. Looking back from these so many years later I think I am safe in reporting it is the biggest and longest climb I have ever made on a hunt. The Mt Creighton country is big country in anyone's book, and steep. But, we were young and fit and we'd seen a couple of nice stags. In those days we'd not invested in spotting scopes, just 7 x 35 binoculars were our only optics; so neither of us could say just how many points each stag carried. We did agree that the largest stag had the widest and longest antlers. And so we climbed…

The stags had dashed up a steep and very long ridgeline leading to what appeared to be a low saddle at the very head of the basin. Within a rather short period of time they were no longer in sight. And so we climbed….

Today I don't recall what the time was when the aircraft ruined the hunt, but it would have been around 7.30am. At 1pm we were still a long way from the head of the basin, a long way. Our problem was the ridge we were climbing offered very little chance to sidle and so ease the climb, instead we were forced to climb the slope head on with the usual straining of hind legs

A 'shot' for the camera, not for the rifle.

and lungs. And so we climbed.

At close to 3pm we had reached a point where we had to decide whether to continue the climb or toss in the towel. The roll of the slope was stopping us from seeing very far ahead. After so many hours of climbing we were both determined to at least complete the climb and see what was over the other side of the saddle. And so we climbed…

That's where we found them. On a bony piece of fine gravel, lacking any form of vegetable there were the three stags, two of them obviously asleep. We must have made a small amount of noise as we eased out of our pikaus and slithered into the prone position. My stag lunged to his feet and paused just for

The author with his trophy Red stag. Beam length 39⅛; spread 38⅖, Douglas Score 250. It was an eighteen hour day.

a second. A fuselage of shots and two stags were down. I never did see where the third and smallest stag went.

Bob had himself a classic 6 x 6 trophy.   Not large in antler length or spreads but neat in its classic Royal form. My stag carried only ten points, 5 x 5, but with a beam length of just over 39 inches and a spread of better than 38 inches I had secured a trophy.

After taking photos we briefly discussed taking the head skins, but neither of us really knew how to do this, and we were very aware of how late in the day it was.

Have you ever worked your way downhill with a heavy load? You have. So you know that it isn't long before your tired legs start to complain and despite a desire to press on, for the sun is fast dropping below the western horizon, you just have to rest your screaming legs and aching back.

By the time we could see that we were approaching the gorge and the lower rim of the basin it had been dark for a long time. To be sure of hearing Roger when we called we tried to stay as far from the stream as we could, knowing that the sound of the water continually tumbling over rocks would prevent us from hearing his response. At the beginning of the gorge there was Roger cold and chilled and obviously anxious at our very late rendezvous. Amazingly he'd heard our shots. He'd had an unsuccessful day.

Now in deep darkness we stumbled our way downhill, until finally we could see the vague ribbon of lighter colour, the Mt Creighton-Glenorchy Road. We still had a distance to travel but we were on a relatively smooth gravel road where we could almost see where next we were placing our feet.

At last we were dropping our gear and antlers at the shearer's quarters. Immediately we stumbled across to the homestead to report our safe return. Mr Key senior simply handed each of us a tumbler of whisky. It was 11pm. We'd been away from camp eighteen hours.

COMMENTS:

One of the ironies of being a professional hunting guide is that many of my clients took much better trophies than my own personal trophies. This was particularly so with Red stag. Believe it or not but I never did kill a better stag than the one detailed in this chapter. I think I can safely state that more than two hundred of our clients secured a Red stag with a Douglas Score of better than 250; such is the joy (?) of being a guide.

While culling Red and non-typical Wapiti in Fiordland I shot a number of lovely 12 and 14-point stags, but as we were allowed to carry only the one trophy out I elected (naturally) that I'd bring out a Wapiti.

Prior to establishing our guided hunting operation at Lilybank I was a school teacher, so was never able to take a couple of weeks off to hunt the prime Red stag trophy valleys in the South Island during the height of the rut. By the time the May school holidays rolled around the stags weren't roaring, they were hard to find.

That isn't to say that, in subsequent years, I didn't see stags better than my Mt Creighton trophy. During a five-day hunt well back in the bush in the Waioweka Gorge we located a supreme 7 x 7 stag, daily resting (with hinds) on an open spur in the bush. The closest we could get was across the valley from him, say 300 metres. In those days I was still carrying my .303 and lacked the experience to have confidence in a killing shot at that range. Today, given the same chance with my 30-06, I wouldn't hesitate. Maybe that chance may yet arrive?

DEER BY THE DOZENS

Often it is not what you know but who you know that opens doors.

For four years from the beginning of 1959 I taught at Hamilton West School, Hamilton. During that period I taught both daughters of Mr Len Gilbert, well-known throughout New Zealand as a racing car driver, who annually competed in the New Zealand Grand Prix at Ardmore. Every one of my peers, plus even the older generation, will know of Len Gilbert.

All the children I taught knew of my consuming interest in hunting and had no doubt told their parents of my weekend and holiday pastime. Early one year, shortly after the summer school holiday, Mr Gilbert arrived at school, just after 3pm, to collect his daughter. We exchanged greetings and during that conversation I noted that his daughter had told me their family had holidayed in the South Island and had been to Queenstown.

In response Mr Gilbert told me of an incredible flight he'd experienced. It transpired that Mr Gilbert had served in the NZ Air Force with Tex Smith who after the war had established a light aircraft charter service operating from Queenstown Airport. Tex had flown Len up the lake from Queenstown then dropping low had flown him the length of a somewhat narrow valley where the river flats were teaming with dozens and dozens of deer.

Mr Gilbert had no idea what species of deer he'd seen; no idea of the property he'd flown over. Our conversation concluded with Mr Gilbert promising to make contact with Tex to discover if indeed I might be lucky enough to gain permission to hunt this deer-chocked valley.

A couple of weeks later Mr Gilbert was once again at the door to my classroom, at a few minutes after 3pm, and that is when he told me that Tex had been in touch with the property owner, that permission had been granted for me and one other to hunt the valley, on two conditions…

1. We were to kill every deer we could.
2. We were to hunt only the valley floor.

I clearly recall thinking to myself… "Often it's not what you know but who you know that opens doors."

In those days Ray Mueller was my constant hunting companion, we were both teaching at Hamilton West. Here were we a couple of young inexperienced hunters, recently having just celebrated our twenty-first birthdays, with an opportunity to hunt in a valley that was seemingly suffering a plague of deer. We would be in Hunting Heaven. Immediately we made plans for a May school holiday hunt.

And so it was that upon arriving at the Queenstown Airport and locating Tex Smith, we loaded our gear into his Cessna 180 and within minutes were high over Lake Wakatipu. The day was a typical autumn high country day, calm, cloudless, tall mountains our horizon in every direction.

When the aircraft banked left and Tex cut the throttle we knew we were close to our destination. Yes, ahead was the

Caples Valley. At a bend in the valley – where the Greenstone River joined the Caples – Tex gently applied the flaps and there before us was the full length of the valley. Immediately Ray and I could see ahead of us dozens of groups of deer racing from the frosted browntop grass river flat to the safety of the beach forest bordering the flats on either side. Tex had informed us before departing Queenstown that he'd fly us up and down the valley; to allow us to gather some knowledge of the valley we'd be hunting for the next ten days.

The valley was a continual series of grass flats, either side of the meandering river, with tongues of beech forest separating each of the many flats. But, it was the top flat that had us spellbound. As the aircraft banked over an area of (say) 40ha we must have seen as many as 60-80 Fallow deer race for the surrounding forest. There was one white deer.

After a gut dropping steep banking turn Tex flew us back down valley with us trying to take a mental note of too much to remember, but I did remember seeing a small isolated clearing away from the river and totally encircled by forest.

Most of that day was spent ferrying our gear from the airstrip to the Birchwood homestead, an old dwelling but perfect for us as a warm, snug base, with a coal range and open fire for cooking and warmth. There was no shortage of firewood. I shall never forget most of the walls were papered with the glossy photo essays from the *Auckland Weekly*.

By about 4pm we'd unpacked our gear, had set up camp and Ray had taken care of dinner preparations. We were itching to go for a bit of a wander before dark, who wouldn't have been?

We had camp meat within fifteen minutes of departing the old homestead. A young female made the mistake of standing and staring at two two-legged intruders in her domain.

Before dawn porridge had been consumed and Ray was about to start the bacon and eggs when I looked out the window. There'd been a heavy frost; the flats across the river were white

A scenic photo of a typical river flat clearing in the Caples Valley. Photo credit to Warren Jacobs

as if covered with snow. As I watched numerous black "blobs" were moving out of the bush into the grass flats. Binoculars. I counted about fifteen Fallow deer happily feeding.

Bacon and eggs were put aside, pikaus on backs, rifles in hand. We pulled off a neat stalk and within ten minutes or so had ourselves in a position across the river from the deer, none of them aware of our presence. At our first salvo the deer came running towards us; we realised the echo of our shooting was confusing the deer and they were uncertain as to the source of the rifle fire.

When the last of the mob disappeared into the beech forest we had seven dead deer scattered across the river flat. Not wishing to get wet feet we returned to camp, intending to skin the carcasses after completing our breakfast and making sure camp was shipshape before heading out for the day.

We were in the act of eating our bacon and eggs when into the homestead walked Archie Sutherland, son of Archie Sutherland senior, owner of the Caples Valley Station. He'd arrived on horseback so we'd not heard him approaching. Archie was very grumpy, wanting to know what we thought we were doing sitting around eating breakfast while six or eight deer were out feeding on the flat immediately across from the homestead! His attitude softened somewhat when we explained that we'd already killed seven deer on that very flat less than thirty minutes ago. My proffered binoculars provided confirmation for Archie. Our offer of a cuppa was accepted. Obviously Archie had ridden in to check up on us.

Ironic as it may sound we repeated our early stalk on that same flat across the river and shot three or four more deer. Now we had to ford the river and start skinning. Prior to departing on the trip we'd decided that we'd skin as many of the deer as we could in the hope of selling the skins, to offset the cost of the trip.

Our trip fell into a pattern. We'd head out from the old homestead at break of dawn stalking the series of flats, taking care to make a wide loop if the wind was wrong for a direct approach onto the next flat. We soon learned that Paradise ducks were our worst enemy for when a pair of ducks took flight with their familiar alarm calls the deer would race for the safety of the beech forest. If we could outwit the ducks we got shooting at each flat we stalked.

We quickly learned that it was not smart to leave carcasses to be skinned later, that fresh-killed deer were so much easier to skin than those left until the following day. We'd shoot, skin, then stalk to the next flat, leaving skin flesh side up to hopefully dry a little. Often we'd find deer back out feeding on a flat we'd shot much earlier in the day. Many a day we were skinning the last of the deer in fast gathering darkness.

Before daylight on about day four we were woken by very heavy rain drumming on the corrugated roof of the homestead, so we shut off the alarm and had a well-earned sleep-in. But, by about mid-afternoon we were both suffering severe 'cabin-fever' so after slipping into our Swanndris we headed out into the still torrential rain. We jointly agreed that we'd be lucky to see any deer out and about in such conditions. The first flat we sneaked up on – yes we outsmarted the ducks – we discovered dozens of deer dejectedly sitting out on the flats. Once again the deer were confused as to the source of the rifle fire and within a few brief seconds we had ourselves a goodly number of deer to skin out.

Our observation was the deer didn't like to be back in the forest with heavy droplets of rain spattering down, they preferred to be out on the flats where the rainfall was a steady continuous pattern.

We also witnessed an interesting phenomenon. When one of our projectiles struck a deer in the shoulder a circular eruption of water was the instant result. The skins of the deer must have been saturated with rainwater for this to occur.

About midway into our trip I'd not yet visited the secret small clearing back in the bush, so the next morning we agreed to separate and hunt solo for the day. Ray wasn't all that interested in trophy hunting whereas a trophy (if lucky) was my primary concern. The only buck we'd seen was one running with the masses of deer on the top flat. We'd not seen, or killed a buck, on the lower valley flats.

It was just breaking day when I stalked with infinite care through the beech forest, seeking the small clearing, knowing the forest floor would be dark and not frosted, while the grass on the clearing would stand out lighter due to the heavy frost.

I finally located the clearing and there in silhouette against the frosted grasses was an exceptional Fallow buck. He was feeding, totally unaware I was about. Against the frosted grass of the clearing his right antler was clear to see, a top- shelf trophy with massive blade. I didn't hesitate for in the next second he could sense me trespassing on his domain. One shot and he was dead as he fell on his left side.

Even today, so many years later, I still clearly recall how my heart-pounding excitement turned to the bitterest of disappointment. Yes, the right antler carried every possible quality of an outstanding trophy Fallow buck. I studied it in absolute ecstasy; I studied it for long minutes thrilled at my trophy. Then I moved to view the left antler counterpart, fully expecting to see a repeat of the right antler. The left antler was about half the length of the right beam; the brow tyne was a short stub about two inches long. The only other points on that left antler were two short stubs at the tip. I had a lump in my throat sufficient to choke me. I walked away from that clearing, too disappointed to even skin the carcass.

We were fully occupied each day "dealing" with the flats closest to the old homestead and as the days passed we never did get to the top flat, the one where there were so many deer. One evening we made a plan. We'd make a super early start, ignore all the flats we'd previously shot, making the top flat our sole objective for the day.

From the safety of well back in the beech forest we both started counting, and after a couple of careful passes with our glasses we agreed there were about 84-85 deer out feeding on the flat. One white one. What to do to maximise our tally? Recalling how deer were confused by our shooting echoing back from the bush edge we made a slow and very careful approach via the river, staying below the banks, which were about a metre high. Once we were in position, not a deer was alarmed, it was agreed that I would try for the buck then we'd both do our best on females.

I dropped the buck in his tracks, the deer milled and raced back and forth (have you ever tried to kill a running Fallow

deer) we didn't make as many kills as we'd have liked to, despite following the deer into the trees, where we tidied up the odd wounded deer. We realised that the fewer the deer on a flat the better our tally. With so many deer racing about it was difficult to settle on a target.

But, I had my trophy and we had deer to skin. That night we were very late back at the old homestead.

By now the area around the old Birchwood homestead was looking rather like a culler's camp – I guess it was! We had skins draped here, there and everywhere attempting to, keep them out of the rain, attempting to dry them as much as possible in the limited time. The day before we were due to fly back out to Queenstown we bundled up the partially dried skins and counted them. We were a couple short of sixty. To make it easier on us on the day of departure we moved all the skins, and some of our gear to the airstrip.

Tex and his Cessna 180 arrived and landed while the frost was still thick on the grass. He showed a measure of surprise at the load we were flying out with, but all he said was…

"You lads did better than we thought you would."

I noticed Tex was stowing the gear with great care, seemingly making an extra effort to balance the loading of the aircraft. Once loaded he taxied to the very furthest point of the airstrip, there was no wind, the tail of the Cessna in the matagouri. He then revved the engine to screaming point before releasing

After Mt Creighton was sold, following Bob Key's tragic and untimely death, the author's company bought Fallow stock from Mt Creighton to establish Fallow hunting at Lilybank, eventually producing trophy Fallow buck like that in this photo. Probable Douglas Score 240+.

the brake. We trundled down that bumpy airstrip, seeming to gather speed at alarmingly slow pace. I was seated beside Tex so could see the matagouri at the boundary of the airstrip looming closer and closer and still we were not airborne.

When I was about to flinch at the real prospect of us rocketing into the metre and a half high matagouri Tex finally pulled back and we lumbered into the air, and that is when some sort of on-board instrument started "bleeping" loud and constant.

It wasn't until some years later, while flying with bush pilots in Alaska, that I learned about the stall warning. A warning the aircraft could drop out of the air due to lack of air speed. Just as well I didn't know this that morning we flew out of the Caples with Tex.

We sold our partially dried skin and almost covered the cost of our amazing Caples cull.

FOOTNOTE:
My trophy Fallow buck was a poor second to the one-antlered buck on the secret clearing, but it was the best buck I'd seen during ten days in Fallow country, so what is a trophy? With a Douglas Score of 190 it was just ten points below the score of 200, the generally accepted minimum score for a trophy Fallow buck.
I entered my trophy in the NZDA Annual Antler and Horn Competition that year, where I discovered it was the only buck entered in the Fallow competition. Apparently no other members had been lucky enough to take a Fallow buck of trophy proportion. You'll be just as amazed as I was when I inform you someone decided a Fallow buck with a Douglas Score of 190 was not good enough to be awarded a National Award, the judges decision will be final, (and all that).
Today those Fallow buck antlers are a wonderful tangible reminder of a

fantastic ten days Ray Mueller and I experienced in that magic Caples Valley. In reality that ten days in Hunters Heaven was the real lifetime trophy.

Porridge & Pipis

The Wapiti bull was bugling almost continually. He was deep in a "Pick Up Sticks" jumble of wind-blown trees covered in snow from the previous night's snowfall.

It was from the floatplane that I fully realised what an expansive area Fiordland is, for no matter which way I looked the area stretched to the horizon in every direction. We'd departed Lake Te Anau, our destination Lake Te Au in the prohibited takahe area. By special permission we were permitted to land on this small lake, large enough to land on, but too small for the take-off of a loaded aircraft at the end of trip. By prior arrangement we would be met by a fishing boat at the mouth of the Irene River, three weeks hence.

We were a party of five with our leader being Allan Harrison, one of New Zealand's Master Wapiti hunters, after countless Fiordland bugle trips stretching back many years. Remaining members were John Bamford, his younger brother Rodney, friend Russell West, plus me. I was the novice member of our party.

In those days, the late 60s, a hunter hoping to hunt Wapiti in Fiordland was required to first take part in an official culling trip, usually in the summer, targeting all Red deer and any other deer that appeared to be hybrids. During the trophy season no Wapiti bull was to be shot as a trophy unless it carried a minimum of twelve points.

The unusual aspect of our party was that due to Allan and John's trustworthiness we were to cull and were also allowed to trophy hunt during the trophy season. Our brief was to cull everything that looked like a Red deer, didn't look like a Wapiti. Each member of the party being allowed to take just one trophy, whether it be a Red stag or Wapiti bull.

After landing safely on Lake Te Au, and watching the floatplane use the entire length of the lake before finally becoming airborne, we shouldered our packs and set off for a hut located on the Robin Saddle. A lashing Fiordland rainstorm kept us in that tiny hut for two days, a hut hardly large enough for two persons, let alone five.

The author entered this photo of a pair of Blue Duck on the Irene River in Fiordland into a national photo competition where the judge rejected the photo as a fake......!!!!! Obviously the judge had never been to Fiordland.

Prior to day one of our trip Allan and John had flown in airdrops of supplies, dropping them on basins above bush line, clearings beside the river, the pre-determined plan being for the party to descend from the Robin Saddle into the Irene River where we would slowly hunt our way downstream, recovering our airdrops from time to time, to finally reach the fiord. This allowed for lighter packs, better eating throughout the trip.

Under Allan's guidance we established a pattern of setting up a tent camp, hunting from that camp for a few days, then moving to a new location close to an airdrop. It is possible that the deer in the valley may have never before seen a man, for we were able to virtually walk up to a group, in the thick beech forest, and shoot a number from as close as forty metres. Our tally quickly rose. From each deer we shot we were required to weigh the kidneys, with and without fat, take body measurements, and also remove the lower left jaw. Securing this data slowed the shooting, but still, with five rifles we built up an impressive daily tally.

With his vast Fiordland experience Allan decreed that during the trip we would light no fires. His rationale being that even a small drift of wind would carry smoke, alerting all the deer. The trouble was that for the duration of our hunt it rained, every

One of our many camps in the Irene River Valley.

For three days our diet was porridge and pipis. Here we have members of the party busy shelling more pipis.

day, and the longest period of bright (warming) sunshine we experienced was just for four hours one day. Consequentially our clothes were continually wet.

Each of us had two sets of clothes, those we wore daily while hunting, always wet and shiveringly cold each morning after reluctantly crawling out of our snug sleeping bags. The second lot, carried in plastic bags deep in our packs, to don once camp was established and we were, at last, out of the rain.

And then there were the sandflies. I had taken an old pair of long-legged summer pyjamas to wear in camp and these were great at depriving the sandflies access to the soft skin at the backs of knees and ankles. I had also cut-down some lightweight gumboots, my "camp slippers".

One night we were all deprived of sleep by five or six Red stags continually chorusing on the opposite side of a river flat where we'd set up our camp on the bush edge. Seemingly they were so worked up with the rut they took no notice of "man smell" on the flat. With the crack of dawn, and the improving light, there was a discussion as to who would – "sort those B….. out…" It so happened that I was the only person who could stay in my sleeping bag and get away a shot or two!! As so often happens on a bush clearing the stags had no idea where my first shots originated from, due to the echoes trapped by the surrounding trees. If I recall correctly only one of the stags made it to the safety of the bush.

So, as each day passed we steadily increased our tally. Often we would be travelling with packs up, yet were able to add to our tally, the deer actually standing and watching our approach, the noise of five men struggling through the always wet moss-draped windfalls apparently attracting the deer rather than chasing them away. Obviously, due to perhaps never having seen hunters before, the deer, mistakenly, figured us for approaching deer?

The deer were not in prime condition and possibly feed was short, for throughout the Irene Valley the deer had eaten the tops off every crown fern, right down to the very stem. Whether the hunting fraternity liked it or not it was dramatically self-evident that every Red deer and hybrid needed to be culled in the hope of a vegetation recovery.

NOTE – Today the Irene Valley is no longer in the Wapiti Area.

Almost daily we were shooting lovely twelve to fourteen point Red stags, with estimated Douglas Scores of between 260 to 270, (all better than my 5 x 5 Douglas Score 250 stag from Mt Creighton), but none of us sought these as trophies, we sought trophy Wapiti. John's brother Rodney was the first to score, a bull that later took third place in the Wapiti Section of the Annual NZDA Antler and Horn Competition.

About the end of week two we woke to a white world, for during the night it had snowed. Our entire landscape was blanketed, even well back in the bush. But, up the slope, back in the bush, a Wapiti bull was bugling, a classic bugle, no sniff of hybrid there. Guided by Allan the pair of us carefully set out to stalk the bull hoping for a shot. After about an hour of slow careful climbing we were within about thirty metres of my possible target.

The Wapiti bull was bugling almost continually. He was deep

in a "Pick Up Sticks" jumble of wind-blown trees covered in snow from the previous night's snowstorm.

Such was the thickness of the tangle of logs we could see little of the bull. We needed to ensure he carried the required number of points before a shot could be taken, and even then the projectile would have to find its way through the mess.

While bugling the bull would throw his antlers back then when finished drop his nose. This gave us fleeting glimpses of his antlers as they moved back and forth behind the screen of snow-shrouded downed trees. Both of us were using our binoculars to get a clearer picture. The bolt of my Husqvarna was closed.

Regularly I'd glance at Allan, awaiting some sort of thumb-up, thumb-down signal.

It may have been three or four minutes that we stood there, uncertain. I glanced at Allan; he was flexing his trigger finger.

I knew my chances of making a clean one-shot kill were unlikely due to the complete jumble of logs between me and the bull, so I decided to rapid fire and hope. I guess I fired three or four shots, the last couple as the bull lunged to our left over a small drop, then out of sight. We stood, still. There was no sound of him crashing away downhill.

You've experienced the thrill and exhilaration of an exciting hunt and a trophy down. Your heart is pounding, your adrenaline is at maximum and, given half a chance, you could float on air. Have you experienced ground shrinkage? I have. I did that day.

It rained every day for three weeks; we were forever soaked to the skin. Side creeks offered hazardous crossings, the sound of waterfalls, torrents of cascading water, could be heard long before they were sighted.

To make a sad story as short as possible, and then move on, my "trophy" Wapiti bull was a dwarf, a runt. When the rest of the team arrived to measure and take the usual scientific data we discovered the bull was over a foot (30cm) shorter at the shoulder than the average Wapiti bull. Everything was short by a foot, even the antlers. I can't blame Allan. The bull was within an awful tangle of downed trees, there was snow everywhere, and who would have stopped for a minute, in such circumstances, to consider the shoulder height of the bull? The bull did carry six points aside, so was a legal trophy, but I couldn't seek a larger bull of normal proportions, one trophy was my allowed quota.

And so we progressed down valley, killing more and more Red stags as they were seemingly moving up valley in some sort of rut trek! We couldn't find our last airdrop.

So it was that on the appointed day before we were due to be collected from the mouth of the Irene River, we set up a more or less temporary camp and that night roasted ourselves, and dried our clothes, around a blazing fire. The shoreline was thick with tide-tossed logs.

The fishing boat didn't arrive. We sat it out all day, our gear more or less half packed, ready at the first sight of the boat down the fiord. No boat. The sandflies were having a banquet. Having been unable to locate our last airdrop we were almost out of food, so early the next morning John and Rodney set off back up valley in the hope of maybe locating it, and/or shooting a deer. They failed on both counts, no airdrop, no deer.

Meanwhile we'd discovered that at low tide we had a

The author's dwarf Wapiti bull trophy, shot in a snow shrouded windfall.

bountiful supply of pipis, so that's what we occupied ourselves with, digging pipis. The only food we had left was porridge so our menu was porridge and pipis.

We'd been at the mouth of the Irene for four days when finally the fishing boat arrived, with the news that he'd battled a hell of a storm to get into the Sound and he'd not be trying to get out until the storm abated and the seas calmed.

There wasn't a lot of room for seven men on that boat, but we were grateful for the shelter and warmth it provided. We went from a diet of porridge and pipis to a diet of Blue Cod, all caught over the side of the moored boat.

After about three days the skipper made an attempt at exiting the Sound, but quickly changed his mind when from the crest of about seven to eight metre waves we could all see the big ones further out. Turning the boat in such adverse conditions was a gut churning experience, for an instant or two we feared we'd be pooped and swamped. Meanwhile, Allan Harrison, who was the world's worst sailor, was pleading with us to throw him overboard…

Finally, six or seven days later than planned we steamed out of Charles Sound, the sea bright blue and smooth as a millpond. How grateful Allan was…

NOTES:

One afternoon, early in the trip, three of us climbed out above tree line to recover our first airdrop. After clearing the bush we soon discovered the clipped snowgrass characteristic of takahe feeding. It was therefore no surprise that we encountered a pair of takahe blithely feeding, paying no heed to our presence. There can be no doubt they'd never before seen humans. Sadly, none of us were carrying our cameras for the focus of the day was to climb light and carry back the airdrop. These birds were well out of the known takahe area, a pleasing indication of range extension, numbers increasing.

I did get some fine photos of Blue duck on two or three occasions, when traversing open grass flats beside the Irene River, we saw pairs of ducks feeding in their usual fast water habitat. Some months later I entered a fine photo of a pair of these rare native ducks swimming on the river, in a photo competition, only to have the photo tossed out by the judge. His view being the photo was a fake. Obviously that esteemed judge had never seen Whio in their native habitat.

In total our party sighted 91 animals and culled 33 Red deer and non-typical Wapiti.

Zis Von Ve 'Ave

He was German and spoke only a few words of English,
I knew about three words of German, learned from watching
World War II movies.
We had no interpreter.

Goodwin McNutt had flown us from the airport at Taupo into the Boyd. It was late into the afternoon by the time Karl and I had settled into the hut and I'd begun preparations for our evening meal. The evening was cool and calm and even from within the hut we could hear the Sika stags starting to tune up for the evening. For a time we sat outdoors listening, both speaking, neither of us understanding what the other was saying. Hand signals were our sole form of communication as we ate our dinner. It was going to be an interesting hunt.

With simple hand gestures, clock in hand, I showed Karl that I'd set the alarm and at what hour we'd arise for our first day of hunting. It was a noisy dark night when we headed for our respective sleeping bags, for roaring Sika stags kept us awake for some time. There seemed to be plenty of them about, so chances of taking a trophy stag seemed promising.

It was before dawn when we headed away from the hut, making for a small valley indenting the bush behind the hut. With careful stalking we had ourselves a Sika stag, raising merry hell in a patch of pepperwood across a small gully. It seemed to me just a matter of time and patience before Karl would sight the stag and have a chance of a shot. It happened. There was the stag strutting and making the sounds only a rutting Sika stag can make.

Karl had seen the stag. With the universal signal of a moving trigger finger I nodded in the direction of the stag. When I heard the succession of metallic clicks I knew we had a problem. The stag didn't even wait to determine the source of these foreign sounds.

With all manner of almost comic pantomime hand gestures, (I was grateful no one was watching us), I finally discovered that the fancy 7mm magnum rifle Karl was carrying had three different safety catches, and, he had engaged each after loading the rifle. I'd seen Karl load his rifle as we departed the hut, but it had been too dark to see exactly what he was doing. The previous evening, while the pair of us were settling in to the hut, I'd noticed the size of the shell cases on his 7mm magnum, they appeared to be almost the size of the .50 calibre machine gun shell I had in my cartridge collection at home. Lots of powder behind a relatively small projectile.

Sitting there in the bush with distant Sika stags signalling their locations, I knew I'd hit a barrier, a language barrier. No matter how ingeniously I mimed all manner of hand actions, while explaining in English what I was desperate to convey, Karl seemed to have no real idea of what I was conveying to him.

We got onto a couple more stags with the same click, click, click result. I could clearly see from Karl's facial expressions he was disappointed each time a stag raced away before a shot could be taken. I persevered for all that day. We returned to the hut at dusk, a very frustrated guide, and an unhappy client.

After dinner that evening, in the light of the hissing Tilley lamp, I asked (with hand gestures) for Karl to hand me his rifle. Yes, it was unloaded. That is when I went through a whole series of gestures in an effort to show Karl how we used a half open bolt, for safety, not using safety catches at all.   I pantomimed the "clicks" of his safety catches, and then demonstrated the soft almost silent sound of the half open bolt being closed. His rifle was beautifully made and indeed the closing of the half open bolt made hardly a sound. After handing back his rifle I sought that he practise and practise always signalling to ignore any of and all three of the safety catches.

His nodding head, and ever-spreading smile, told me that tomorrow could be different, successful. Yes, the Sika stags kept us awake for a time.

Once again we were well away from the hut before the faintest touch of pink and gold began to etch our skyline to the east. That morning we headed across the airstrip and finally entered the beech forest more or less to the north-east of the hut. I'd chosen this direction due to the sounds of a number of stags in that section of forest, but also I'd felt a slight breeze on my face when looking north.

It was about mid-morning when we finally sneaked up onto a wide shallow valley within the forest, the beech trees not so thick, and visibility perhaps sixty metres. Unseen as yet, somewhere across this shallow forest valley, was a noisy Sika stag signalling to us, and all other stags, his location.

Taking Karl's arm I indicated that he should do as I was doing and sit. I then signalled that he should close his half open bolt and be ready.   For maybe ten minutes nothing happened, other than the stag continuing to make no end of noise. The gentlest of breezes was in our faces. Everything seemed to be in our favour, I didn't wish to move.

We both saw him at the same time, the stag standing broadside on, but the major part of his body hidden from us by a beech tree with a trunk about thirty centimetres wide. That is when Karl breathed…

"Zis von ve 'ave'. Raised his rifle and squeezed the trigger.

I couldn't believe what I witnessed. The trunk of the beech tree seemed to explode into hundreds of pieces of shattered timber; a nice 4 x 4 Sika stag staggered through the shards of timber to fall dead on the beech leaf debris of the forest floor.

Rising to my feet I reached to shake Karl's hand, drawing him at the same time to his feet.

"This one we have," I said, while pumping his hand.

His eyes were bright. You should have seen his smile.

Forty Year Trophy

The Sambar stag was seventy metres away, standing broadside to me in the middle of an open clearing.
Why wouldn't the bolt close on my trusty .303?

One of my earliest hunting companions was Garry Seddon who lived immediately across the road from my parents in a suburb of Hamilton. I was teaching at a local school, living at home, for the cost of flatting was too high for me a struggling young teacher earning twenty-nine pounds a month (yes, a month).

Our twenty-first birthdays were close; we jointly decided it would be a great idea to have roast venison for the celebratory party. But, we neither of us had any form of transport, and, we really had no idea where we might seek out some venison.

After much "research" we set on a plan to hunt the narrow strip of land between Lakes Tarawera and Rotomahana. This decision was founded solely on the fact that by taking a NZ Road Services bus to Rotorua, a taxi to the jetty at Lake Tarawera and the regular tourist launch across the lake to be dropped off at Hot Water Beach – where there was a substantial hut – we'd be in hunting country.

Thus it was that by noon on a cool May Saturday we were deposited on the shore of the lake at Hot Water Beach. Needless

to say it wasn't long before we settled in, had a good lunch and with hopes high set about finding a deer.

Those of you who know your New Zealand history will recall that in June of 1886 Mt Tarawera erupted, smoothing the surrounding landscape for many square kilometres with hundreds of metres deep volcanic ash. Some time shortly after the eruption the area suffered days on end of torrential rains, which washed deep gutters through the new soft volcanic ash. As the years passed native vegetation began to heal the wounds of the eruption so by the time we arrived in the later 1950s the mixture of native vegetation was beginning to take hold, mostly

A placid scene of Lake Tarawera home to giant rainbow trout. Sambar and Red deer plus wild pigs plentiful in the bush and scrublands surrounding the lake.

only knee-high. Most of the razorback ridges were still bare and on each we found distinct deer trails.

It was while climbing a ridge, and following a deer trail, that out of the vegetation clothing the deep ravine there exploded a Sambar spiker. No need to explain in detail, two very excited young hunters more or less emptied their magazines at that hapless deer. We had our venison.

After inexpertly butchering the carcass we return to the hut very satisfied with our first foray into Sambar country.

We'd made no plan for being picked up by the launch on Lake Tarawera for on the Sunday there was no scheduled tourist trip on the lake and we simply couldn't afford the cost of a charter. The launch operator had informed us that at the head of the main wash (valley of fine sand) there was a walking track that provided access through to the thermal area of Waimangu and finally the main road connecting Taupo and Rotorua.

Finally arriving at the highway we "thumbed down" the first NZR bus heading for Rotorua, and then boarded the first Hamilton bound NZR bus later that afternoon. None of our fellow bus passengers seemed in the least concerned at two rough looking lads with blood-spattered clothes, carrying rifles, joining them as passengers.

As my financial situation improved and I could finally afford my first small car – a 1937 Morris Series. E. – groups of us made numerous trips to Hot Water Beach for along with Sambar deer there were Red deer, pigs and in the lake large rainbow trout. A party of three or four could afford to hire a large dinghy, with outboard, so by getting away from Hamilton immediately at 3:05pm we could be safely at the hut at Hot Water Beach well

Wash day in the bush! My grandmother told me cleanliness was next to holiness!

before dark on a Friday evening. (On two occasions we shot a deer from the dinghy while cruising the shoreline to our destination).

During these many trips to the area I slowly gained more and more understanding of where to locate Sambar, and it was while "exploring" that I found what I called "The Amphitheatre." This was an open area of sand, devoid of any vegetation, with many deep cool vegetation chocked ravines radiating from the clearing, exactly like the spokes of a wheel. The Amphitheatre was well hidden off the beaten track and surrounded by much taller vegetation than elsewhere on the peninsula between the two lakes.

Mt Tarawera and it's crater, the result of a catastrophic volcanic eruption in June 1886. With his new Husqvarna 30-06 the author shot a Red spiker in the crater, his first kill with the new rifle he'd be carrying for his Alaskan adventure.

When I first discovered this secret haven I also discovered the tracks of a large Sambar stag. So each time we spent a weekend at Hot Water Beach I would very carefully stalk my way in to The Amphitheatre in the hope of finding the owner of the big footprints. It was well known that Sambar stags are largely territorial and will spend months in a relatively small area, given there is a good food supply and they aren't disturbed.

These many years later I can't tell you how many times I sneaked into The Amphitheatre and failed to sight the stag. But, on the Saturday afternoon that is still imprinted sharp and clear in my mind, there was the Sambar stag standing motionless broadside to me at seventy metres, looking me straight in the eye. Frozen on the spot, never taking my eyes off the stag, I very slowly dropped my right hand to the bolt of my .303, intending to close it as silently as possible from the safe half-open position. The bolt wouldn't close!!!!!!

Somehow, in setting the bolt in the safe half-open position I had unwittingly lipped the rims of the .303 cases, the upper most cartridge rim being behind the rim of the cartridge below. SHIT.

Slowly I dropped to my knees. Screened by some short manuka, and with desperate hands I managed to rectify my problem, but aware that no matter how careful I was I was making foreign metallic sounds. Gently I closed the bolt on a round then slowly raised my head. The stag had disappeared. I never saw him again.

However, on subsequent visits to The Amphitheatre I did have a number of "contacts." In an effort to outsmart the stag I changed tactics and by starting much earlier in the afternoon I would work my way towards my objective via the high ridges surrounding The Amphitheatre. It was on one such sortie that I discovered a very large recently used wallow. Mr Big's bathtub.

Very early one morning, on a later trip, I sneaked in ever so slowly on the wallow. At about twenty metres, flat on my stomach, all I could see was four very black mud covered lower legs, the body of the stag invisible to me due to the thick manuka scrub. I was carrying my newly-acquired .348 loaded with 200 gr handloads, but as I didn't have a clear shot at a vital area, and not wishing to wound and lose such a fine trophy I didn't fire a shot.

Still working on the theory that coming in from high above and working downhill onto The Amphitheatre I found myself very late one afternoon seated on one of the many razor backed ridges contemplating my navel and wondering just what I had to do to get a shot at the stag that was now becoming something of an obsession. Utter silence prevailed, not even a whisper of a breeze, when from immediately below me came the sounds of an animal tearing at vegetation, I could hear him chewing.

The gully was chocked with all manner of thick regrowth, including Five Finger; I could see nothing of the body of the stag (?) Ever so slowly I stood, picked up a large rock, and after judging exactly where the sound was coming from dropped the rock through the canopy. I distinctly heard the "whomp" of the stone hitting the body of the deer. With bolt closed and not breathing I waited for the stag to break cover and (hopefully) dash across one of the many open spaces. He didn't. That stag just raced down that deep gully while I stood there listening to his antlers smashing through the supplejack.

Once again working on the theory of coming onto The Amphitheatre from above, to provide a better view, I was working my way infinitely slowly down yet another razor back ridge when there below me, on my right, was Mrs Pig with six or eight perfect roasting size piglets. What to do? Bird in the hand…? I nailed a couple before they figured the source of the noise.

After hauling each gutted carcass up on to the ridge I wandered about thirty metres to a large pine tree that I had ideas of climbing for a better overview of the surrounding area. Standing beside the trunk I glanced to my left and there in the

sand were the footprints of a stag. I didn't need to see the stag to interpret the sign. He had obviously been walking slowly down the sand bed of the gully when I had fired at the pigs. With the discharge of my first shot he had lunged immediately into a mad charge to disappear into yet another of those accused supplejack-chocked gullies.

Would I have got a shot at the stag if I'd not shot the pigs? Guess how many times I've asked myself that very question over the past forty odd years.

It was soon after this incident that we formed a company and took over Lilybank Station at the head of Lake Tekapo and for the following twenty-two years were busy developing our professional hunting guiding business. (NOTE – read my book *Bulls Bucks and Bureaucrats* for the full Lilybank story.) Seldom during those years did I have a chance for any recreational hunting for myself, but when we sold Lilybank in 1992 I was once again in a position to seek and add to my personal trophy collection.

By an intriguing set of circumstances I found myself in Sambar country, hunting private property, escorted by Mr Sambar himself Craig Ferguson. We saw a few deer, but never a stag. Craig was giving me his time FOC so from time to time he needed to take care of his own business, so left me to my own devices, to explore and learn. That is how I discovered yet another secret location where a Mr Cervus Unicolor was living. It screamed of recent sign. I found a large wallow, a couple of rotten tree stumps that had been thrashed into wood pulp, and droppings almost everywhere. Every second step I took was sign of recent browsing. Yet, I didn't see the Sambar stag.

It was dawn on a Saturday morning that Craig and I braved almost horizontal rain, driven by a lashing southerly, to return to camp soaked through to the skin and frozen half to death. Even my Swanndri wasn't enough to keep out that driving rain. A hot shower, change of clothes and lunch kindly provided by the farmer's wife finally drove the chill out of my bones. Craig meanwhile has driven home for his own hot shower and change into dry warm clothes.

My host had a roaring fire blazing in the hearth and was about to settle down to watch an All Black test match. He invited me to join him, he having to raise his voice against the storm still lashing his home and pounding on the windows. I had a choice to be made. A man could watch an All Black test many times in his life, but how often would he get a second chance at a trophy Sambar stag. I chose to once again face the southerly storm.

What influenced my decision to hunt in the storm? From time to time North Island hunters from the Manawatu would pass through Lilybank on their way to hunting Tahr in the Upper Godley, Mount Cook National Park. Upon returning from the Godley they would always courteously drop in at our lodge to inform us of their safe return. A cuppa was always in order; conversation would flow back and forth. That is how I learned that local Manawatu Sambar hunters always hunted their quarry during a southerly storm, for they had learned that the sounds of the storm would drown out any noise they made. The deer wouldn't hear them.

So it was that at about 4pm – clad in every stitch of warm clothes I had with me – I took a slow tour around the perimeter of the gully containing all the stag sign, but quickly realised that despite the sounds of the lashing wind and driving rain I'd still make excessive noise fighting my way through dense gorge, blackberry and ferns. Best to find a place to sit, and pray, and hope…

With a convenient large and thick gorse bush to partially shelter me from the still raging lashing southerly I sat with my Husqvarna across my knees fully loaded and safety catch off. (I wasn't going to get caught out a second time.) In the breech of the 30-06 (rimless case) was a special load I had made up for Elk hunting with 190-gr projectiles.

How long did I sit there? I don't know. I can tell you that it wasn't very long before the rain had driven up my sleeves, down my neck, even up the legs of my shorts. Yes, I'd mistakenly figured shorts would be fine for a North Island hunt!

I do recall I was sitting in a puddle of very cold water. I waited.

With the hood of my 'Swannie' pulled well down over my head, and dropping my head forward I was doing my best to shelter my face from the driving rain. From time to time I would look up, study the terrain within view. Nothing. Head down, suffer the misery a few minutes more, look up…

There he was. Not thirty metres on my left a Sambar stag was walking slowly directly towards me. The 190gr Hornady projectile hit him in the centre of his brisket. His legs folded, he slumped to his left. He was dead before his body hit the ground. After forty years I finally had my trophy Sambar stag. With an antler length of 28 inches he was just two inches short of the magic thirty inches.

OBSERVATIONS:

Let me begin by firmly declaring I am absolutely not an expert on Sambar deer. Yes, I have had some (really) limited experience and from that I'd like to make a few (helpful) observations.

Hunting in a severe storm worked for me and works for the local Manawatu hunters, so maybe it will work for you. First find where a stag is living then seek him out in a storm. It may take more than one storm!

I am satisfied, based on my own personal experience and the observations of Sambar hunters, that a Sambar stag is a creature of habit. Given that he has a plentiful food supply and he isn't disturbed, I suggest that if you see a stag in a certain area you'll likely see him there again. And his chosen area may not be all that large.

Sambar are largely nocturnal, spending virtually all the daylight hours in deep cover, maybe even much of the night in the same deep cover if there is a sufficient food supply.

They are very difficult to see in thick under brush such as manuka. Their zoological name is *Cervus Unicolor* (a deer of uniform body colouring) so that dark grey is perfect for blending in, especially in deep shadows with mottled light.

The size of their ears tells you that their hearing is their first line of defence. I have no doubt that many an aspiring Sambar hunter has been continually unsuccessful because the deer have heard him approaching. (That's why it is suggested you hunt during a noisy storm.)

Success at last. Forty years after missing out on a Sambar stag trophy the author finally nailed this guy, only the second Sambar stag he'd ever seen.

Also I make the observation that a Sambar stag is much like a bull Moose in that if they have heard a hunter approaching and feel comfortable that they've not been seen the stag/bull will stand perfectly still in deep cover and allow the hunter to walk past him. His nose will be raised, his antlers laid back possibly resting on his back, his nostrils flared to take in any scent. His eyes will be following your every movement, and if you don't look directly at him he'll let you blithely walk past.

A fully mature Sambar stag is a big bodied animal so PLEASE don't go chasing after a trophy stag with a rifle smaller than .30 calibre firing a nice big heavy projectile. Craig Ferguson – who has hunted Sambar all his adult life – hunts only with a .375. It's the old story – 'When in Rome do as the Romans do…!!'

ANOTHER FIRST (THE NEXT GENERATION)

We watched as the Chamois buck raced towards the skyline rim of the gorge.
Would he stop before disappearing?

It was seldom that our children's Correspondence School lessons ran through a day without interruption. Growing up at a hunting lodge, where almost daily a happy hunter returned to the lodge with yet another trophy, made it impossible for their teacher to hold her pupil's attention, let alone stop them from racing out of the classroom to view the results of yet another successful hunt, guided by their dad.

By the time son Stephen was eight or nine he was asking when he'd be allowed to tag along on a hunt. With a client's approval Stephen was invited, from time to time, to accompany his father as "assistant guide" carrying the spotting scope.

It's no wonder he hated boarding school, for he was missing out on the hunting successes, interacting with our hunting clients who came from many different countries, missing out on the daily activities and conversations, all largely relating to hunting. However, when home during school holidays he had no commitment to school lessons, so each day hoped he'd once again spend his holiday days as "assistant guide". He did, but always with the approval of each client.

It is an indisputable fact that young people learn by what I term – "a process of osmosis". That is, provided they are deeply interested, they take in all that is happening around them without consciously being aware they are learning.

Example – If a client was to tell Stephen all the details of his rifle, his handloads, what trophies he'd shot in Africa, our son would be able to repeat all that information, many weeks later, word perfect. BUT, despite my every effort he never did learn all the sequence of the elements of Mendeleev's Periodic Table!!!

Looking back I don't have recall of how many days I guided clients accompanied by my son. He conducted himself in a very professional manner and as a father I was proud while enjoying sharing my professional function with my son.

Both Stephen and Julie were skilled with a skinning knife long before they were sent off to boarding schools. Many a client watched in a highly nervous manner when either Stephen or Julie was instructed to skin out a trophy for a full body mount. The client's nervousness lasted but a few minutes for off came the skin with not a gram of flesh attached.

When Stephen was twelve years old we arranged for an inbound client to carry with him a Remington BDL rifle, in .243 calibre, that I had bought in the States. Having seen so many spoiled kids really not valuing and appreciating such gifts Sue (my wife) and I were determined Stephen would "earn" his rifle. An "agreement" was entered into, Stephen would buy the rifle from his father by doing all manner of chores, each hour worked earning a "credit" of one dollar per hour. The rifle had cost $487.

Sell a boy a rifle and the next you know he (naturally) wants to use it. Unbeknown to me clients had gifted Stephen small gratuities for his services as "assistant guide" so the next we knew he had enough money to fit his BDL with a x 4 scope. As Stephen wasn't yet old enough to legally own a firearm I accompanied him on short outings "culling" the local rabbit and hare population. On the infrequent occasions that we had a need to cull a deer Stephen was happy to be the marksman.

I'm sure you are guessing the progression that developed. The next question I got was – "Dad, when can I shoot a trophy…?"

It was the August school holidays, son and daughter were home from boarding school, our hunting season was over, Dad – the guide – was free from client commitments. Stephen had by now been the very proud owner of his .243 for two years. He'd been extremely patient. He was fourteen years old.

So it was that on a mild early September afternoon we went looking for a trophy Chamois. I'd not considered looking for a Tahr for my professional opinion was (and still is) a .243 has insufficient energy to be sure of making a good clean kill on a mature bull Tahr in full winter coat.

That afternoon we cruised the Macaulay Valley, in the Toyota, employing our usual "modus operandi" searching with binoculars then studying a sighted Chamois with the much more powerful spotting scope. During the afternoon we located four buck Chamois, but a stalk on two was unsuccessful; they gave us the slip and we never did discover how they'd disappeared off the mountain face. On our way back to the lodge, with fading light, we sighted a buck high above us. Stephen missed the shot.

That evening I decided we might as well make a "real" expedition of it so that evening and the following morning we

The author with his wife Sue, plus friend Kingsley Field (from Hamilton) at the old Waterfall Hut. Years before a hunting client secured a nice trophy Chamois buck shooting from the door of this hut.

sorted and packed gear, organised our food, and after an early lunch set off for the Waterfall Hut in the Macaulay. It took us about an hour to get our gear set up in the hut, the fire lit.

About 3pm we made the climb into Waterfall Basin, which is immediately above the hut. Chamois often frequented the Waterfall Creek gorge, close to the hut, but despite climbing carefully and glassing the gorge continually we saw not a single Chamois buck. All we saw that afternoon was one solitary female Chamois, and far across on the opposite side of the valley, one bull Tahr. The rapidly failing light chased us back to the hut. The day was gloriously fine, but promised a frosty night.

We woke to a very cold hut, however once the open fire was

The true right, mid-section, of the game-rich Macaulay Valley, Waterfall Gorge and Basin in centre, Lower Tindall Basin on the far right. Father and son stayed in the Waterfall Hut, son secured his trophy Chamois in the Lower Tindall.

ablaze we soon warmed up. I had discovered the hut to be in a very untidy state, a real mess in fact. A tramping club had used the hut on an irregular basis during the winter and their standard of care (of a hut they didn't own) was far below our standards. After breakfast Stephen and I set about rectifying other folk's mess.

It was 1pm before we had the hut, as it should have been, so off we went, heading for the Lower Tindall. Like the Waterfall

Creek I knew we had a chance of locating Chamois in the lower gorge of the Lower Tindall. The Tindall has two streams, which join about half an hour's climb from the river flats; so first we carefully explored the true right branch. Nothing.

Back to the confluence of the streams to slowly work our way towards and into the lower gorge, working our way towards the first waterfall. We'd seen no game. Without warning, unexpectedly, a buck Chamois exploded from behind a large boulder to stand atop it looking back at us. Stephen had time for a hasty offhand shot. A miss.

It was then I saw an example of my son's "osmotic" learning for he immediately reloaded, shook off his day pack and using the pack as a fore-end rest settled into a steady shooting position to follow the Chamois in his scope sight. We watched as the Chamois buck raced towards the skyline rim of the gorge. Would he stop before disappearing?

When a Chamois buck is about to stop he will often drop his rear end, take two or three steps, then stand looking back. It is the dropping of the rear end that is the advanced signal to be ready for a quick shot. We both registered the signal that indeed the buck would stop and look back before cresting out.

Stephen was settled into a very good shooting position, but by now my guess was the buck was closer to 350m away than 300m. I quietly told Stephen it was a very long shot and asked how he felt about it.

I got no reply. Instead the .243 shattered the silence and as I watched through my binoculars the Chamois dropped from sight. With the buck not visible to our searching with binoculars it was a nervous pair who climbed to where we'd last seen him.

Stephen Joll, aged 14 years, with his first-ever hunting trophy a 9 inch Chamois buck. He worked-to-earn his .243 Remington BDL at $1 per hour labouring for his father.

No need for nervousness for there between two rocks we found Stephen's trophy buck Chamois, his first ever trophy.

There we were, father and son, and we'd both secured our first trophies on Lilybank. I'd shot my 13⅞ inch bull Tahr in 1959 at the age of twenty-one, Stephen had shot his 9 inch trophy buck Chamois in the Macaulay at the age of fourteen, twenty-seven years apart.

Sad to report the nine-to-ten-year-old buck's skin was in very poor order; in fact the buck was in low body condition, obviously having suffered through our severe winter. After a series of family album photos we removed the head from the carcass and began our tramp back to the hut. Stephen led the way and I couldn't help noticing he had a great spring in his stride. Each time he looked back at me he had an ear-to-ear grin…

COMMENTS:

Never, never, never shoot at a running Chamois. Your first shot will move him into top gear, your second will move him rapidly into over-drive, your third he'll probably cut in the after-burners and he'll never stop running.

Do as Stephen had "osmotically" learned to do. Set yourself up in a comfortable prone position (if you can) and wait for the buck to drop his arse. You'll have a second or two to make a killing shot after he'd taken two or three more steps. I say drop into a prone position, if you can, for in camo gear and flat on the ground it will likely confuse the buck for he'll probably have trouble locating your position, thus giving you a fraction more time to place a clean kill shot.

In my experience it is very difficult to locate Chamois in adverse weather conditions. They seem to be rather sensitive and fragile animals that dislike strong gusty winds, very hot sunshine days, very cold days, snow storms or heavy rain. I've spent an entire day, hunting Chamois, after a heavy snowfall and not seen a single animal. Forget hunting them in a nor'west gale.

Their behaviour during the rut is worthy of reporting. Many times I sighted buck Chamois racing across a mountain, obviously moving from female group to female group seeking females in oestrous. Twice I have experienced bucks running all the way down the mountain to my client and I, to be shot at close range. In his testosterone charged state did the buck think we were other Chamois? On the second occasion this occurred the buck was the biggest and best trophy Chamois we'd ever take. With horn length of 10⅞ inches and an SCI Score of 29 it placed as Number One in the SCI Record Book.

I have no doubt that Chamois have preferred locations within their home range. It is usual to see Chamois in the same place, from time to time, but it could be that the group you see on a favoured spot this week may not be the same group you sighted there last week. If there wasn't a buck with the group of females and young last week don't assume there'll not be a buck there this week. If my observations are correct Chamois groups move, from one favoured location to another, a sort of rotation.

Twice during my hunting career I have found buck Chamois with their horns caught in tall snow tussock, the tussock twisted into a thick rope. No escape. The first such buck I located had been long dead; the second was very much alive and fighting for his life. My client and I climbed far up the mountain where we cut him loose. He was a trophy-class 9½ inch buck, but who wants their trophy lassoed before making a kill.

Those who kill female Chamois claiming it is impossible to determine if a Chamois is male or female annoy me immensely. The female has much slenderer horns than the male and the hook is far less pronounced. A mature buck's horns will make 180 degrees of a circle, a mature female's horns never will. If you are so blind as to not be able to determine the above through your binoculars just sit back and wait for the animal to take a pee!

FOOTNOTE:

In the years since Stephen shot that first Chamois trophy the .243 700 BDL Remington has undergone a number of modifications. The stock has been replaced by a Hogue rubber over melded Tactical. The original scope has been replaced by a Custom Leupold VX 3 4.5 to 14 by 40 long range matched ballistics mil dot reticle. A Gabe Zigleani suppressor has been fitted, also a Harris S series 9 to 13 bi-pod.

Stephen has spent many hours improving and perfecting his hand loads. Today his load is 46.5 grains of Winchester 760 ball powder, driving a Hornady 2442 87-gr hollow point. He's using Federal 215 Magnum primers. Best group was five shots at 100 metres – 11mm outside to outside. His longest shot – verified by two witnesses – is a 447 yards shot on a rabbit.

Our son is very proud of his 700 BDL and is quick to tell that he paid off his rifle by labouring for his parents for 487 hours at $1/hour. Enjoyment with the rifle = $ priceless.

The Trials & Challenges Of A Professional Hunting Guide

QUOTE: *"It is a self-evident absolute that there are no degrees of Professionalism.*

"Professionalism is a complete way of life, a mind-set and attitude..."

It was dark; we could see nothing but the first faint flush of dawn in the eastern sky etching the peak of the 2310m mountain high above. Around us numerous stags were roaring lustily. The chance for a shot would have to wait.

We'd departed the lodge a couple of hours before daylight and after driving up valley I'd parked the Toyota and walking slowly, stumbling over unseen obstacles, we began to climb the slope in the dark. With me were man and wife clients from North Carolina. We were looking for a trophy stag for the wife. The previous dawn we'd made an attempt to stalk onto the numerous stags holding hinds on the face but soon discovered the open nature of the mountainside offered too little cover and we'd blown every stalk I'd attempted. This morning I was trying a new strategy by attempting to be high on the face long before the arrival of dawn. A sort of pre-dawn ambush.

The tussock face we were slowly climbing stretched for five kilometres and rose from the valley floor for about 700m as a gentle gradient until meeting the buttresses of greywacke rock bluffs, a mad jumble of cliffs, home to many a trophy bull Tahr. My problem was lack of cover to provide successful stalking, for the vast slope was basically smooth, broken only by a few shallow old watercourses. The matagouri was sparse and low.

Progress was slow for I'd decided that our best chance of possible success for the wife was to climb the slope via one of the deeper gullies, a gully just deep enough to hide us if we climbed while leaning forward, sufficient to keep our heads below the gully rim. My client, a retired international airline pilot, was not very fit, perhaps not even as fit as his wife, so frequent, very frequent, rests were required. But, my heart was pounding for from either side of us, and above, was a chorus of countless Red stags roaring.

The couple had booked a two-on-one three species hunt (Tahr, Chamois and Red stag), but during the drive from Christchurch to our property the husband had informed me he would not be taking a Red stag for he'd killed a magnificent 12-point Royal Red stag on an estate belonging to the Dutch royal family. He'd hunted there as a guest. We'd hunted Tahr and Chamois first – I always hunted the hardest species first – and without fail each day my male client reminded me that he wouldn't be taking a stag with us for the quality of stag in New Zealand couldn't possibly measure up to his Royal stag from Holland. I honestly confess I got tired of his running down our stags, especially so as at that point in the hunt we'd seen few stags for we'd been targeting Tahr and Chamois.

And so it was that we finally crawled carefully across frosted tussock onto a small elevated knoll, the three of us flat on our bellies, stags all around us roaring, still too dark to see any possible target. Each time I slowly lifted my head to gauge the amount of light I was grateful for the frosty chill on my cheeks from the night time thermal. No stag above us on the slope would have picked up our scent.

For perhaps twenty minutes we lay there, awaiting the arrival of sufficient light, the frost rapidly creeping into our clothing, chilling us. The wife was shivering. But with each passing minute more and more of the surrounding landscape was becoming visible, the roaring of the stags reaching a crescendo…

From almost immediately above our position we had a stag with a particular deep chesty roar, but he seemed to be content to stand his ground. Whispering in Joan's ear to thumb off her safety-catch, and be ready for my call, I pulled my roaring horn from my shirt front, and keeping it low and close to the ground, to confuse him as to our exact location, I offered a short "invitation" to the stag.

That stag instantly accepted my 'invitation'. Suddenly, less than fifty metres on our front stood a fantastic 7 x 7 fourteen point stag, an Imperial of classic form. One glance and I knew we had an incredible trophy stag for my lady hunter. I was on Joan's right, her husband on her left. As I was whispering to her to place the crosshairs in the centre of the chest and squeeze, her husband leapt to his feet and in the one motion jerked the rifle out of his wife's grasp!

Spinning to look directly into my face he rasped – "She doesn't need to kill a stag of that size…"

It all happened so quickly I never did see what the stag did; I was speechless, struck dumb. If the morning was cold and frosty the chill factor out there on that gentle knoll dropped to an extreme chill factor as man and wife glared at each other, neither saying a word.

I said nothing. I indicated to the husband that he should hand me the rifle. I unloaded it. With a nod of my head in the direction of the Toyota I indicated we should return to camp… You don't need me to explain do you? Upon seeing that Imperial stag materialise the husband knew instantly that his wife was about to kill a stag much superior to his Dutch Royal. His fragile male ego couldn't handle such a situation.

One of the problems a young professional guide has is guiding men who are many years their senior. Men who because of their age are inclined to think they know more about hunting than their guide a couple of decades younger than themselves. They forget they are hunting for the first time in foreign land, a land where they are unfamiliar with the species being hunted.

Karl was from Pennsylvania, of German extraction. As I had done in the above story he and I had climbed the slope in total darkness, waited for dawn and then successfully located an excellent stag. This stag however, was determined that we would have to come to him, he wasn't coming to us. After a whispered discussion as to the range I instructed Karl to aim for the centre of the shoulder. I knew instantly by the reaction of the stag to the shot that Karl had not aimed where I told him.

In such a circumstance where a client has not complied with my instructions and so seriously screwed up a fine stalk, resulting in the possible loss of a trophy, and painful death of a fine stag, my professional diplomacy is inclined to evaporate…

Doing my very best to smother my anger I said – "You didn't aim where I told you to. Did you?"

His reply was – "I thought you had misjudged the range, that the stag was much further away and so I held high…"

While this short sharp exchange of words was occurring I was watching the stag with my binoculars, as he climbed higher and higher up the mountain to crest out in a shallow saddle, to finally disappear into the adjoining valley.

We had a wounded stag. My professional responsibility was to make every possible effort to first locate and dispatch the stag, secondly, conclude the mess my disobedient client had dropped us both in to. Back at the lodge I saddled two horses, packed food into the saddlebags and off we rode.

First we had to zigzag climb our way to the low saddle where last I'd seen the stag. This took about four hours. I left the horses on the saddle and from that point on Karl and I very carefully studied every possible hiding place in that adjoining steep valley. We searched unsuccessfully all afternoon. An hour from sunset we still hadn't located the stag. We were still high on the ridge but close to where this side valley joined an even larger valley. If the stag had travelled downhill, as I had expected it would, we would never locate him should his stamina have carried him into the large main valley.

Yet, I had this gut feeling that with every half hour the stag travelled the wound high on his shoulder would be starting to seize up and he'd likely got to ground in an attempt to ease his pain. But, light was fading fast and we were one hell of a way from the lodge…

I had deliberately stayed high for that would give us a better view down in to likely places the stag might seek to rest. That's how I located him. He was at the confluence of the two valleys, far below us on the opposite side of the valley, snug in a matagouri thicket. We'd never have sighted him had we not retained the advantage of height. The spotting scope revealed a flesh wound high on the shoulder. This was indeed Karl's stag.

What to do? We couldn't climb down from the ridge for our first step onto the slope would place us in full view of the wounded stag. Karl had one option, and one option only. Take a shot from the ridge. My guess was the range was about 300m at a very steep downhill angle.

After explaining our limited options I asked Karl to take up a very comfortable prone shooting position, using my daypack as fore-end rest. When he was well settled and comfortable he turned to me and asked… "Gary, where should I aim?"

"Place the horizontal line of your crosshairs exactly on the lowest point of his brisket. You need to be aware that this is a one-shot deal, for if the stag gets up and runs darkness and thousands of acres will win."

Karl made a one-shot kill. It was 1am when we finally arrived back at the lodge, Karl's trophy antlers with cape across my shoulders. Yes, he did thank me with genuine sincerity.

Hand-loads have always been a most interesting topic in hunting circles. I myself have hand loaded all my own centre-fire rifles for many years, so when a client arrived with his own handloads it always added a further dimension to the hunt and conversation. So it was that I was down at the range with a newly arrived client from Alaska, the yellow plastic cartridge containers a sure hand loader giveaway.

When you've stood safely behind some hundreds of clients at the range bench rest, while checking their rifle is suitably sighted, one has become familiar with the noise of discharge of the various calibres. Although I was wearing earmuffs the discharge was incredibly loud, the rifle recoil greater than I'd seen even on a .505 Gibbs!!! As I was slowly gathering my senses, much puzzled by such recoil and extreme noise from a 30-06 my new client was struggling to open the bolt of his rifle? He couldn't?

As he struggled unsuccessfully with the rifle bolt I learned he was a new hand-loader, that these loads he had with him were his first, loaded just a couple of days before the hunt. My usual questions about the type of powder and grains used triggered extreme alarm bells in my head. Meanwhile my client had still failed to eject the spent cartridge. He hadn't test-fired his new loads to determine accuracy, he hadn't used a Reloading Manual, he hadn't used scales to measure the power loads, and he'd simply filled the cartridges to the brim and then seated the projectiles. Yes, honestly, that's what he'd done. That ignorant man was placing his life (and mine) in fatal jeopardy by expecting to fire compressed loads in his rifle.

We had quite a serious discussion there at the bench rest, with me adamant that he would not be firing that rifle again while I was his guide. It wasn't until I had found a short hefty tree branch that I was able to hammer open the rifle bolt, and as I worked the bolt back the primer fell out onto the table top. Close inspection of the base of the cartridge showed impressed milling marks from the bolt face. In the simplest of terms each of that man's cartridges was a lethal bomb. We concluded a successful hunt with my client using one of our rifles, our hand-loads.

Staying with the theme of hand-loads I need to tell you about a unique hand-loader, unique in the strictest sense of the word, the only instance I ever experienced. This client, from the United States, arrived at the bench rest at the range with four of those rubber five-shot cartridge holders threading onto a belt. I noticed each group of five shells had a different colour code marking on the shell face. Obviously this prompted me to question my client. (Are you ready for this?) Each group of five shells had been hand loaded for best effect at different ranges. The first group of five was for shots out to 100m, the next for shots from 100m to 150m, the next 150m to 200m, the next 200m to 250m, and the final five shells for all shots over 250m. I kid you not…..

The problem I encountered on the hunt was that upon sighting (say) a stag and determining that the range was 250m my client would load his rifle with the appropriate ammo. If the terrain allowed I would then work carefully to reduce the range, to be sure of a better shot. BUT, once we'd reduced the range to about 200m the ammo in the magazine had to be removed and the 200m-range ammo loaded. I love to stalk, that is my daily challenge, so once again, terrain allowing it, we'd stalk even closer. Yes, once again the magazine would have to be unloaded and the ammo replaced. That's all very well, but there comes a point when a stag finally hears all this unloading and reloading of rifle magazine and decides to depart for safer much more distant pastures. Stalk blown.

What to do? Apply psychology. After one or two aborted

stalks I took care to note what particular ammo wasn't in the cartridge holders. That told me the anticipated range. It was simple, regardless of whatever the distance was I would call it as the same as the loads in the rifle. It worked. My man killed Red stag, Tahr and Chamois.

The ten-day hunt was successful with a day or two up our sleeves so off we went chasing Wallabies, fine sport for an American hunter who has never chased them before. But, hunting Wallabies generated a tremendous dilemma for my client. What load should be used? I suggested the fastest with the lightest projectiles. He killed some Wallabies and was a very happy hunter.

While talking of psychology I need to tell of yet another hunt where I applied this science, even though I confess I don't have any formal qualification on the subject. My client on this hunt was a fine retired bank manager from the eastern part of the United States. His usual mode of hunting was to sit in a tree stand and shoot a Whitetail buck when it passed below him.

On the first day of the hunt my client fired a whole box of ammo at a number of bull Tahr and didn't so much as draw blood on any of them. On the long drive back to the lodge, after a long and disappointing day's hunting, my client informed me that he simply couldn't hit anything over one hundred metres. (He was shooting a Remington 30-06!!)

The client of the author had a real quandary in deciding which of his many specialised hand-loads he should use on his Wallaby hunt!!

Next morning, at crack of dawn, we had a fine buck Chamois standing looking at us at about 200m. My client asked me the range. I told him that in this very early dawn light I couldn't be sure but my guess was 95m. One shot, one dead Chamois buck. Over the following six or eight days my client killed a Red stag at about 250m (a one-shot kill), and a good bull Tahr at somewhere in the 250m+ range, (also a one-shot kill), with me always calling the range at a little under 100m. All in a days work for a professional hunting guide. At the end of the hunt did I tell my client about my applied psychology? No I didn't. My job was to secure the client his trophies and that is what I did. Upon consideration I felt it best not to confess to my client that I had deliberately mis-called the range (lied!) to ensure his success.

If I were to sit down under a shady tree one summer and trawl through all my old diaries I am sure I'd find enough material to write an entire book on rifles and those who use them, but here are a few snippets for your consumption.

Very early on in my career I learned to be on the watch-out for clients who did more shotgunning than rifle shooting, for almost without fail I'd get them on the range and have a small bet with myself that they'd jerk the trigger. Bingo, right again, round holes in the target four or five inches to the right. With such clients I would have to be constantly on the alert when they were about to fire at a trophy, reminding them to "squ-e-e-eze" not jerk. Then there were the clients who were using rifles with serious recoil such that they obviously flinched each time the trigger was activated. I can recall actually watching one hunter sight on the target, turn his head away, close his eyes, then pull the trigger. No shots on the A4 sheet of paper at 100m.

The most difficult situation arose with man and wife hunting two-on-one, couples I called Pigeon Pairs. They would be dressed in the very same camo outfits, both carrying the same make of magnum rifle. The husband would have no trouble with the severe recoil, the poor wife obviously afraid to fire her rifle. She was hunting solely to please her husband. It was extremely delicate for I would have to ever so gently work towards the wife leaving the magnum at the lodge, using our son's .243 instead. Those ladies shot that little rifle with incredible skill, once they had overcome their fear of punishing recoil with every shot fired.

Why the odd client arrived with a twin gun case, two rifles, I never could decide. No doubt it was insurance against one malfunctioning, and sometimes a rifle did. One very fancy custom rifle was so finely tuned that the firing pin travelled too short a distance to strike the primer with sufficient force to ignite it. On that occasion I spent a consuming half hour on the phone talking to the USA rifle maker, (we'd called him collect), while he worked me through the steps to overcome the problem.

Another rifle had probably never ever been cleaned for at the range I was immediately aware the firearm was hang-firing. After I'd spent a diligent hour in our gunroom cleaning the rifle, flushing and cleaning the bolt, we had no further problems.

Scope sights offered me many a challenge, particularly so when a client insisted that the scope was fine, it had been "spot-on" two years ago when he'd hunted Mule deer in Mexico. Quite often a client would oppose my making any adjustment to the scope, saying that if it was out slightly he would compensate. It was on such occasions that I would simply invite my client to visualise a scene where he and I have climbed for six hours to the top of a mountain where we finally have a 14 inch+ bull Tahr in our sights. He fires a dozen shots at the bull and misses every one. The next day we are on the range correcting the scope sight, so why not make the correction today and not miss an outstanding trophy tomorrow…? Subsequent to my insistence we'd have a highly successful hunt and almost without fail my grateful client will quietly thank me for my professional insistence.

Mention the word "safety catch" to me and even today the hairs on the back of my neck start to prickle. Countless times I had to remonstrate with my client for walking behind me with a rifle fully loaded, the "safety-catch" applied (maybe!!!!). Their excuse always was that they may have to take a sudden jump shot and they'd not have time to work the bolt. There were clients who would sneakily reload their rifles, even leave the "safety-catch" disengaged, while walking a couple of steps behind me. They only had to stumble and fall and if the rifle accidentally discharged who would likely be DEAD?

If a given client committed this "indiscretion" a second time I would ask him to sit on a convenient rock and tell him I was going to allow him ten minutes in which to mentally compose what he would say to my wife Sue that evening when he walked in to the lodge to tell her he'd killed me. After the appropriate amount of time I would explain that we didn't need to carry a rifle in a state of readiness in the open mountain terrain we were hunting. I'd then demonstrate the safest "safety-catch" of the lot, the half open bolt, activated only when on final approach. I would gently explain that both of us would know the state of the rifle visually without the need for words to be spoken. Few of the hunters I guided were familiar with the above safety practice.

Rifles are made to kill and one mistake is likely to not only be fatal to the person the hunting projectile strikes, but also fatal to a professional guide's future business. During my many years as a professional we were constantly diligent with all aspects of safety and I am proud to report we had not one firearms incident.

Earlier I wrote of the difficulties for a young guide guiding a client many years older than himself, especially when the elder was inclined to think he knew more about New Zealand hunting and our outdoors than his young guide. Two illustrative incidents come to mind. I was guiding a well-known American hunter, well known for his prowess as a sheep hunter. As previously mentioned I always tackled the Tahr hunt first, while my new client was fresh and full of energy. My normal practice was to drive the valley and spot for a likely bull, watching him until he settled for the day, then climb to the known location, probably making a kill late afternoon.

But, my world-famous sheep hunter thought he knew better than me. We'd stopped to look for a good bull when upon noticing a basin high up close to the top of the mountain my client informed me that if he was hunting sheep he'd be heading for that basin, and that was what we were going to do.

My explanation of locate and stalk a known bull fell on deaf ears, my client virtually ignored me and set off to climb to the basin! I had no choice but to follow. I knew the day was wasted for the client was unaware that we were climbing that tall mountain with the daytime thermal "up our arses…" Hours before we could reach his chosen basin all the Tahr on that mountain would have winded us and removed themselves to a different mountain.

As was almost always the case my client was nowhere near as fit as me; I had to teach him two subtle lessons that day otherwise he would screw-up the whole ten-day hunt. I set the pace up the mountain. Without trying to I would draw away from him, increasing the distance between us. When I became aware of his not being close behind me, (I couldn't hear his rasping breathing) I would stop. I'd allow him to close the distance between us, give him a short minute to catch his breath, and then set off again. It goes without saying that my companion puffed his way up that mountain for hours on end and when we did finally clamber over to the rim of the basin not a Tahr was to be seen. After that we went back to Gary's usual modus operandi and yet another ten-day three species hunt was successful.

Here's a short story relating to four-wheel-drives. As a change (for me) I decided to locate from one of our huts well towards the head of the valley, hunting fresh ground for trophy Tahr. My client was a retired earthmoving contractor from California so knew all there was to know about vehicles, four-wheel-drive his (apparent) speciality. Throughout the two-hour drive to the hut my client kept up a running litany of instructions on handling the Toyota. I wasn't about to offer him the steering wheel for it was patently obvious to me he clearly had no knowledge or experience of South Island high country valleys and rivers. We hunted out of the hut for a couple of days and were successful, the Toyota parked at the hut and not used. I figured one more day could see us with a Chamois, but that night the skies opened and boy oh boy did it rain. At daylight the next morning the river was in ragging, roiling dirty flood.

It rained all that day, forcing us to remain indoors at the hut, watching the river rise and rise. Next day dawned fine but the river was at its wildest worst, a day perhaps to find a Chamois, but certainly not to try and depart down valley. Ironic as it may sound my client shot a Chamois from the hut door just on dark that evening.

I'll not dwell on the four-hour (normal time two), trip down valley the following day. At times we had water over the door handles, much of our gear in the back of the vehicle wet from deep river crossings. I can however tell you that throughout those four hours of tortuously navigating a still flooded river my earthmoving contractor from California uttered not a word, not a single word…

Many years ago I attended a talk by Rex Forrester, the then Hunting & Fishing Officer for the Government Tourist Bureau, Rotorua. Rex was the consummate raconteur, he told many a great tale of his days as a professional guide. One section of his address I shall always remember, he informed the gathering that the profession of professional guide was the most demanding and all-encompassing profession of any on earth. He made it clear that a professional guide required the skills of fifty-odd professions all rolled into one. A guide needed to be all things to all men.

Rex couldn't, in his wildest dreams, have envisaged the true story I am about to tell to close this chapter.

Once again we were guiding a man and wife team, two-on-

one, each seeking trophy Red stag, Tahr and Chamois. By Day Eight we had all six trophies down with Day Nine set aside to take care of final knife work on capes, before getting all skins into the salt and skulls boiled out. That evening my male client informed me that he now regretted not having his Chamois skinned for a full body mount, the same as he'd done with his Tahr. Could we get another Chamois?

I was aware that the weather was deteriorating rapidly so suggested that the best remedy to fulfil his wish would be to bring in a chopper and seek out a very good buck Chamois. As would be expected the question of additional costs were fully discussed with me drafting out this addition to his bill on a separate sheet of paper.

The chopper was with us within an hour of daylight. We flew in seriously marginal weather. In a distant basin we finally located a buck Chamois and after playing a lengthy game of hide-and-seek in thick fog-like conditions the Chamois was secured. On foot I had been unaware of how rapidly a southerly had advanced up the valley; it wasn't until my client and I boarded the chopper that I realised we were in a virtual whiteout. The conditions had deteriorated to such a degree we flew, at snail's pace, out of the basin with me handsignalling the pilot as I recognised familiar landmarks virtually off the tips of the rotating blades. By now the bubble of the chopper was opaque with streaky raindrops.

Somehow I managed to guide the chopper pilot, with further hand signals, until at last we were low in the main valley and able to follow the river back to the lodge. My afternoon was fully occupied with attending to the skinning of the buck Chamois for the full body mount and finalising all the paperwork for the

conclusion of the hunt. My client and his wife were invited in to my office, before dinner, to settle up the account, for we'd be heading for Christchurch early the following morning, to arrive in time for their flight departing for the States.

As was always my practice the full details of the account were presented, along with the additional account for the second Chamois plus chopper hire. The wife wrote me a cheque for all outstanding amounts. Now it was time to party.

But, standing in the door of my office my male client launched into a vitriolic tirade about professional hunting guides and how they were always ripping off hunting clients. To this day I have no idea where his venom came from for I'd not charged him one dollar more than that detailed on the documentation I'd provided in advance. His timid wife was roughly grasped by the upper arm and forced down the passage to their room. Their bedroom door was slammed shut!

Sue had dinner almost ready, a special dinner for that very day was the male client's birthday and the wife had asked Sue to make a special effort for dinner, even asked for a birthday cake. Sue had willingly complied and was in the final last-minute dinner preparations when the "eruption" occurred.

Over the following hour Sue and I knocked on the door of our guests, informing them that dinner was ready, asking if they'd be at the table shortly. We could hear the wife sobbing, the husband demanding that she not answer us! They didn't come to dinner.

Sue and I, plus two other hunting clients, ate our lovely three-course dinner in silence, the birthday cake left standing, uncut, on the dining room table when we all finally retired to bed. The following morning our client stalked out of the lodge, ignoring Sue's invitation to enjoy a breakfast, threw his and his wife's luggage into the back of the Toyota, then climbed into the back seat of the four-wheel-drive, and sat silently waiting. With Sue and the other two clients aboard we headed off on the three and a half hour journey to Christchurch. Throughout that entire trip to the city our two-Chamois-client remained silent, never once responding to our collective attempts to engage him in conversation.

I had dangerously put my life on the line for that man the previous day, solely to get him his second Chamois, always seeking to have very happy clients depart after a fully successful hunt. What lit his wick? Was it that it was his fortieth birthday and he was suddenly feeling old? Was it that his wife had expressed an unwelcome negative opinion on his taking a second Chamois? It certainly wasn't that I'd over-charged him. These years later I'll still have no idea.

All I can say is that the life of a professional guide was never dull, was always demanding, no two days the same. I love to hunt with a consuming passion, always relishing the challenge of yet another stalk. What a perfect vocation it would be if we weren't dealing with the vagaries of the male human being. Yet, for every "difficult" client I guided (and there were few), the compensation was the many dozens whose company we enjoyed, lifelong friendships formed and cemented.

Editor's Note – Gary Joll was the founding President of the New Zealand Professional Hunting Guides Association Inc and the first professional hunting guide in the South Pacific to be recipient of the prestigious Safari Club International Outstanding International Professional Guide of the Year Award in 1992.

SECTION TWO

– Australia

Dust to Mud

Of Barramundi, Buffalo & Banteng

Sitting Up a Tree All Day !!!!

Dust To Mud

It was like an invasion in a science fiction movie.

It sometimes happens that events, additional to the success of the hunt, are remembered long after the mounted trophy has been hung on the wall. An example of this was my Chital hunt inland from Townsville, Queensland, Australia.

Sue and I were planning our annual trip to the United States, to attend the usual round of hunting conventions, when we learned (by chance) that a ridiculously cheap add-on fare to our Sydney-Los Angeles QANTAS Business Class flight would allow us to take a side trip, to anywhere on the east coast of Australia.

And so it was that a few months later we were airborne and on our way to Townsville to hunt Chital on Niall Station, guided by Noel Brown. Noel met us at Townsville Airport and soon had us settled into a spare bedroom in his home. We were to overnight with Noel and his wife for it was far too late in the day to set off for Niall Station, a long four or five hour drive inland.

That was the evening we were introduced to cane toads! Before the evening meal Noel took us into his backyard, for the "introduction"! Neither Sue nor I knew such "monsters" existed in North Queensland.

The drive inland to Niall took longer than I had anticipated so it was somewhat late into the afternoon before we arrived at what was to be our hunting camp for the next few days, a low shed, with just three walls and a roof (naturally) and concrete floor. It was comfortable, well-equipped and highly adequate. The camp beds were comfortable. The weather was very hot and extremely humid so the "open plan" living took advantage of whatever breeze there might be. Sue was nervous of the fact that lizards of various sizes and colours seemed to be permanent residents amid the roof rafters.

Who sleeps well the night before Day One of a hunt at a new

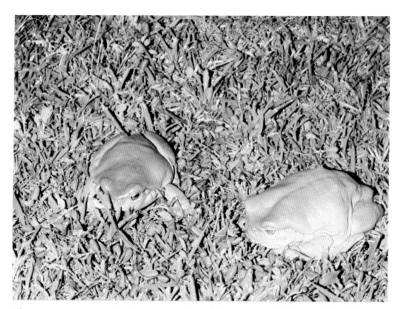

The venomous cane toad was introduced in to Australia from Hawaii in 1935 to try and control a native cane beetle. Weighing as much as 1.8kg and about the size of a large human male hand it is estimated the Australian population is 200 million and increasing.

location, hunting a new species? Add to this extreme humidity, very high night time temperature PLUS no end of many strange noises in the night, PLUS a nervous wife, and I would guess I slept little that night. With the shed not having a fourth wall the early rising of the sun denied any further chance of sleep.

Sue was happy to enjoy breakfast in bed, offered by Noel, then off Noel and I went.

The beautiful red-coated white spotted Chital (or Axis) deer had always fascinated me. All deer are graceful when they move, but to me the Chital epitomised absolute grace and beauty. I learned much about Chital during the next hour or so. When we came across the first small group Noel shut off the engine and my lessons began.

That's when I learned that unlike temperate deer species worldwide the Chital had no annual calendar of behaviour. The rut took place all year so fawns could be born on any and all months of the year. Growth of antler occurred through the year so on any given day a hunter could see stags with very recently cast antlers, antlers in every stage of velvet growth, newly striped pale antlers not yet rubbed and colouring up, fully coloured antlers, the stag rutting. BUT, the other piece of information I learned early that morning was the fact that very often, due perhaps to the environment, many stags suffered broken tynes, even smashed main beams, within a few days of colouring up their antlers.

All this information, relating to antlers, meant that while a trophy hunter may view fifty stags during a day of diligent hunting, the law of averages allowed that maybe only a handful were in full coloured-up antler and without any breakages.

It was easy for the Chital to play hide and seek in this type of landscape especially so after they'd roll in the red dust then stand like statues in the dappled shadows of the ever present gum trees.

I was also amazed to learn, that morning as we studied each new group of deer encountered, that despite the fact that the deer had a bright red colour with bold white spots, they weren't that easy to see. The terrain at Niall is red earth country, very red. The deer apparently rolled in the dust regularly. Place a group of deer with red coats and white spots, having rolled in red dust and standing in the dappled shade of the inevitable gum trees, and the deer simply seem to disappear!

The terrain was generally flat, with patches of brush, many a gum tree, with the flat plains interpersed with deep dry gulches where obvious excessive rains, during the wet, had gouged these

67

meandering "gutters" many ten to fifteen feet deep.

These gutters allowed for relatively easy stalking for when a distant group of deer were sighted, with a prospective trophy stag, Noel was able to guide us, via connecting gutters, to within easy shooting distance.

So it was that by about 11am we were taking the usual photos followed by careful skinning of the cape. Back at camp in time for lunch. That afternoon Noel took care of the caping while, after a siesta, Sue and I had a very refreshing swim in a nearby billabong. We had a second or two of excitement when Sue sighted a small garter snake swimming between the shore and us. Swimming was terminated when we felt many "somethings" nibbling at our legs! Noel informed us the "nibblers" were tiny harmless fish.

Late into the afternoon we did our best to be as tidy as possible for Mick Anning and his wife had invited the three of us to dinner at the homestead. Sue and I'd never seen a dwelling like the Niall homestead before. Most of the exterior walls, and also interior walls, were completely open for the lower couple of feet and it seemed that all were clad in corrugated iron.

Rustic as the dwelling may have appeared to us the dining room table was far from rustic. Mrs Anning had set a lovely table and what a fine dinner we enjoyed with those fine outback folks. Much conversation flowed for we were visiting outback Queensland for the first time in our lives and how different their

The author's trophy Chital stag. With their striking beautiful red coat and white spots the author considers the Chital to be the prettiest and most graceful of all the deer species.

way of life was to ours in the remote New Zealand Southern Alps.

Towards the end of the meal, maybe when she rose from the table to make coffee, our gracious hostess stepped back from her chair and uttered a soft – "Damn!"

It was like an invasion from a science fiction movie, for silently moving across the concrete floor of the dining room were a multitude of tiny frogs. They were everywhere. Mick and his wife, and Noel, were used to such night time invasions, Sue and I were not. No-one actually informed Sue and I why we were experiencing such an invasion, I guess because it was so much a part of their lives it wasn't all that noteworthy of comment.

Our last surprise for that day was when we departed the homestead. Noel flicked the headlights of his station wagon on high then drove in a wide arc around a large flat, of forty or fifty hectares or more, immediately in front of the house. Dare I say I saw two hundred deer in the headlights?

During the evening meal Noel has expressed to our host that he'd been a little disappointed that he'd not got me a real Top Shelf trophy. In response Mick suggested that perhaps we should make an early morning hunt in the hope to sighting two or three very good stags, whose location he explained to Noel.

It was going to be yet another short night. It was, for no sooner had we turned off the lamp than it started to rain. Rain!! It hammered on the roof with such volume and violence conversation (and sleep) were impossible. It drummed on the roof all night like a thousand drummers drumming, a cooling fine mist drifting onto our faces.

What a new world we looked out onto at dawn. The ever-rising dust of yesterday was now a glutenous clinging red mud today. The dry "gutters" which had aided us in making a successful stalk yesterday were today bank to bank with roiling red torrents of water that looked more like thick red paint than water.

Between the Niall homestead and our camp was a very deep gutter across which was a bridge constructed exactly like one of our steel pipe cattle stops. There was no sign of the bridge; it was many metres underwater. Noel and Mick were having a shouted conversation, trying to hear each other above the roaring of the torrent. It was still raining.

The gist of the conversation was that Noel felt sure he had a snowball's hope in hell of getting back to Townsville, in his two-wheel-drive station wagon, after such a deluge, could he make use of one of Niall's Toyota 4 x 4's? Mick readily agreed, but, all the four-wheel-drives were on his side of the inundated bridge! Noel (plus Gary and Sue) would have to wait until the bridge could be crossed. Back to camp, and wait two days.

With one of his members of staff walking ahead of him Mick drove his brand new 4 x 4 Toyota Land Cruiser across the bridge while there was still about 30cm of flood water covering it. Incidentally the Niall member of staff was a very fine looking Aborigine. Sue, standing there in the mud and rain, felt it only polite to speak to the lad. He replied in the most perfect English. Further conversation informed Sue he'd been raised in a very strict Catholic school where only "proper" English was accepted.

As mentioned above, Mick Anning's four-wheel-drive was brand new, he'd taken delivery the same day we'd driven from Townsville, arriving at Niall after us. Noel and Mick agreed

The previous day this watercourse was dry and dusty, not a sign of water. After a night of torrential rain the bridge between the hunting camp and Niall Homestead was under 5-7 metres of water.

that with the onset of "The Wet" chances of successful hunting was gone for it would be impossible to cross any of the flooded gutters. Best that Noel, Gary and Sue pack up and head for Townsville, Gary driving the new Toyota, following Noel, and if he got stuck Gary could pull him out of the mud and back into the hard. That was the plan. No one asked Gary if he minded having the responsibility of driving someone else's brand new

Two days after the cloud burst heralding the beginning of the wet the access bridge to Niall Homestead was still covered by knee deep water, however, Mick Anning successfully crossed in his brand new Toyota.

vehicle in rather adverse conditions. We made it to Townsville without Noel once getting stuck in the mud. I sensed that my co-driver was nervous much of the time.

NOTES:

As mentioned previously the Chital, or Axis, deer is one of the prettiest of all deer species, the name 'Chital' arising from the Hindi word for spots – cital. Often this species is referred to as "the spotted deer". If a trophy hunter were to have just one of the species of South Pacific deer life-size mounted there is only one to consider.

With a shoulder height of around 36 inches (91cm) and a body weight of 180 to 200lb (82 to 91kg) a Chital stag is almost the same weight and size as a Fallow buck – shoulder height 36 inches (91cm), weight 150 to 200lb (68 to 91kg) – but perhaps longer in the leg, shallower in the chest, less bulky in the body.

As is typical with most Asiatic deer Chital stags will carry six point antlers, 3 x 3.

OF BARRAMUNDI, BUFFALO & BANTENG

This billabong was about one kilometre in length and from 70 to 80m wide, not a large tract of water, but home to about 200 crocodiles, many barramundi and catfish which the crocs fed on.

Ray Allwright spoke from the bank behind me.
"Gary, turn around very slowly, try not to make any ripples and get yourself back to dry land."

In response to this clearly urgent instruction I turned slightly and gave Ray a questioning look. His response was – "This billabong may be only 1km long and no more than 70m to 80m wide but our best estimate is there are more than two hundred crocs living here. And, we've seen one that is about 5m long."

Needless to say that upon hearing Ray's words I obeyed his instructions with some measure of alarm. At home in New Zealand I always trout fish in shorts and light boots, never waders, and as a matter of unconscious habit wade where ever I can to get a better cast at a likely spot for a trout.

But, I wasn't in New Zealand, I was having a sort of busman's holiday with Ray Allwright, part owner of Wimray Safaris, based out of Darwin, Northern Territory, Australia and this morning we were fishing for barramundi. I had figured the fish were likely to be on the outside edge of the weed bed so a cast along that frontage should prompt a strike on the Nils lure I was using. This being my very first visit to the Northern Territory I hadn't given the slightest thought to crocodiles!

For some years we had worked with Ray and his company promoting trophy hunting in the South Pacific, so when Ray made the suggestion that when our New Zealand guiding season was over I should visit the Territory to gain a first-hand understanding of his operation, to better promote it at our joint booth at conventions in the United States, I accepted immediately.

Early that morning we'd taken the alloy dinghy and motored to the furthest point on the billabong from Ray's Wildman Camp. While Ray was busy securing the dinghy I'd waded into the tepid water, a creature of habit. Ray's warning was a gut-wrenching wake-up call for me for I had sufficient knowledge of crocs to know that they attacked by stealth, never offering any form of warning!

Why were we fishing for barramundi? Later that day Ray and his team had a busload of tourists arriving to stay the night at their bush camp and dinner would feature fresh-caught barramundi. Ray and I had a commission to catch enough good-sized fish to feed thirty people. For the next couple of hours we fished from the shore or from the boat, not once did I put even my big toe in the water!

And, boy, we caught fish. We were fishing with Nils lures. Ray obviously knew exactly which coloured lure to use – he'd lived his entire life in the Territory – for I was catching a fish with almost every second cast. The strike was light, more like a kahawai than a trout, the fight nothing like rainbow or brown trout, or kahawai. And, I was learning that although I hadn't seen one, there were indeed crocs in that particular billabong, for periodically there would be an eruption of water close-in against the water lily beds. Imagine the scene. It is perfectly quiet, the only sound the soft call from numerous multicoloured birds, no intrusion of "civilisation"…

Then, too close to the boat for comfort (for me) an eruption followed by a brief thrashing, then quiet. Ray explained that the crocs were catching fish, but as a croc is unable to swallow under water they have to surface to do so. Amazingly I never did actually see the crocs when they surfaced for it all happened too quickly.

We were catching fish in the 6lb to 10lb class, so when Ray was content that we had enough for the evening meal we motored back to camp where the fish were taken care of and

The author is all smiles for in hand he has two ten pound barramundi, caught in a croc-infested billabong.

I had the afternoon free to relax. I had a swim in the pool and even took a siesta for the heat was starting to cause me some degree of discomfort. Ray had told me that I must drink a litre an hour, and if I didn't pee every couple of hours I wasn't drinking enough!

Soft drinks and Coke was freely available in the camp fridge but within a few hours I was suffering from too much sugar and feeling rather "queasy", so I made me a very large pot of tea, and refrigerated it. Cold tea was my constant drink of choice for the remainder of my visit to the Territory.

For the next couple of days I was "camp boy" and general "dogs body" and I had a great time. I would serve at table, wash dishes, help keep camp tidy AND go catching barramundi whenever a fresh supply was required. Wimray Safaris – the name of Ray and his partner's outfit – ran a very professional

Sensing that the author didn't believe his comment that the billabong contained perhaps 200 crocs, Ray took Gary spotlighting late one evening.

operation, a fine camp.

Over the duration of a couple of days fishing on the billabong I hadn't seen hide nor hair of a croc so (politely) asked Ray if he was giving me the usual tourist pitch about the crocs? His response was to ask me if I was game to take the dinghy and a spotlight and have a tour of the billabong long after dark. I was intrigued, obviously, so immediately accepted…

We saw crocodiles, dozens and dozens of crocodiles in the spotlight. They were literally everywhere along the shoreline of that billabong. I lost count of how many I saw during my thirty minute "Croc Safari", but more than fifty wouldn't be an exaggeration. Like all good tourist guides Ray kept his best croc story up his sleeve until we were safely back on dry land. That's when he asked me to help him tip the dinghy on its side? He then switched on the spotlight and pointed the beam at a series of regularly spaced indents in the hull, indents very like those made by a very hard strike with a ball-peen hammer. That's when he informed me this very dinghy had been attacked by a 6m to 7m salt water croc and the indents where from the croc's teeth…

Noel Bleakley was Ray's partner in Wimray Safaris and he would be my guide and mentor for the next chapter of my Northern Territory Safaris. We departed Wildman Camp by Toyota at 6.30am and would travel for ten hours before reaching Ray and Noel's Buffalo hunting camp on Gimbat Station. That's the day I learned just how vast the Northern Territory is and how HOT. Throughout that entire day we didn't see a petrol station, country store, township; the only sign of civilisation was the road we travelled. I don't recall seeing a single homestead.

Most of the day we seemed to drive through mile after mile of burned over gum forest, not a blade of green grass to be seen, the only relief being the incredible variation of colours of the rocks and soils, flashes of colour from birds in flight.

Our "air-conditioning" in the Toyota was to have every window open, in the hope that the breeze would cool us down. It didn't cool me at all. No doubt Noel, who had also lived many years in the Territory, was used to the heat, I wasn't. It is really difficult to combat extreme heat, unlike extreme cold. I've spent a few days in the Antarctic and part of a winter in Alaska, where in both cases it is possible to dress appropriately and stay warm. How do you dress appropriately to stay cool in severe heat? Within hours I was bathed in excess sweat and sticking to the vinyl seat. This "stickiness" was overcome when I asked Noel to stop and I draped my towel over the vinyl, both to stop me sticking to it and absorb the sweat. When the opportunity offered we would both very slowly and gently wade, fully dressed, into creeks we crossed, where we would soak our clothes thoroughly. Over the next hour or so the evaporation of muddy creek water would have a cooling effect.

Finally at Gimbat Camp we settled in and before attempting to prepare a meal we both had a good soak and soap in the Katherine River, always trying to make as few ripples as possible…

Day One of my Buffalo hunt was twelve hours of Toyota travel beginning at 6am. We cruised mile after mile of country, seldom on any form of track, seeing very few Buffalo, little recent sign. The terrain was a copy of what we'd travelled through the day before with dense burned-over gum forest always restricting

The outback in Australia is not dissimilar to the bush in South Africa. This is a scene typical of the country where the author hunted Buffalo. He noted that the Buffalo were in much better body condition than the domestic cattle.

any opportunity of a long view of more distant country. The landscape lacked any hills or hillocks so we were never offered a chance of gaining a high point and glass for game. As had happened the day before the heat was really starting to distress me. I was drinking mug after mug of cold tea from the Esky on the back of the Toyota, and we were regularly dunking in whatever water we came across, offering relief for an hour or so. Indicative of how hot it was is the information that a burn would result from touching any part of the body of the Toyota, touching a part of the metal of the rifle would also burn. I was deeply concerned for the film in my camera for I knew extreme heat was not kind to film.

The one observation that remains in my mind is the fact that the few Buffalo we did see looked to be in much better condition than the domestic cattle!

On Day Two Noel changed tactics. That's the day we cruised close to the Katherine River, never far from the water, and we saw a lot more game. The day was divided into two parts, morning hunt, late afternoon hunt, with a siesta during the hotter mid-part of the day. We saw a lot more game, than the day before, even a couple of immature bulls, not yet with large enough horns to be classed as trophy.

Day Three and yet another change of tactics by Noel. We were hunting in October, the last Buffalo hunt of the season for Wimray, so the area had been hunted almost continually for six months and Noel figured the Buffalo had become wary of the sound of vehicles. That morning we didn't hurry to depart camp for Noel had observed that it was about 11am that we'd seen the most game the day before, all very close to the river. We crossed

the river and turned left instead of right and after cruising for a time departed the vehicle and began a slow wander along the bank of the river.

The ground underfoot was soft sand; we made virtually no sound as we moved slowly forward. That's how a Buffalo bull came walking directly towards us! His head was down in the typical Buffalo carry of head while wandering, no doubt his mind fully occupied with thoughts of his first thirst-quenching drink for the day.

Fortunately the bull didn't see us slip off to the side, so as he ambled past us I was able to put a .338 projectile neatly into the base of his neck from a range of about thirty metres. As I hastily worked the bolt, for I'd expected the bull to drop dead in his tracks, the bull spun, offering the other side of his neck. That's where I placed my second shot. This was the first time I'd used a .338 (provided by Wimray Safaris) and I suspect a .375 or .458 would be better medicine for Buffalo bulls. However, at last I had a nice trophy Buffalo bull on the ground.

Noel knew I'd had more than my share of experience skinning out trophies so after the photos were taken he set off to bring up the Toyota, while I made a start on skinning. That task went smoothly, smoothly that is until I tried to roll the bull over to skin the underside. No matter what I tried it was as if the bull was glued to the ground. I struggled to get as much skinning done as I could until Noel arrived… He didn't arrive? An

Gary with his trophy Buffalo. The real work began with the removal of the cape and skinning preparatory to salting it down. With the extreme heat (40°C) a cape will spoil within a very short period of time if not cooled and salted as quickly as possible.

76

After many months of being continually hunted the Buffalo at Gimbat sought distant pastures at the sound of a vehicle. This bull was the exception, giving the author a chance of a photo of a bull in typical Buffalo hunting terrain.

appreciable period of time elapsed after I'd done all the skinning I could and yet I could hear no approaching Toyota? Sitting on a dead Buffalo bull, in the middle of nowhere in the Northern Territory, in utter silence, slowly works on a man's imagination to the point where he starts into the 'What if's…?'

When I finally heard the vehicle approaching, a couple of hours had elapsed, and I do admit to feeling a wash of relief upon hearing the slow beat of the diesel motor growing slowly louder. It transpired that in attempting to cross the river Noel had got the Toyota stuck in a patch of soft sand, he'd spent a couple of hours winching it forward on to hard ground.

Noel expertly used the vehicle winch to roll the carcass of the bull, so we could complete removing the cape. It was a two-man task to heft skull plus cape onto the back of the Toyota. The Esky provided us with a much-needed intake of liquid and food.

That morning, as we had departed the Gimbat Camp, I'd taken note of the fact that we were travelling in the direction of the shadows from the trees cast by the morning sun. After we'd loaded my trophy bull into the back of the vehicle Noel started the motor then informed me next stop would be camp. Fine. But, within minutes I checked the shadows cast by the trees to clearly see that according to my observations we were heading away from camp!

What to do? Noel had lived most of his life in the Territory, I had been there just a few days, yet my every instinct told me we were not heading towards camp. Remember, the whole landscape for hundreds of kilometres in every direction looks exactly the same; a man could go hundreds of kilometres in the wrong direction without knowing it if he wasn't taking note of where the sun was at that time of the day. (Noel wasn't carrying a GPS)

So strong was my gut feeling, that Noel was heading away from camp, I finally casually asked if he'd seen any familiar landmarks, for him to immediately respond to the negative and also ask me if I felt we were heading in the right direction? Bingo! After telling Noel about my taking note of the shadows from the trees as we'd departed camp Noel immediately turned the Toyota around and for maybe thirty minutes we travelled in silence, each searching for some indication to confirm our present route.

It was with palpable joint relief that we came onto wheel tracks we'd made earlier in the morning, a quick inspection of the tread marks confirming we were indeed heading for camp on our current course. Even with my very limited experience of the Australian bush I can easily understand how persons can get lost, for to the inexperienced person there are no distinguishing features to set a course from. No doubt the modern GPS will alleviate future fatalities in the Aussie bush, provided everyone carries one when hiking or hunting.

With my Buffalo cape finally in the salt, after about four hours joint effort by Noel and myself, my Territory Safari was more or less concluded. I had a further three or four days to spend with Noel and Ray before my return flight to Sydney and New Zealand, so what to do with the available time? We'd roughly measured the trophy as scoring 94½ for SCI, a Bronze Medal. It was late that evening that Noel confided that I was his first Buffalo hunting "client" and this was his first visit to the Gimbat Camp hunting area. Aware of this information I have to say he did extremely well.

Wimray Safaris had a concession on the Coberg Peninsula for the hunting of Banteng, but all ten of their annual permits had been pre-sold with the last hunt of the season due to begin within the next forty-eight hours. No I'd not have a chance at a Banteng this time around.

After we'd tidied camp and washed our meal dishes Noel got busy on the radio. It was well after dark when he informed me of "The Plan". Next morning a pilot would fly in with a light aircraft, take over Noel's Toyota and set off for Darwin. Noel would pilot the aircraft and take me scenic flying over the Northern Territory, including Kakadu National Park. Great.

And that's what we did. From the air a man begins to comprehend just how vast that Northern Territory is. Yes, I flew over Kakadu, marvelling at the landscape, the landforms, the colours. It was while we were high over the East Alligator River that I spotted what appeared to be a dozen or more very long dugout canoes drawn up at a bend in the river. I pointed these out to Noel and commented that I had no idea the Aborigines had the skills to make such canoes. Noel said not a word, he just tipped the Beechcraft Baron on its left wing and down, down, down we went.

We were only a few hundred feet above the river when we flashed over the "dugout" canoes. Christ, they weren't canoes they were gigantic salt-water crocodiles. Pulling lots of "G"-forces we made a steep banking turn after which Noel applied the flaps to bring us slow and low over the crocs once more. I have no idea how big those giant reptiles were but 6m to 7m in length wouldn't be a bad guess. For a few minutes we stayed low over the river, following its many bends and sweeps, seeing more and more such giants.

Finally, Noel pulled power and with a gentle banking turn we set course for Darwin. From time to time Noel was busy on the radio, but as I wasn't linked in with the radio system I had no idea of his conversations. But, after fifteen to twenty minutes, after apparently setting course for Darwin, he made a modest change of course to our right and after settling the aircraft on this new course turned to me, and over the noise of the engine shouted that we were making a change in course. Smith Point was our new destination.

I knew Smith Point was Wimray's camp on the Coberg Peninsula where they hunted Banteng under a permit system operated by the Aborigine tribe owners. Conversation in a light aircraft is not all that easy so I just sat back in my seat marvelling at all that was unfolding below. I wasn't surprised to see Ray Allwright in the airstrip at Coberg, there ahead of his last Banteng hunting client for the season.

It wasn't until I had been shown to my well-appointed cabin, with front door view of the sparkling ocean, and had been told how to operate the hot water solar showers, that Ray stopped me in my tracks with a question.

"How would you like to take a Banteng trophy?" He rushed on to explain that one of his arriving party of two had decided against taking a Banteng. This left Ray with one pre-paid Banteng permit unexpectedly available at the very end of his season, with me his only prospect of using the permit.

The permit was mine. If I wished to accept his offer, we would hunt at daylight the following morning for the hunting party had arrived in Darwin without their luggage and there would be some delay before they arrived at the Coberg. This gave Ray and I time to seek out a trophy Banteng for me. Did I accept Ray's wonderful offer? You know the answer to that question.

We departed Smith Point Camp with the first light of the new dawn. Under local Aborigine regulations no Banteng are allowed to be shot until after 18km from the village. (The point marked by a 44-gallon drum.) Banteng were actually feeding on the nearby airstrip, but local regulation had to be adhered to. So, we cruised the roads on the Coberg seeing small groups of Banteng, some immature bulls, nothing that screamed "trophy" at us.

Later I learned we'd driven 80km before we turned off on to a sidetrack that led down towards a shallow lagoon. The Banteng sign here was clear to see in every direction, but a very large tree, down across the track, stopped any further forward progress. We had no choice but to backtrack and continue searching the main access track. We were continually seeing Banteng, many more sightings than Noel and I'd had of Buffalo, so it figured on the law of averages that we would eventually sight a trophy bull. We did. He was well off the track and seemingly not greatly concerned about us slowly stopping the Toyota and sneaking off into the trees, me rifle in hand.

That's when I discovered the floor of the gum forest on the

The author with his Silver Medal Banteng. In 1849 Banteng were introduced to the Coberg Peninsula to provide sport hunting for a garrison of British troops. It is probable that the author's trophy was the first taken by a Kiwi hunter.

Coberg was deeply littered with potato chip crunchy dry gum leaves. Even the most careful placing of a foot resulted in a crisp "crunch". Trying our best to be as quiet as possible we used the tree trunk to mask our approach, but although I guessed we'd not been seen we were clearly heard by the bull for after looking towards our direction he started to move slowly away. That is when we threw caution to the wind and moved as fast as we could to follow the bull as he retreated.

From time to time he'd stop and look back towards his back trail, knowing something was there but not sure yet what? Weaving between the many trees we had closed the distance between us to about 100m when he stopped again to look back, this time slightly quartering to his left, exposing his ribs to a slight degree. Hastily I settled the crosshairs on his last rib and touched the trigger. I heard the bullet strike.

Amazingly the bull didn't race off at breakneck speed. He moved off, carrying on in his previous direction, but not at great speed. We were able to successfully chase after him, and the next time he swung his head to look back at his back trail I had time to pause the crosshairs briefly on the left side of his neck and squeeze. He dropped. But, he was still thrashing about so I raced up and at short range drove another .338 projectile into the other side of his neck. At my feet was possibly the very first Banteng ever shot by a Kiwi. When officially measured the horns were 18⅝ inches, Bases – 13½ inches. SCI Score – 64¼ an SCI Silver Medal.

A reader may wonder why I took neck shots on both the Buffalo and Banteng? It was because I had a strong feeling that the .338 (kindly provided by Ray & Noel) just didn't seem like enough gun to drive a killing shot deep into the vital organs of a very large beast such as Buffalo and Banteng. I felt the neck shot offered the best chance, for the projectile had to travel but a short distance through skin and flesh before shattering the bones of the neck.

For the balance of that day we were busy taking care of the Banteng cape for in the heat a cape could spoil within a short span of time. I was a very happy chappy, for I'd be arriving back in New Zealand with a prized and most unexpected trophy, the Banteng, plus a notebook full of memories of so many new and unique experiences.

Despite the Smith Point Camp being right beside the ocean, where there was sometimes a gentle breeze, I was still suffering from the heat, to the point where my whole back had erupted with severe heat rash. Ray and Noel would be busy taking care of their last hunt for the season so a young pilot was instructed to fly me back to Darwin where Ray's wife Diane would take care of me until my due departure. The pilot had been told of my discomfort with the 40ºC+ heat and high humidity, so to provide me with a measure of comfort he set course for Darwin then climbed the aircraft to 10,000ft where it was hoped the air would be cooler. It was while the aircraft was gaining altitude that from time to time the propeller would strike something and make the most unexpected chaff-cutter noise! My pilot shouted to inform me there wasn't a problem; the prop was striking gum leaves lifted into the air by wind up-drafts. Guess what the temperature was at 10,000ft. Yes, 40ºC.

NOTES:

1. Beware of crocodiles.

2. Be VERY alert for crocodiles whenever you are close to water, fresh or salt.

3. When hunting Banteng and/or Buffalo carry nothing less than a .375 with heavy projectiles.

4. Judging horn size on Buffalo is not easy, so rely on your guide.

5. The Northern Territory has just two seasons, "The Wet" and "The Dry" Book your hunt to take place in "The Dry".

6. If you're not used to tropical heat you (like me) will suffer much discomfort. Drink plenty of non-alcoholic, non-sugar drinks, for dehydration is a real risk. At 40 degrees Celsius the heat is a constant and very unpleasant companion.

7. Be fully aware that the heat will ruin a cape within a very short period of time. To cool my Banteng cape we soaked it in the sea for a lengthy period for the salt water will do a cape no harm.

8. Beware of fire ants.

9. Along with barramundi the Northern Territory offers wonderful fishing for a great variety of saltwater game fish.

Sitting Up A Tree All Day….!!!!!

I was confused!

My host and guide was telling me that breakfast would be at 9.30am, two and a half hours after daylight!

Why not a pre-dawn start?

After crossing the Tasman and an overnight in a hotel in Melbourne Jamie Bell's wife Lara collected me early in the morning to drive me to my Hog deer hunt destination away north on the coast of Victoria not far from the New South Wales border. It was to be virtually an all day trip, and I do recall how smooth the road surfaces were.

Late into the afternoon we finally arrived at the marina of the small holiday resort of Metung on the northern shore of Lake King, a very long, but relatively narrow, saltwater bay protected on its seaward side by a string of many low sand islands, all apparently inhabited by varying numbers of Hog deer. One of these islands, Boole Poole, was my hunting destination.

During my long trip from Melbourne I'd learned from Lara that Jamie wouldn't be guiding me, as he was busy with another hunting party, my guide would be Dennis Crane who owned the island I was to hunt on. The fact that Jamie wouldn't be my guide didn't bother or concern me too much, for I figured the guy who owns the land probably knows more about the deer and trophy prospects.

After brief introductions my gear, plus boxes of groceries, were loaded into Dennis' cabin cruiser for the fifteen to twenty minute trip across the saltwater lake. As we approached the island I noticed that indeed the land was very low with plenty of the expected gum trees, tall tea tree, plus large areas of waist-high fern. Other than the airstrip there seemed to be very little open grasslands, but plenty of sand. Even before we had landed I saw the first of the many kangaroos inhabiting the island.

Dennis' "camp" is four adjoining motel units, all very nicely equipped and maintained. I could see that on my Victorian trophy hunt I would not be "roughing it". After dumping my gear in my assigned unit I found myself with a cool beer in hand, to be shortly followed by a fine meal prepared by Dennis' wife Pat, "camp mother" for the duration.

It was after dinner that Dennis set out the plan for Day One of my hunt, telling me there was no need to set an alarm for breakfast would be at 9.30am! Yes, two and a half hours after sunrise! One of my pet hates (as a professional hunting guide) is a newly arrived client who, within the first couple of hours of arriving in camp, bombards his guide with a multitude of questions. So, I sat back and listened, figuring that the passage of time would reveal everything to me. I retired for the night, lulled by the soft sound of waves breaking on the shoreline just 100 metres from "camp".

Having deliberately left the drapes to my room open I was fully awake with the very first flush of light in the eastern sky. How could a man sleep-in on Day One of a new hunting adventure on foreign soil? Dressed in my camo gear I quietly let myself out the back door of my unit and with slow gentle steps made my way towards the tall tea tree brush not twenty metres away. I found a track to follow, my footsteps almost soundless on the soft sand. I wanted to discover a little more about my surroundings before breakfast.

The track meandered through the tea tree but in the soft pre-sunrise light I could see that a clearing was coming up. With absolute caution I took one last step into the clearing. About a dozen pairs of eyes were watching me. Just for a second. Then that dozen or more kangaroos exploded into action, crashing through the tall fern, racing to the far side of the clearing to disappear into the tall tea tree. What a racket those 'roos made. Before me was a clearing of about 20ha completely surrounded by tea tree about three times the height of a man, the clearing covered with knee-high bracken fern. If this is Boole Poole, how does a man secure a trophy stag? How does he actually see a Hog deer? How does he avoid the ever-present kangaroos?

When I presented myself at 9.30am for breakfast my host/guide's first comment, he was grinning, was - "You went for a little walk at daylight? I guess now you know why it is impossible to hunt hoggie's by stalking." Dennis went on to explain that a fully adult stag would stand no more than 26 inches (.66m) at the shoulder and weigh no more than 40kg. With all the kangaroos about, and the Hog deer being shorter at the shoulder than the height of the bracken fern a man would have to be extremely lucky to even see deer in such terrain.

He continued: "Gary we hunt these little rascals from tree stands. I've used heavy equipment to create a number of water

Typical Hog deer habitat at Boole Poole, coastal northern Victoria.

holes close to suitable trees where we have built tree stands. The deer come to these to drink between about 11am and 2pm, so if we are up a tree stand well in advance of 11am we'll have every chance of seeing a stag or two." Dennis went on to explain that poaching on the property was a continuing problem so he'd built his tree stands as high as he could, reached only by using extra long ladders that he removed from each tree stand whenever he wasn't using them.

We were in our first tree stand about 10.30am. Dennis had provided comfortable folding chairs, an Esky with cold drinks and food, so we settled down in comfort to wait. One of Jamie Bell's .270 Sako rifles was loaded and within easy reach. I was

dressed head to foot in appropriate camo gear, including camo hat and gauze face mask. This particular tree stand was exactly 100m from the man-made waterhole. I guess we were towards the edge of a 50ha clearing fully bordered by tall gum trees. There was not a lot of tea tree but the entire clearing was carpeted in bracken fern, virtually no grass to be seen.

With the water hole 100m away Dennis and I were safe to hold whispered conversations for the wind was blowing from the direction of the waterhole. That's how I learned Hog deer didn't like adverse weather conditions such as a cold wind or driving rain. The easterly wind that day was somewhat bone chilling, even if it was only 1st April, so in five hours we saw just eight deer – three small stags, one spiker, four females. Yes, a slow day, but highly enjoyable for it was the first time in my life of hunting that I'd sat in a tree stand, passively watching deer coming and going absolutely unaware of our being up the tree.

On Day Two we were up the same tree stand at the appointed hour, but within an hour it was clearly evident something was amiss for we saw not a single deer. Poachers? Dennis was restless with this lack of success, so about 11.30am we climbed down from the stand and after travelling about ten minutes in Dennis' worst-for-wear old Toyota, we arrived at another tree stand.

We'd hardly settled ourselves into our chairs before deer started appearing, obviously having moved away with the arrival of the old Toyota, but returning as soon as the motor was cut and silence returned to that section of landscape. Here the ground in front of us was largely sand, with the fern some distance away,

Hunting was from tree stands. This is one the author used during his successful hunt.

The author thoroughly enjoyed watching and photographing deer from tree stands for the deer were completely unaware of guide and hunter watching them.

we'd seen so far. The stag was very interested in a couple of adult hinds contemplating the waterhole so I had plenty of time to study him with my binoculars. He was about forty metres away. Before Dennis and I could have a "conference" the stag chased after a female, across the clearing, and was gone.

That's when Dennis and I had our "conference". Dennis assessed the antlers as being minimum of 14 inches, real trophy class, but we both agreed that it was only Day Two of a five-day hunt so why be hasty? More deer were coming and going and I was getting some great photos. The deer would hear the camera shutter trip, but if I remained perfectly still after taking the shot,

The owners of the property had used heavy equipment to dig water holes for fresh water is extremely scarce. Fresh, salt-free, drinking water certainly attracted the deer. Note all the sign…

the clearing once again surrounded by the usual scattering of tall gum trees and tea tree. Behind us, the direction from which the deer began appearing from, was burned-over tall tea tree.

I was enthralled. Within thirty minutes we had a dozen or more deer coming and going to the waterhole. I had a sense of intruding on their privacy for they hadn't the slightest inkling that Dennis and I were in the tree stand. I guess my personal reaction was that of a peeping tom.

My blissful part daydreaming was broken when Dennis gave my elbow a nudge and inclined his head to our left. From the cover of the burned tea tree walked the biggest set of antlers they soon lost interest in the source of the noise. I think also the fact that the sun was directly behind us was a factor.

Perhaps fifteen minutes later Mr Big returned from the other side of the clearing to once again spend time showing mild interest in each of the adult females "taking the sun" close to the waterhole.

But, as he'd done before, the stag sauntered off into cover after a relatively short time in the open. Dennis initiated another "conference". The core of the discussion revolved around whether or not I considered the stag a trophy worthy of securing. It transpired that I was about the first 'client' Dennis had ever guided for Jamie Bell, so was not accustomed to making an assessment and decision to make a kill. He knew I was a professional guide of many years experience, BUT, nil experience in assessing a Hog stag trophy. We were at somewhat of an impasse.

However, I had a pretty good idea of the direction Dennis' thinking was tracking when he started whispering about the fact that the weather report for the coming two or three days was for gales, heavy rain, electrical storms with thunder and lightning. All elements that would hold all Hog deer in dense cover until the weather mended.

But, Mr Big had walked in and out of the clearing twice already, so would he be coming back today? The clock ticked past 2pm and not a stag were we seeing. I'd got one or two more neat photos and was framing another photo when into the view-finder walked Mr Big….

Author with his fine Hog deer stag, shot from a tree stand. A new experience for this very experienced trophy hunter.

One glance at my host/guide and he's flexing his trigger finger. "Bird in the hand…?" At 40m it was an easy shot, the stag never ever knowing we were up that tree.

It turned out that Dennis' assessment of the antlers was very accurate, displaying his knowledge of the deer, for the tape showed an antler length of 14¼ inches, but what set this trophy apart from many others was the fact that the tip-to-tip measurement was 13 inches (usual tip-to-tip is 7 to 8 inches) There was no doubt I had me a real neat trophy Hoggie…

Dennis was correct; the weather packed a sad for the next three days.

COMMENTS:

My first and only experience of hunting from a tree stand was fascinating. It was rather like shooting from a mai mai, but no need to be constantly searching the sky. It created excellent wild game photo opportunities. The fact of being very close to deer, for a long period of time, their never knowing they were being observed, was something I enjoyed, and never tired of.

Hog deer are small with a body not unlike that of a pig, barrel-bodied and short legs. Are their short legs the reason for their name? I daresay there are some who have successfully stalked Hog deer, but since my hunt virtually everyone I have spoken with has shot their trophy by climbing a tree and watching game trails, or have done as I did with Dennis, used a tree stand.

With a uniform body colouring (not unlike Sambar) Hog deer are very hard to see when amongst the fern or tea tree. The fact that they have a whole series of tunnels under the tall fern also means that often all a hunter sees is the fern shaking!

If you are planning a trophy Hog hunt give very careful consideration to rifle calibre. My view is a .243 plus heavy projectile would be minimum, for with the dense cover the last situation you need is the stag running off one hundred metres before he dies. If that happened you'd likely never find him. Be sure to nail him and drop him on the spot.

Hog deer hunting in Victoria is expertly managed by the authorities with a legal hunting season. Be sure to comply with all the associated rules. We were legally required to check my trophy in at a local Checking Station where many details were noted and recorded. Poaching is almost a way of life for a certain segment of Victorian deer hunters, best to not get conned into an out of season hunt. Stay legal.

When hunting Rusa in New Caledonia I observed the deer moving about either side of midday and wondered if they were doing so to drink. It seems Hog deer are similar to Rusa for they share this same propensity to seek a drink around the noon hour. One wonders if this is a trait of all Asiatic deer?

SECTION THREE

– New Caledonia

A Two Trophy Hunt

A Two Trophy Hunt

I had a dilemma.

Does a man squeeze the trigger on a trophy on the first hour of the first day of a seven-day guided hunt?

My flight had arrived at Tonto Airport, Noumea, New Caledonia, long after dark the night before. I'd been met by my guide, not asked if I'd had dinner. I hadn't. At a few minutes after 11pm I was deposited in a motel room, with little ceremony, to be told I'd be called at 4am the next morning. It was after my guide had disappeared into the night that I discovered the motel lacked any facilities, I couldn't even make a cuppa. As you can easily imagine it was a short night and my disposition had somewhat deteriorated. As a professional hunting guide with many years' experience in my craft it was not the way I'd have treated one of my newly arrived clients, but all I could do was "go with the flow".

Pierre, my guide, was hammering on the door of the motel at the appointed hour. I was hastened to dress in my hunting gear, and while my pack was thrown into the back of a sedan I was handed one small French bread roll and a mug of coffee. Breakfast! After a period of dashing through city streets we appeared to finally arrive on a highway leading out of the city. The speed of the vehicle increased appreciably. Fortunately, Pierre a

native Frenchman, had a reasonable command of English, so as we raced through the dark he explained that he wanted us to be on the top of a forested ridge, overlooking a large area of mangrove swamp, close to the ocean, with the arrival of the dawn. He further explained that during the night the Rusa deer fed in and around the mangroves then with the first signal of dawn in the eastern sky would depart the mangroves to climb up through the forest to bed down deep in the forest. Our mission was to intercept the deer as they travelled the ridgeline.

We had climbed up through the still dark forest to arrive on the ridge and wait for sufficient light to glass the mangroves below. We didn't see a single deer! Clearly my newly met guide was disappointed that his strategy hadn't worked, so in an effort to salvage the morning we started a slow stalk into the wind along the ridge.

The very first Rusa deer I'd ever seen in my life in the wild was a very good stag standing staring at me from about 35m. As one Pierre and I each slipped behind a convenient wide tree trunk, me to use my binoculars to assess the antler, Pierre to begin his exaggerated Frenchman's signal for me to make a kill…

What to do? Don't be hasty, for there are literally seven days of hunting ahead for me. My glasses tell me that the right antler on this stag is somewhat shorter than the left. The right-hand trez is long but the left trez is many inches shorter than the right side counterpart. The brow tynes are short, very short. Nothing pisses off a professional guide more than a client who doesn't follow his guide's directions and instructions, but before me was not a truly top shelf trophy Rusa stag.

You should have seen Pierre's face when I gave him the

Landscape typical of where the author hunted. The brush choked gullies offered wonderful stalking opportunities for both rifle and camera.

Despite the minor language barrier I knew Pierre was not at all pleased with me, so to smooth and improve Kiwi-French relationships I suggested that Pierre and I have a quiet sit and a chat. My hunt was booked with Murray Cameron, a fellow Kiwi and a fine gentleman I'd known for years. I'd just done six months of continual guiding at home at Lilybank Safari Lodge and had arranged to hunt with Murray after my own season closed. I would be Murray's last client for his season. I expressed my surprise to Pierre that Murray hadn't met me at the airport?

I learned from Pierre that he wasn't a professional hunting guide but a French game scientist studying the Rusa deer on New Caledonia. He revealed that Murray was delayed by a group of extremely difficult Australian hunters who were making his life utter hell. Pierre had been asked to meet and take care of me "for a few days" until Murray could get rid of the obnoxious Aussies. That little diplomatic chat, on the ridge overlooking the universal thumbs-down sign followed by the open palm signal for him to stay still and not move. Concealed behind my large tree trunk I slowly removed my day pack and from it drew my 35mm Pentax camera, the 400mm tele lens already fitted. Using my convenient tree as a camera rest I proceeded to take a number of fantastic shots of the Rusa stag as he stood in confused puzzlement at my actions and the noise of the focal plain shutter. When he finally turned and dashed off I was happy that during the very first hour of the very first day of my seven day guided Rusa stag trophy hunt I possibly had an outstanding trophy, the best wild game photo I'd ever taken in my life. Yes, a true trophy.

The author observed Rusa deer regularly moving about late in the morning and early afternoon, offering wonderful opportunities for camera action.

This trophy Rusa stag was photographed in the first hour of the first day of the author's seven day New Caledonian hunt.

mangrove swamps, cleared the air for us both and melted any international discard that could have arisen.

So, for the next three days Pierre "escorted" me to a variety of different properties, always seeing plenty of deer, seeing no stags even slightly approaching the trophy quality of the one I'd photographed. At that time New Caledonia was in the middle of a rather nasty revolt by the natives, such that no one was permitted to carry a firearm in a vehicle on a public road; all vehicles were to be off the roads by sunset. Yes, a full curfew each night. At each property I was offered the use of the property owner's rifle, but because every cartridge had to be formally accounted for I was never offered the opportunity to test-fire a rifle.

By the time I finally met up with Murray at his base camp I'd had some great encounters with Rusa stags. On one property the teenage son was obviously a master at stalking these deer for in dense cover he stalked me to within fifteen metres of an exceptional stag. Like Pierre he gave me the silent nod to make the kill. Like Pierre he was nonplussed when I signalled no. What the lad hadn't seen, or perhaps it didn't matter to him, was the fact that the left brow tyne on this stag was broken off, leaving an inch-long stub. With hand signals, for we were too close to speak; no point in trying to speak either for the lad knew no English and my French was at the level of high school Third Form. Today I am sure that lad still talked about the idiot Kiwi who wouldn't make a kill.

I finally met up with Murray late into the afternoon of his last day of enduring the difficult Aussie clients. I could see that these three had really got under Murray's normally gentlemanly

Rusa are creatures of habit witnessed by well-worn game trails throughout their habitat.

verbally rubbishing all professional hunting guides. I let them rabbit on for they were Murray's guests, and they'd be gone the next day. No need to create even more aggravation for Murray.

Their major gripe was that they'd paid Murray X amount of dollars and in seven days he'd not shown them a Rusa stag any better than the ones they poached out of the Royal National Park on the edge of Sydney. I've been around many a hunting camp in many a country, but never have I experienced such gauche, uncouth and ungrateful rednecks. It was only after the party had finally departed the following morning that Murray explained that he had guided these guys onto some exceptional trophy stags but they all refused to shoot, saying Murray was bullshitting them as to the size of the stags, they knew Rusa stags and Murray was a dishonest bastard.

Murray Cameron is one of life's gentlemen, ethical and honest to the very core of his being, so to be treated in such a manner, for a whole week by these three, Murray required a day or so to recover. He and I had a relaxed day of looking over (maybe) a couple of hundred deer, I got lots of photos, and Murray recovered to his own urbane self. It was that evening, after an excellent meal, that Murray told me he had a particular stag that he hoped we could successfully stalk, a stag the obnoxious Aussies had turned down twice. The stag fed after dark out in the middle of a vast flat plain, retreating to dense cover with the first inkling of the dawn of the new day. The hunt strategy was to be out in the middle of the plain in the dark in the hope of intercepting the stag as he made his way back to cover in the pre-dawn.

Our attempt the next morning was a failure, we were too

skin and they soon got under mine. To this day I have no idea if they knew who I was, that I was a professional hunting guide, but as they guzzled can after can of Murray's beer they set about

It was easy to use lots of film on game photography for the large numbers of deer offered opportunities such as above.

late. So, the next morning we were out there on the plain long before dawn, in fact in total darkness. There was no need for Murray to make any sort of signal for out there at about 200m, in silhouette against the dawn sky, was the biggest set of antlers

I'd seen while in New Caledonia. The stag was on his way back to cover, moving left to right across my front. I was prone so had to ease the weight off my right elbow to following the stag while at the same time swing my body position slightly. As the crosshairs

Gary with his outstanding Gold Medal Rusa stag trophy. This is the trophy that three rumbustious Aussie hunters turned down as too small, yet this very trophy placed number twelve in the SCI record book. Guess who were very poor judges of trophy quality?

settled near the front of his brisket, I touched the trigger. That first shot dropped him in his tracks, I gave him a second for he was still moving slightly, for as I'd not been able to test-fire the rifle I had no idea just how accurate it might be.

Ground shrinkage is a term familiar to us all. We walk up on a fantastic set of antlers only for them to seemingly shrink with every step that takes us closer to our downed trophy. I can tell you for sure that that morning, as Murray and I walked up on that stag, the reverse of ground shrinkage occurred. On the ground at our feet was a monster set of antlers, exceptionally thick and heavily pearled, Murray's guidance and my patience had been fully rewarded; my New Caledonia hunt had produced two fine trophies – one with a camera, one with a rifle.

The absolutely gratifying postscript (for Murray) to my successful hunt is that the stag I killed was one the Australian party had turned down as being too small. I guess it is appropriate for a professional guide to close the story of his hunt with words of advice – "Listen to your guide, he probably does know his craft; is without doubt a better judge of antler than you…. Think about it…."

FOOTNOTE: With beam length of 31 inches and trez tynes at 13 inches my trophy easily qualified as an SCI Gold Medal trophy, in fact placed #12 in the following issue of the SCI Record Book.

COMMENTS:

1. Hunting in New Caledonia today is like it used to be here in New Zealand in the 1950-1960s for on a good day it wasn't uncommon for me to see well over two hundred deer.

2. With such numbers be patient and selective before you squeeze the trigger for there are still many outstanding trophy Rusa stags being shot on guided hunts currently. (Many better than my trophy)

3. Rusa seem to be creatures of habit, clearly indicated by the deeply rutted game trails criss-crossing open plains area and along the edges of cover.

4. As with all deer hunting dawn and dusk are the prime times to be out and about with your rifle, but my observations showed that there was a lot of movement by the deer from about 11am until 1pm. I'm not sure if this movement related to a need to drink, but when most of us would be back in camp after a morning hunt, perhaps even having a pre-luncheon siesta, the deer were up and moving.

5. It was this mid-day deer activity that gave me many chances for great shots with my Pentax and 400mm lens. The lighting was great, plenty of deer to stalk successfully, and not interfering with dawn and dusk trophy hunting.

6. Other than some properties where there was rather thick forest, on steep, (but not high hills) the Rusa hunting terrain on New Caledonia is not at all demanding for older hunters. There is a real need to stalk slowly and be observant, so no need to go racing about and get puffed. Hunting Rusa on New Caledonia is similar to plains game hunting in South Africa.

7. With French the official language some consideration needs to be given when booking your New Caledonian hunt. You have a choice of booking with a local resident guide who has a very good command of English, or you book with one of the Kiwi or Australian guides who offer guided hunts on the island. If you speak fluent French then you have no problems.

8. Since I hunted with Murray Cameron the regulations regarding firearms have been relaxed, so today you are allowed to carry in your own rifle. I would suggest a .270 be the minimum calibre.

9. If you are looking for a wonderful family hunt/overseas trip, New Caledonia is the perfect father and son/daughter hunt destination. Wives really enjoy a week in Noumea shopping.

SECTION FOUR

– Alaska

M·BAILEY

How it Came to Be………..

Ursus Horribilus & Supper Interruptis

Success in a Storm

Camera & Caribou

Running Bull

Walk the Man Down

United States Of America – Alaska How It Came To Be

I held the letter to the light, the better to read the spidery, irregular writing as it climbed across the page with grand disregard for line or spacing.

The address was Palmer, Alaska, USA and the signature – Johnny Luster.

Laboriously I read, word by word, silently cursing Johnny for his English-cum-Indian pigeon grammar. But the meaning was clear:

…you come work for me, I no pay you, you no pay me. You work – you hunt.

After a few years as a primary school teacher I got restless, reached the point where I had no wish to spend much of my adult life within the four walls of a school classroom. I loved hunting and had a hankering to be a professional hunting guide in New Zealand.

But, in those days – the very early 1960s – there was just the one professional hunting guide in New Zealand, Rex Forrester, and he didn't need a trainee.

My reading of such magazines as the American publication – *Outdoor Life* – informed me that countries such as India, Africa and North America had professional guides, so I figured if I could somehow spend time, in no matter what capacity, with a professional guide somewhere, I must learn much before attempting to establish my own guiding business in New Zealand.

Over a period of months I wrote to professional outfitters in the three countries mentioned above. The only reply I received was from Johnny Luster.

That's how Bob Hart and I arrived in Alaska during the (Alaskan) summer of 1963 and started working for Johnny Luster. First we helped Johnny with horseback summer treks into the boondocks with non-hunting customers, but once the hunting season was close at hand we became fully involved with hunting and hunting clients, and our own trophy hunting.

Read on.

Ursus Horribilis And Supper Interruptis

I was about to commit to the three things I'd been told never to do, but under the prevailing circumstances I had no choice.

It had taken us four hours to catch, saddle and load the fifteen packhorses. Our last tasks were to cover each load with a tarp then secure each with a diamond hitch. After tailing-up the horses into two strings, our final action was to tail-up the front packhorses to the tails of our riding horses.

We were a party of four, Charlie the horse wrangler, Walt the client, Bob Hart my Kiwi hunting companion and myself. Walt would lead us out, Bob and I would ride the horses leading the two strings of packhorses, Charlie would take the tail-end-Charlie (no pun intended) watching ahead to be alert for any problems occurring in the pack-strings.

Departing our temporary base camp at Leila Lake we immediately started the long climb up Squaw Creek to where it saddled with Caribou Creek. We then worked our way down, heading for the wide gravel beds of Caribou Creek, far below.

Our brief was to ride as far up Caribou Creek as we could until locating a suitable campsite. The chosen site must have plenty of firewood and be close to the river (for water supply), with the most important factor being that it be handy to a wide expanse of riverbed with sufficient length for a bush pilot to land

a balloon-tyred Super Cub.

After thirteen hours in the saddle we finally found a great campsite that would satisfy all our needs. When trekking with a pack-train it is wise to not stop, for packhorses are notorious for tying themselves in knots, often around trees, when the tension comes off their lead rope. So, by the time we arrived at our proposed campsite it had been eighteen hours since we'd had food or drink.

I guess it took us well over an hour to unpack each horse, hobble those known to wander far during the night, bell one or two of the mares. While Bob, Charlie and I were busy with the horses Walt had got a good fire going and soon had the smoke

First pack string departs Base Camp at Leila Lake, heading for Caribou Creek where the main hunting camp was to be established.

blackened coffee pot on. We decided that due to the late hour we'd cover our sleeping bags with packhorse tarps that night, erecting tents the next morning.

It was about twenty minutes before dark when we finally sat down to enjoy the warmth of the fire, our first mugs of coffee since our pre-dawn breakfast. Walt had been busy at the fire, for after topping up our coffee mugs a couple of times he dished us each a plate of grilled Moose steak, mashed potatoes with green peas.

Bob's bladder was the first to complain at too much coffee. Excusing himself he walked a discreet distance from the fire to "answer the call." We paid him little attention for we were hungry and the Moose steak succulent and tasty.

He had our full attention when he whispered from the edge of the firelight.

"Hey! You guys want to see a Grizzly bear?"

Bob was standing about twenty metres from us, somewhat out of view against the trees forming the edge of the clearing. As one we dropped our half finished meals and moved quickly to join him. He pointed to the steep gravel face about 180 metres distance on the north bank of the creek. Various species of brush and berry bushes dotted the gravel face, many shades of greens. We sighted the bear instantly, it was moving slowly to our right. What a sight. The coat of the bear can only be described as the shade of pale golden honey, with legs and across the shoulders a mid-golden brown. The fur appeared to be long and soft for with each movement of the bear it rippled and shone, caught by the very last rays of the setting sun.

We had no trouble identifying the bear as a Grizzly, for the characteristic shoulder hump was clear to see. All four of us stood, somewhat transfixed by our very first sighting of *ursus horribilis…*

Standing there in the slowly gathering darkness, watching the bear, I was aware of something triggering in my brain, the thought that the bear seemed to be stalking, like a cat would stalk a bird. Stalking? Prey? A couple of quick steps to my left brought instant realisation. I'd not noticed them before, due to the screen of thick brush, but at the foot of the steep bank were two of our packhorses, innocently grazing. The instant I sighted the horses the intent of the Grizzly was patently clear.

Bob had been the first to sight the bear, so under our hunting agreement it was his trophy. (We both held Grizzly Bear Tags). The light was fading, night would be upon us shortly, so Bob would have to dispatch the bear before darkness fell, otherwise we'd be certain to lose at least one horse during the night. After studying the bear for some time with his binoculars Bob declared he didn't wish to kill this bear. As a hunter was allowed only one bear in any given season, and a tag was $US75 Bob didn't wish to rush into killing the very first Grizzly sighted on our hunt.

But there was a salient fact that couldn't be overlooked. If we didn't kill the bear we'd lose some horses. The bear had to be "dealt with". From the time Bob had asked us all if we wished to see a Grizzly I'd viewed the bear with a detached sort of aesthetic/scientific interest, knowing it was Bob's trophy. However, with one short sentence from Bob I was forced to smartly readjust my thinking.

"You take him Gary…"

A myriad of thoughts flew through my head – 'Bob clearly

didn't wish to attempt to kill the bear under the prevailing conditions. The bear must be killed before dark. Bob and I were the only members of our quartet who held Bear Tags and Bob had bowed out.

Once again I studied the bear, which now was slowly reducing the distance to the nearest horse. The colour was attractive, but (as far as I could judge) it wasn't a super large bear. Thoughts like – "bird in the hand; may not see another one; would make a lovely floor rug;" raced through my head. My heart was pounding. Hastily I returned to camp, picked up my 30-06 Husqvarna and checked the magazine. Full. Five extra rounds handy in my pocket. Asking Bob and Walt to back me up if the need arose, and cautioning them to cover my every move, we eased from the cover of the brush close to camp to make our way, bent double, as silently as we could, through the shoulder high brush on the edge of the river flat. Trying to move forward without a sound, fully aware that bears have excellent hearing, I set a course to place me somewhat behind the bear. The hope being that the bear was less likely to see us, while he was intent on stalking the horses.

By now a deep twilight was blanketing the landscape. However, the very light colouring of the bear made it easy for me to follow his movements, for he stood out boldly against the dark grey of the gravel bank. At seventy metres I ended my stalk for in front of me was an extra tall and thick sapling, a perfect rifle rest. Closing the bolt of the Husqvarna with infinite care I slowly raised it to rest the fore end on a convenient fork in the branches. Breathing deeply, to charge my lungs, trying to still my pounding heart, I settled and sighted. Through the scope the bear appeared enormous.

While fighting to keep the scope crosshairs motionless on the neck of the bear my mind was crowded with the many stories we'd hear of hunters being killed or mauled by bears. I was doing everything wrong, I was about to commit to the three things I'd been told not to do while hunting bears, but under the prevailing situation I had no choice.

Johnny Luster our outfitter and mentor had told us time and time again: -

1. Never shoot at a bear that is uphill from you.

2. Never shoot at a bear in dense brush for he'll be on you before you know it.

3. Never tackle a bear in the fading light of approaching darkness.

For a minute split second I was tempted to lower my rifle and sneak away, to gamble on the hope that the bear wouldn't succeed in killing one of our horses. But then it was all taken out of my hands and conditioned reflex took over. The bear turned and looked directly at me. A short breathe. Steady sights on neck. Squeeze trigger. With the blast of the rifle the bear turned end-for-end and raced back the way he had come. Within seconds I'd reloaded and as the bear appeared to dive into a thick brushy gully I triggered off another shot.

Not a leaf stirs. No bear in sight. I searched, my every nerve screaming to give me first warning. Nothing! Risking my very life I opened the bolt of the Husqvarna and thumbed in two fresh cartridges, replacing the two I'd fired. Still silence. Still no sighting. All I could hear was my own heartbeat. We'd been told a bear could stalk a prey soundlessly. I strained my eyes

The author with his first Alaskan trophy a blond Grizzly that was, with obvious evil intent, stalking one of the outfitter's pack horses. Rifle is a Crown Grade Husqvarna in 30-06 calibre with x4 Nickel scope.

The author shows a comparison between his hand and the front paw of the Grizzly bear.

searching the brush ahead, on either side.

At last I saw a small movement of a lighter colour amid the thick dark brush at the head of the gully the bear had disappeared in to. I blessed my Nickel scope for its wonderful light gathering ability for I could see the bear coming downhill towards me. Not taking my rifle from my shoulder I rapid-fired three shots into the front of the advancing bear. Work bolt again.

As that fourth cartridge seats home ahead of the closing bolt I saw the bear more clearly. He was in the open and coming downhill. Without the aid of the rifle scope I can see he was badly hurt, but still coming. I needed to stop him before he

reached the thick brush just thirty metres ahead of me for once within the brush the next time I'd see him he'd be on top of me. He was front-on so this time, I held just under his chin and sent yet another, and another, 180-gr projectile on their way.

The bear began to roll, faster and faster, until he finally disappeared into the waist high brush ahead of me.

"You've got him, you've got him," shouted Bob and Walt as they raced up to me. Walt wanted to hurry over and view the downed bear but I restrained him, for now it is virtually dark and the bear, even if seriously wounded and not dead, held all the advantages.

After loading my rifle with my three remaining shells we

back-tracked about fifty or sixty metres, climbed the gravel face well away from where we'd last seen the bear, filled our pockets with stones, until finally we were standing above the smashed brush the bear had broken during his final tumble downhill. Many stones thrown into the brush registered no reaction. With nervous caution we eased our way down the slope. There below, pale amid the dark brush, was the bear. I had my very first Alaskan trophy.

Have you ever skinned your very first bear by torchlight? Difficult isn't it. After sending Charlie back to camp for torches Bob and I set about skinning the bear. As it transpires we made a terrible job of it for we'd been told the skin of a bear was very much like that of a pig with the hair follicles coming all the way through the skin. We'd been told to be most careful to not cut the root of the hairs for if we did the hair would all fall out during the tanning process. Next morning, in the full light of day, we discovered that in taking care not to cut any hair follicles we'd left an excessive amount of fat on the skin!!

Much of our next two days, along with setting up camp, were spent with our Green River skinning knives, sharpened to razor-sharp, shaving all the fat we could off the bearskin. It was a time-consuming tedious protracted task. Fortunately the weather was cool to cold so no risk of slippage before the skin was salted down.

NOTES:

My bear trophy was not large. The largest grizzlies will "square out" at as much as nine feet whereas mine was just on eight feet. A very large Grizzly could weigh as much as 750lb, so mine would have been about the 600lb mark. Boars are much larger and heavier than sows.

It wasn't until I was in Alaska that I learned there is a wide colour variation in grizzlies. Most bears are shades of dark brown, but mine was a honey-blond, while bears with coats the colour of butter have been sighted.

Near our temporary Leila Lake Base Camp was Gunsight Lodge. On the wall in the bar was the skin of an exceptionally large boar Grizzly that had killed four men. The story was that the men were out flying after a heavy snowfall and they'd sighted where a bear was coming out of hibernation. They'd landed and with a long pole prodded into the bear's den. He'd come out of the den in a very angry state of mind and killed all four.

Did you know that bear fat is a wonderful boot dressing? For the duration of our time in Alaska that is all we used to preserve the leather and keep our feet dry.

Bob and I both carried 30-06 rifles and I would have to say this is a minimum calibre for killing bears. We were using Norma 180-gr projectiles, as a general load for all Alaskan game. Most guides who guide on the large grizzlies and even larger coastal Brown bear use .375s and larger. One of our client (in Alaska) killed Grizzly and Black bear, each with one-shot kills, with a .338. The very first time we'd ever seen this calibre, (in 1963).

You never know when you are going to come upon a bear for they wander a lot and are totally unpredictable. There was a rule in camp that we were never to walk any distance from camp without carrying our rifles. If we were going to the river with a bucket for water we either carried a bucket in one hand, our rifle in the other, or two persons went for water, one carrying two buckets, the other a rifle.

The author on the left, Charley (camp help) centre, Bob Hart (Kiwi) on right, with Gary's Grizzly bear skin. Many hours would be spent de-fleshing the skin after hasty skinning by torchlight.

ready switched on our torches. At first frantic sweeps we saw nothing? Slower and more searching sweeps of the torch illustrated a porcupine on his nocturnal camp visit!!!

After we'd been in our Caribou Creek camp a few days, and got it all set up, Bob and I were woken at night by "snuffling" sounds outside our tent, plus the sound of something being dragged across the ground. By then we'd been fed all manner of stories about how dangerous Grizzly bears were, so we were certain that out there, on the other side of our tent wall, was a hungry Grizzly sniffing for a Kiwi meal. We endured two or three nights with this bear(?) visiting our camp after lights out! Finally, one night, we didn't get undressed for bed, we left the zip on our tent unzipped (for quiet exiting) and had our torches and loaded rifles beside us. When we were once again aware of the bear(?) snuffling close to our tent we sneaked out and with rifles at the

Success In A Storm

We should have stayed in camp where we'd have been warm and dry, but you don't find a trophy while huddling in a tent…!

It was Don the bush pilot who'd taken Bob and I aside to quietly tell us that in flying out from camp, down Caribou Creek on a more direct route to Anchorage, he'd sighted a dozen or more Moose, one of which (in his words) was a giant bull. The Moose were on a large swampy clearing in the middle of the spruce forest.

What with Don flying in numerous clients and Johnny having arrived with a number of guides and a couple of long pack strings of horses Bob and I were busy with a multitude of camp chores for a number of days so could do nothing about the information from Don.

On this particular day we'd taken care of all our camp chores by late morning, all the guides were off and away with clients, we finally had a free afternoon. However, the weather was miserable. Heavy cloud blotted out the sun and blustering winds blew from first one direction, then another, rattling the trees. Rain squalls, chased by the often-screaming wind, drove across the landscape.

All the riding horses were out with guides and clients, so after dressing in our warmest and most weatherproof gear we

Bob Hart in the 'kitchen' area of the Caribou Creek hunting camp. Neither Bob nor the author switched on a light, sat in a chair, or flushed a toilet, for the duration of the hunting season.

set off to walk down Caribou Creek. We were happy to walk for it would warm us and also we'd be less likely to be sighted by any game in the area, two men on foot being far less obvious than two on horseback. The weather really didn't bother us for the sound of the wind buffeting the trees would cover any sound we would make, but how does a hunter find success in such a storm, where the wind is constantly changing, one minute up your arse, the next driving rain into your face?

It took us about an hour and a half of fast walking to finally reach the heavily forested lower slopes of Gunsight Mountain. Somewhere above, we had no idea where, was a clearing and swamp surrounded by dense spruce forest. We soon discovered that the forest was in fact a series of terraces, so decided to climb high in the hope of coming upon a high point where we'd, hopefully, be able to determine where the Moose-swamp was.

Progress wasn't fast for we soon discovered that each of the forest benches was basically a swamp, always a struggle to walk through, the trees less dense, the brush thicker. On the rise to the next bench the spruce trees grew thickly, there was little under-storey of brush. We had no wish to race through the forest for at each next step we could perhaps sight the trophy Moose. Our adrenalin level was high.

For more than an hour we climbed, constantly alert for surely somewhere in the forest was a trophy for one of us. At last we could see that ahead the forest was thinning, we'd finally reached timberline. That's where the force of the storm really hit us, for deep in the spruce forest we'd been sheltered from the full blast of the wind and lashing rain. Standing in the treeless open landscape above the forest verge we quickly realised that the wind had been chasing us from behind. We'd spent all afternoon with the wind driving our scent ahead of us. No wonder we'd seen no game! We'd seen no swamp either?

With the vast panorama of the above timberline landscape opening above we continued to climb, hoping that somehow with further elevation we might, by chance, find our objective. By 4.30pm, we were a good halfway up the mountain the timberline far below, the skyline ridges still a long way off. Up there on the steep cliff faces under the summit we could see the tiny white dots of small herds of Dall sheep. Gunsight Mountain was a sheep reserve, no hunting, so we made no effort to determine what rams were with the ewes and lambs. Driving rain squalls and the constantly buffeting wind made our binoculars virtually useless.

Looking back, in the general direction of camp, we could see low gathering dark grey clouds with rain showers rolling towards us carried by the still swirling, almost gale force winds. We agreed that if we had wet arses now they were going to be soaking wet before we finally reached the comfort of our camp. Camp was a good three and a half hours away; we decided to return to its warmth and comfort.

The full force of the gathering storm hit us full in our faces as we turned to begin descending the mountain. As often happens

View down Caribou Creek from Base Hunting Camp.

with gusting winds there are periods when conditions are almost calm, calm that is until the next gust strikes. It was during one such lull that I happened to look back up the mountain, that's when I sighted the Black bear.

High on the slopes of the mountain, higher than we had climbed, we could see the bear moving across a wide dark grey gravel slide, above which was a narrow dark canyon. Had the bear spent the day in the canyon sheltering from the gathering storm? Was he now out and about seeking food?

Huddled in the sheltered lee of an extra large boulder we sat studying the bear through our binoculars. We watched as the bear moved quite quickly across an area of gravel until reaching a flat terrace beside a narrow dark canyon where he slowed and began moving very slowly, his head always down. Feeding? Although we couldn't say for sure we agreed that perhaps the bear was feeding on berries, and that being the case he'd likely stay on the berry patch for some time.

The impending storm was gathering, the wind moaning around the rock we were sheltering behind, carrying our scent ahead of us. Our only chance of success was to approach the bear from a position where our scent was likely to be funnelled into a confined area and not wafted all over the mountain face. Our attention focused on the narrow canyon beside the flat where the bear seemed to be feeding. We would have to cross two other shallower canyons, before reaching the third, (our objective), but if we climbed in the bottom of the canyon there'd be a chance our scent would be funnelled, pushed by the ever increasing wind force, up and away from the bear.

All our hopes were based largely on the wind velocity increasing, our scent being blasted up the canyon without being dispersed. Any noise we might make, within the canyon, would hopefully be covered by the wind. Once within the canyon would we be able to climb out onto the bench where the bear was?

I was nervously aware that for much of the time we'd be making a blind approach, the bear out of sight for a long period of time. But…nothing ventured, nothing gained. By now cold water was trickling down the back of my neck – maybe we should have stayed in camp where we'd have been warm and dry, but you don't find trophies while huddled in a tent.

It took us threequarters of an hour to work our way across the mountain, cross the two smaller canyons, drop into the third then begin our climb up the sandy floor. Before we'd started our approach we'd marked a lone cottonwood tree as our final objective before making a stalk onto the bear. As far as we were able to judge the tree stood on the rim of the canyon and slightly higher than the terrace where the bear was last seen. If our judgement was correct we would be slightly above the bear thus having an elevated over-view of my target.

The canyon wall comprised crumbling rock and a succession of ledges, all offering plenty of foot and hand holds. We hauled ourselves up to the rim to finally slither over the crest, pausing as we lay flat breathing hard. According to our joint calculations the bear should be below us and no more than ninety metres from where we lay.

Raising our heads ever so slowly we could see neither berry patch nor bear? With my breathing now back to normal I quietly loaded the Husqvarna and edged forward. Bob did the same. Our hope was to sight the bear before he sighted us, a perfect

Author with his Black bear, finally killed within the dense brush in the immediate background.

removing live rounds from the actions of our rifles, closing bolts on empty chambers.

Shit! Not forty metres below the Black bear was racing for the nearest brush-chocked draw. Obviously he'd been feeding, out of sight below, hidden from our view by the roll of the slope, for the entire time we'd been on the canyon rim. Frantically I worked the bolt of my rifle, swung it to my shoulder, hastily sighted. Squeeze. An eruption of grasses immediately about the shoulder of the bear told me that in my haste I've not allowed for the steep downhill angle.

Reload. Bear almost in the thick brush now. Sights on shoulder… Swing well forward… lead… squeeze. The blast from the rifle is flat and muted as the wind whips away the sound. I watched as the bear collapsed. He struggled to rise. He's up and before I could chamber another round he crashed into the thick jungle of brush in the narrow gully. Silence, except for the roaring of the wind as it harasses the lone cottonwood tree on the ridge.

Now we were in trouble. We had a wounded bear on our hands and we can't leave him. I was responsible for not killing the bear; I was responsible for resolving the matter! But, in thick brush? Hell what a mess! With a major storm closing in on us, creating an early dusk, finding a Black bear in dark brush, in poor light, is going to be nervously interesting. I knew before I took my first step into the brush-chocked gully that I'd not see the bear until he moved.

If the look on my face was the same as Bob's I must have looked really frightened. I was afraid. I had myself an unhealthy situation no matter how I approached it, and approach it I must.

ambush. We were out of luck. Ahead, and slightly below us, (we'd read the ground perfectly) was the small bench covered entirely in berry patches. No bear. We sat, disappointed. Together we searched every likely hiding place for a Black bear, to finally agree the bear had probably moved down the mountain to a brush-chocked narrow gully a short distance below the berry flat.

Determined to not be defeated we sat for a further ten minutes diligently searching every possible place a bear may be? On the open ridge top the wind was tearing at our wet clothes, bringing tears to our eyes, our discomfort further exacerbated by disappointment. We'd made a valiant effort. We stood, both

We have a brief conference. Bob would station himself at the lower end of the short gully, killing the bear if it breaks downhill or to our left. I would make an approach from the upper end and also cover the right. We were sure the bear wouldn't leave the security of his hiding place.

My feet rattling stones as I crossed a small gravel slide brought me a memory recall. As a youngster I'd been taken Wallaby hunting in the hills west of Timaru. The older hunters in our party showed how they'd roll large boulders down steep slopes to flush Wallabies from cover. "High Country Huntaways" was their term for these rocks. Could I employ a similar ploy? I filled my pockets with the largest stones at hand. Once close to the upper edge of the small gully I began systematically tossing stones into the thick brush, trying to cover every square metre. A dozen tossed stones scored me nothing, except for a heightening of tension, for with each stone thrown I couldn't be sure that the next second I'd see a very angry bear set on chewing on me.

Stone number fourteen brought a result, a heart stopping deep-throated growl, enough to chill the blood. The next few stones brought the same response, along with the thrashing of one small patch of brush. Bear located. My scalp prickled for with the bear now located the next move was mine. With the bear located I couldn't delay any longer. I had to go in after him. I was very nervous for I knew the bear would certainly hear me approaching long before I sighted him. He would have the initiative.

I knew that there was every chance I would almost step on him before he made his move.

Judging that I had about nine metres to cover before being close to the wounded bear, I shouldered my way into the thick brush, rifle at my hip, ready. Darkness closed in around me as if someone had drawn the blinds. I stood, allowing my eyes to accustom to the lesser amount of light. I stood, willing my senses to reach out in front of me, searching. The vegetation was thick all right, so thick it was going to be difficult to swing my rifle, left or right, without lifting the muzzle. One step at a time I advanced. Time had no meaning now. I could hear nothing but my own pounding heart and the roar of the howling gale as it lashed the brush all around me. Another step. Wait. Look. Listen. Nothing.

My nose brought me first warning. I'd taken yet another hesitant step when I smelled bear! Where is he? Just 1.8m ahead of me a black featureless shape rises up out of the darkness and lunges towards me. For just a split second I paused, settling myself. From my hip the Husqvarna barked. The bear dropped, still an indistinct mass. I could touch his nose with the muzzle of my rifle, without moving my feet.

I shouted to Bob, he raced up to me; we unashamedly hug and do a silly dance. As I said earlier, you're not going to get yourself a trophy huddled in your tent away from a storm…

NOTES:

Of the different species of bear native to North America the Black bear has by far the greatest range. Black bear can be found in virtually every state, ranging from Florida to distant Alaska. Largely nomadic the Black bear wanders far and wide. This makes hunting them a bit of a lottery for it is not easy to predict where a trophy boar may be found. Often such bears are taken as the result of unexpected encounters.

Within this extensive range there is much variation in weight and size with a very large boar weighing up to 600lb and standing up to 40 inches at the shoulder.

Not all Black bears are in fact black. The Glacier or Blue bear, found on a limited range on south coastal Alaska, has a blue steel grey pelt. The Cinnamon bear has a reddish-brown or even yellow-brown. From time to time white Black bears are sighted.

Black bears may not have the reputation for the aggression of the Grizzly, but all bears should be treated with respect and all persons in Black bear country should be acutely aware of just how unpredictable bear can be. During the six months that Bob Hart and I were in Alaska six fishermen were killed, by Black bears, while fishing streams for trout. It was suggested that as the berry crop that year had failed, all Black bears were hungry and so sought food at the trout streams. Seemingly the bears considered the fishermen as trespassers on their private fishing ground.

CAMERA & CARIBOU

Camera in one hand and rifle in the other, while slithering on my belly through low brush was impossible. Propping the rifle against a convenient bush I continued my stalk, intent on getting even closer and better photos.

High above camp, a good three hours climb, was a vast open basin that was on the fall Caribou migration route. We'd been told that Caribou regularly gathered in this basin before making a run down into Caribou Creek, up and over into Squaw Creek to finally cross the Glen Highway to spend their winter in the Nelchina Basin, an area apparently largely snow-free during winter.

We'd already made one exploratory hunt on the eastern rim of the basin and Bob had killed a nice Caribou bull. With the knowledge that the population of Caribou holding-over in the basin was ever changing we decided that we should make another visit, in the hope of finding a trophy bull Caribou for me.

So it was that in the earliest dawn light, before anyone else in camp had stirred, Bob and I set off, heading for the creek bed we'd previously discovered was the best route for the initial part of the climb. Travel was slow for the rocks and boulders in the creek were slick with a crust of ice. The morning was the coldest we'd experienced so far; it was obvious winter was close. We'd learned to climb within creek beds as much as possible for the lower slopes of the mountains were soft with muskeg; climbing was somewhat like climbing a sloping very soft mattress. Such underfoot conditions caused us to lift each leg very high, to clear the spongy muskeg, try it sometime, you'll discover it is quickly very tiring.

It was within the creek that we stumbled onto our first "game", a porcupine snuffling his way through possible choices for his breakfast. All our previous sightings of porcupine had been when they were up trees, so this time we have an excellent opportunity to get a closer look at these overgrown hedgehogs.

The 'Nursery Slope' above Base Hunting Camp so named due to there always being cow Moose and their calves encountered on this vast open mountain face. It is far above the 'Nursery Slope' that the author secured his trophy Caribou.

We'd been warned to never get too close to these rascals for a reflex action in the tail allowed for lightning fast strikes, left and right, leaving twenty to thirty painfully stinging quills imbedded in flesh. Ouch!

At the fork in the creek we followed the left branch, having taken the right the day Bob had got his Caribou bull. This fork was wider and more open. Imprinted in the sand we regularly came upon prints of both Caribou and Moose, and beside one ice-covered side pool a solitary bear print. Our hopes of a successful day were heightened by the fact that some Caribou tracks were imprinted on the still ice-crusted sand.

When the creek finally narrowed to a trickle, chocked with brush and blueberry bushes, we climbed the left bank and soon were hunkered down in low brush on a small hillock. When searching for game with binoculars my habit is to take it carefully and slowly, working to a pattern. First we carefully searched all the country below. Yes, four cow Moose and their calves on what we had named the Nursery Slope for virtually every time we'd looked over this section of country we'd seen Moose cows with the calves.

We didn't hurry our searching, for Caribou have a habit of feeding in shallow depressions, where they are well hidden from wolves, or observation by hunting parties. Eventually the Caribou will show themselves for they have a habit of not staying long in one place, very often running from one location to the next. Alaskans call Caribou "The Ghosts of the Tundra" due to their uncanny ability to seemingly disappear on an open mountain face.

Satisfied that the landscape below held no Caribou we set about glassing the upper section of the basin. Within minutes we had located two bulls high above, skylined in sharp silhouette. They were too far away for our 7 x 35 binoculars to provide a clear assessment of their antlers, so wasting no time we set off, hoping that we'd not have direct personal experience of "The Ghosts of the Tundra".

It took us about ten minutes to cross an open section of the basin until we were safely out of sight behind a long shallow ridge which we hoped would keep us out of sight of the bulls until we were within rifle range. Now on fine gravel, away from the energy sapping spongy tundra, we pushed the pace. Yet, threequarters of an hour later we were still too distant from the Caribou for a shot. It was big, big country!!

Both of us were puffing hard. Exchanging nods we dropped to the ground, a five -minute "breather" was required. Does a hunter have some sort of sixth sense, or is it habit that makes us forever search in the hope of sighting game? These many years later I clearly recall some inner instinct that caused me to sit up and scan the country below, a new landscape we'd not previously searched. With my naked eye I immediately located two bull Caribou, their faces and lower tynes hidden by the low bushes they were feeding on.

My binoculars told me that the bull on the left had small antlers, not worthy of a second glance, but the bull on the right looked to be carrying antlers of trophy proportion, worthy of closer inspection. Forgetting the two bulls far above we set about closing in on our new quarry.

By crawling and using the low brush to our full advantage we closed to within about 350m of the bulls. In those days neither of us owned spotting scopes so we had to stalk close enough to a prospective trophy to be able to evaluate with our 7 x 35s. Jointly we agreed that the larger of the two bulls carried antlers with thick beams and very good upper tynes, we couldn't tell much about the shovel tyne, for both bulls were so intent on feeding they'd not once lifted their heads for the duration of our having them under observation. Perhaps there was a chance for some good wildlife photography for the lay of the land looked to offer the opportunity for a good stalk, bringing us to within just 30m of the feeding animals.

Matching actions to our decision Bob pulled his Super 8 movie camera from his pikau; I pulled the Pentax from my pikau and screwed on my 225-tele lens. At first we had easy stalking, the folds of the ground and tall brush effectively screening us from the two bulls. Bob began to work his way slightly higher than me, hoping to get some footage of me stalking in, Gary and Caribou in the same frame. I could hear the Super 8 whirring, the Caribou still feeding, not alarmed.

At about 55m from the bulls the brush was only about 30cm tall and I was having trouble. Camera in one hand and rifle in the other, while slithering on my belly through low brush was impossible. Propping the rifle against a convenient bush I continued my stalk, intent on getting even closer and better photos. With some twenty metres behind me I now had the two un-alarmed Caribou within easy distance for a great shot or two with the 225-tele lens. I was on the very rim of a shallow depression the Caribou were feeding in; the slight elevation would make for a better photo.

Raising myself with infinite care onto my elbows I was able to frame the two bulls and trip the shutter. Pentax cameras have a focal-plane shutter, a shutter somewhat noisier than those on other makes of cameras. In the hope of being undetected I froze motionless after the shutter had tripped. No reaction! Meanwhile I can hear Bob's Super 8 working with its soft whirring.

Emboldened by the apparent deafness of the two Caribou I dropped once more onto my belly and snaked another ten or fifteen metres closer. Once more I slowly lifted my upper body, once more framed the two Caribou. Glancing back I could see Bob had continued filming. (NOTE – when processed Bob's movie showed the Caribou and me in the same frame. That's how close I was.)

Whether it was the tripping of the Pentax shutter, the sound of Bob's Super 8, or a slight back-eddy of wind, we'll never know, but without warning the smaller bull threw back his head, snorted, and began racing for the far rim of the basin, his characteristic high knee trotting action quickly increasing the distance.

A second series of snorts brought my attention back to the larger bull. He also was up and running, but… hell… the antlers! They were the biggest set of Caribou antlers I'd ever seen. Talk about trophy class, these were supreme.

I was frantic, for at first glance I couldn't see the Husqvarna? Dropping both camera and pikau I raced back, unsure of just where the rifle was? Glancing back I saw the giant bull was high-knee trotting in the opposite direction to his small companion. I was trying to do too many things at once. With fumbling hands, and pounding heart (not from exertion), I loaded the

30-06, rolled into a prone position, settled my eye to the scope, to discover the surrounding brush was too tall for me to take a prone shot.

How long does it take to move from a prone position to sitting? I don't know. It takes as long as it takes a running bull Caribou to increase the range by thirty or forty metres. By now the trophy bull is out there about one hundred metres and going faster. Crosshairs on shoulder, (make it a smooth swing Gary) and touch off.

I clearly heard the dull "thwack" of a hard hit. I saw the bull stumble and drop. I saw him rise to his feet turn and stumble off downhill. This time I took the time to settle, crosshairs on the neck, swing smoothly. Trigger. He was down and dead.

For a moment or two I sat, trying to re-assemble the sequence of events, wondering where my camera was? Meanwhile Bob was shouting…?

"I got it, I got the lot…"

He had filmed the entire sequence with his Super 8.

We were both ecstatic for on the ground before us was without doubt a likely very high scoring Barren Ground Caribou trophy.

Now the real work began. Alaskan Game Laws demanded that all edible meat (bear exempt) must be handled with care, recovered and consumed by humans. It was an offence to not butcher and cool a carcass, not recover a carcass from the field and store in such a manner to not allow the meat to spoil. We

The author with his outstanding trophy Caribou – beam length 53½ inches, spread 42 inches, number of points 37. When measured for Boone & Crockett the Score of 418⅛ placed the trophy fourth best shot in Alaska that year (1963) and twenty-seventh in the Barren Ground Caribou B & C listings.

had a big afternoon's work ahead of us.

After we'd removed the cape I made an immediate start on skinning out the head skin, determined to carry it back to camp with us, to ensure it wasn't damaged by bears or wolves during the night. Meanwhile Bob had started skinning the back half of the carcass. Once all skin was removed we broke the carcass down into the usual sections. After cutting a large pile of springy brush we set out layers of meat and in between each section a bulky layer of brush. This would prevent one section of meat resting on another, resulting in spoilage. The layer of brush also allowing for any wind to pass through, thus enhancing the cooling process. With the edible meat all taken care of, and set so as to not spoil, we finally cut more brush and spread this over the pile of meat. This was to discourage all manner of scavengers including the Blue Jays. (birds). I left the antlers hidden within the pile of meat to be collected the following day when we'd return with packhorses to carry out the meat.

Returning to camp is always easier for generally it is down hill all the way. Once we'd had our couple of cups of coffee, and taken care of any camp chores awaiting our attention I settled to completing the turning of ears, skinning of lips, all preparatory to having the skin ready to be salted down once the skin had cooled completely.

Back to the Caribou Basin tomorrow with packhorse.

NOTES:

A fully mature adult bull Caribou could weigh more than 300kg and stand as tall as 1.5m at the shoulder, so weighing about the same as a Red stag, but taller at the shoulder. As mentioned in the text they have a characteristic high-knee trot that is fast enough to out-run wolves. A most unusual characteristic is that with each step they take there is a "click" within the foot structure.

Both sexes of Caribou carry antlers but those of the females are rudimentary in structure and much smaller than those carried by the bulls.

Caribou behaviour is characterised by their seasonal migrations, where a herd may travel many hundreds of kilometres between summer and winter locations. It is during this migration that an observer, located close to a known migration trail, may view many hundreds of animals in one day.

On the day that Bob Hart shot his trophy Caribou we watched one bull Caribou run in a very large circle, it taking almost an hour for him to finally arrive back at his start point. We had no idea why he thought he needed the exercise.

During our Alaskan hunt we learned much; we saw helicopters in action for the first time in our lives. The Alaskan Game Department owned a number of Bell choppers and used these to visit hunting camps, checking for violations. They had also picked up in the fact that by flying low over areas where hunters may have made a kill they would flush the Blue Jays (birds) off a carcass. The Game Wardens would then check the carcass to ensure all regulations had been adhered to.

My Barren Ground Caribou was indeed an outstanding trophy (no credit to me).

After the statutory sixty-day stand-down period a Boone & Crockett Club Official Scorer measured the antlers. With a B & C Score of $418\frac{1}{8}$ my trophy was the fourth largest shot that year in the state of Alaska and when it was entered into the Boone & Crockett Record Book it placed twenty-seventh in the all-time rankings.

Running Bull

Hope sprung strong within me. I veered to run on an intercept course.

Ahead, a gap in the trees.

As the cows crossed my front I stood firm, dry-firing at each to judge my timing, my swing. The bull. I led and squeezed.

Just after 8am Walt and I had loaded the Caribou sections on two packhorses, the front quarters plus antlers on one, the hindquarters on the other. It had still been dark when we'd cooked ourselves a good breakfast and caught two riding horses, two packhorses. Bob wasn't feeling at all well so Walt had offered to give me a hand to recover my Caribou antlers and meat.

With virtually a whole day ahead I had no wish to return immediately to camp for we had a fine location for looking over a vast expanse of country spread out below. After mounting I suggested to Walt that perhaps we should ride to the western rim of the basin where we would likely gain a view of the lower slopes of Gunsight Mountain where the big Moose was reputed to be. Walt agreed with my suggestion immediately, reminding me that he had his x30 spotting scope in his saddlebag.

By now the sun was warming the air, it was rather pleasant riding conditions. The full expanse of Caribou Creek lay far below with the south faces still in frozen shadow. The spruce trees appeared starkly black against their companion trees, frost encrusted willow and cottonwoods. The terraces on the lower slopes of Gunsight Mountain basked in the bright early morning rising sun, every detail finely detailed by the low angle light.

Arriving at the rim of the basin I dismounted, dropped the reins and after making sure the lenses of my binoculars were clean I wandered over to a large boulder, warmed already by the rising sun, a cosy and steady back rest for glassing. It was a perfect day, I marvelled at the beauty and stillness of the morning. Walt remained on his horse, not bothering to dismount.

Working from my left I methodically began searching for game. Nothing to be seen on Caribou Creek. Nothing on the saddle of Squaw Creek. Nothing on the slopes immediately below. Lots of small white dots on the rock faces of Gunsight Mountain, Dall sheep. Adjust focus for distant spruce forest on lower slopes of the mountain. Nothing. Wait! What's that flashing? Back up a bit… steady… juggle focus… MOOSE!!!

"Walt," I called. "Walt, Moose, Moose everywhere. Come and look, they're everywhere!"

Dragging his spotting scope from the saddlebag Walt quickly set up atop my back-rest rock. After describing just where to focus the scope I watched his face for his expression when he sighted the Moose in the x30 scope. He started counting…

"One, two, three, four, five, six, seven, eight, nine, ten… ten Moose. Sonavabitch… Never seen anything like that in my life…"

My turn with the scope. With the x30 magnification I'm easily able to identify six cows and four bulls ranging in size from a (probable) two-year-old to the largest of the four bulls carrying quite large antlers. Then, something drew my eyes slightly higher and to the right…

"Walt," I found myself whispering. "I see him, I see the granddaddy of them all…"

Almost entirely obscured by thick spruce, but feeding into an opening as I watched, the trophy I'd been seeking stepped into view to fill the scope. Massive, compared to the smaller bulls, the bull's head was crowned with great pale white serrated butterfly wing-like antlers. As I watched, speechless, he fed directly towards me and I saw the full expanse of his antlers, contrasted against the dark swamp. Obviously, it had been the sun reflecting off the pale antlers, which had drawn my attention.

"Man-o-man, he'll make 'The Book' for sure Gary. That is if you can make a successful stalk." Walt was whispering now!

We were back in camp before noon. Bob was sitting close to the fire having a cup of coffee. He poured a cup for Walt and I. Camp was virtually empty, all guides away guiding their clients. We quietly told Bob what we'd discovered, doing our best to control our excitement. Suddenly, Bob was less unwell than he'd been before sunrise. He'd spent the morning cooking up a large Moose stew, so while we refuelled he set about changing the saddle on one of our packhorses, he'd join the Moose hunt.

After a last-minute check of our gear and donning our warmest clothes we three set off down Caribou Creek on our horses. Side-by-side we visited and re-visited the sighting of all the Moose, the sighting of the grandfather of them all. We really couldn't work out a hunt strategy for first we had to locate the swamp, move onto it with the wind in our faces, pray that the Moose hadn't moved to pastures greener during the late

morning, early afternoon?

As had happened the day I'd shot my Black bear the skies started to cloud over, the sun disappeared, the temperature dropped. As we progress down the creek the cloud slowly turned a darker and darker grey. Ominous. My concern was that with a dramatic change in the weather the Moose would not feed on the swamp that evening, but would seek the shelter and warmer conditions within the spruce forest. Dark clouds, no sunlight, dark trees, dark Moose, would make for very difficult conditions.

Chances of success were swinging against me.

It was well over an hour before we finally arrived at the canyon we'd marked as a likely access route to the spruce forest above. Our plan was to leave the horses at the canyon mouth progressing on foot from that point. With the horses well-tethered to suitable trees, we set off up the floor of the canyon, to discover immediately there was a well-defined broad game trail traversing the bed of the canyon. Prints of Moose, Caribou and bear were numerous.

But, upon entering the forest a deep gloom closed in around us lowering contrast, making it most difficult to distinguish details. As we moved slowly forward we well knew that should a bull Moose sight us he'd move off in the gloom with us having not the slightest knowledge of his presence and subsequent flight. We'd had enough previous experience with Moose to know their great bulk and antler spread was not the slightest hindrance to silent and stealthy flight.

Viewed from the rim of the now distant Caribou Basin the spruce forest had looked relatively open, but once in it I realised my mistake. Reluctantly I had to face the fact that my Moose hunt wasn't going to be the "cake walk" I had first thought. The dark forest, thick and silent, the dull sunless afternoon, the dark coat colouring of a Moose, all weighed against possible success.

At the top of the game trail I stopped to re-assemble my thoughts. By my reckoning the swamp and Moose had to be to our east, however we were in a poor stalking position for the odd gentle gust of wind was coming from the west. We needed to veer north-east, seeking higher ground, hoping to arrive at a point where we could overlook the swamp. The uncertainty, and risk, was that the Moose herd had fed into the wind since we'd last sighted them. My hope was that a bountiful supply of preferred food on the swamp would keep the Moose close to where we'd sighted them that morning.

We began stalking carefully, slowly. Not wishing to obstruct each other's forward view we spread out in a line, about ten metres apart. Stepping cautiously, constantly watching each other for hand signals, we advanced, but terribly slowly. We couldn't move too quickly for any mistake would trigger flight and a lost opportunity for a shot. Haste would not gain me a trophy for a bull Moose motionless amid the dark spruce trees would be virtually invisible.

I had no way of slowing my pounding heart, for with every step we took I expected to see once again those massive white antlers I'd studied through the spotting scope that morning. Glancing to my left and right I could see that both Bob and Walt were also highly alert, (their hearts also no doubt pounding), each working at his best, not for themselves, but for me.

How long we eased through the dark spruce forest, expecting to see the great bulk of the bull Moose ghosting away from us through the gloom I have no idea, but we were seen first. It was almost as if we were deaf for a cow Moose moved soundlessly off to our left. She spared us just the one backward glance before melting in to the dark spruce shadows.

We had a quandary! If the cow was a lone female we had no problems, but if she were the tail-end-Charlie of the herd, to continue the hunt would be pointless. We would never find an alarmed and alert Moose herd in that dense and gloomy forest. Alternatively, if she was the vanguard of the herd containing my (hoped for) trophy bull, did we have a chance of sighting the rest of her group shortly? I'd read where a group of Moose travelled with a matriarch as leader with lesser cows following her lead, the younger bulls behind the cows with the patriarch last in line. Were other cows following this lone cow, would we see the master bull parade across our front?

Signalling the others to stand still I eased myself against a spruce and began searching. Maybe five minutes ticked by, accompanied by the hammering of my heart. Nothing stirred. Next I cautiously began climbing the tree I'd been resting my back against. All I could see was more and more spruce trees. The land seemed to rise ahead, maybe from somewhere up there we'd finally locate the Moose swamp we'd failed to locate. Had we somehow got disorientated in the thick gloomy forest and missed the swamp entirely.

Dusk was already slipping, un-noticed, into the shadowed folds. The "Hunters Hour" was at hand – that time when the game departs their daily hiding places to feed in the gathering dark, then into the night. Instinctively I knew we should continue to remain hidden and watchful. If only we could gain an elevated location. At last fortune smiled.

We'd been advancing cautiously for about twenty minutes when we became aware that the land was rising slowly ahead, the forest trees thinning. Five minutes later we were standing on a low open hummock. Turning to overlook the ground below we discovered we were overlooking the swamp.

Grateful, relieved, excited anew, we sank to the ground. But this afternoon the swamp was different, it was empty of Moose! We three searched and searched, nothing? No Moose. There we were, three dejected, tired and deflated hunters. We'd found the Moose swamp at last, but fate had played the final hand. No Moose.

For perhaps fifteen minutes we sat still and quiet while night fingered its way across the landscape. Contained by my own thoughts I tried to recall all I'd been told about the habits of Moose. I'd been told that unless disturbed Moose were highly likely to feed, early morning and late evening, at virtually the same location. By all the rules the Moose should be on the swamp ahead of us feeding, especially with the early onset of dusk. If there were no Moose on the swamp within the next ten minutes we'd know that (unwittingly) we'd alarmed them.

Elbows on knees I glassed that swamp back and forth, back and forth, slowly, slowly, all the time reluctantly telling myself that today would not be the day I collected a great trophy Moose. With the gathering darkness my spirit dropped even more, but I was determined to stay there until it was too dark to see. We'd worry about getting back to camp later.

Walt wanted to move off, get back to the horses; I pretended not to hear him. My binoculars never left my eyes as I slowly swept that swamp, willing it to show me a Moose. In the failing light I found myself studying each dark spruce tree, every paler bush, a pattern of dark tree, lighter coloured bush, dark tree, light brush, dark tree, light brush, dark tree, dark brush. Dark brush? Dark brush??

My glasses revealed six cow Moose, in ghostly silence, materialising from the light brush edging the swamp.

My mouth is suddenly very dry, but I manage to whisper – "Moose".

Walt and Bob were now wide-awake; I distinctly heard their joint in-drawing of breath.

But, where are the bulls? I go back to where the cows had appeared from as if by magic. Yes, standing motionless, just within the brush fringing of the swamp, are the two smaller bulls. As I watch they slowly move out on to the open swamp, their places taken by the two larger bulls. I now have four bulls in view. Four, not five?

Precious minutes tick by before a great black shape detaches itself from the gloom of the forest to stand with those fantastic butterfly wing antlers sharply etched white against the background of dark forest.

Sudden movement by the Master Bull brings realisation. It's the rut and the younger bulls are trying to cut-in on his harem. Fascinated – all thought of shooting forgotten for the moment – I watched the giant bull charge a small bull, tossing him aside with a vicious side-sweep of his antlers. A general scattering then occurred with the smaller bulls forming a dejected group off to the side, closer to us, the Master Bull herding the females further out on to the swamp.

Walt has been busy with his spotting scope…

"Gary," he whispers, "he's a record breaker. Seventeen points a side and a spread of better than 60 inches."

As we watch we see the Master Bull herd his harem out towards the middle of the swamp. If I am to get a shot I'll need to do so within the following ten minutes, for even the fantastic light-gathering ability of my 4 x 81 German Nickel scope-sight can't cut through total darkness.

I have one chance and that is to follow the bull out onto the swamp and hope for a shot. With a nod to Bob we load our rifles and move down from the hillock. Walt will stay behind, on watch.

It had been a long day. I was nervous and mentally tired. After having taken just a few steps onto the swamp I realise I had yet another problem, I sank almost to my knees in a sloppy, swampy slurry. We next stumbled onto a small bull Moose half-hidden in an isolated stand of spruce trees. I hand-signalled for Bob to stay back close to the other bulls in the hope that he may get a shot after I've nailed my trophy.

I struggled on almost knee-deep in the swamp slurry. I couldn't see my bull, but continued on heading towards where I'd last seen him. My breath is rasping in my throat, my heart pounding even more loudly with the effort of struggling through hindering mud. In front of me tracks, deep tracks signalling the passing of the bull and his cows.

Searching the gloom ahead I followed the deep-set furrowed track made by the seven Moose. Through a screen of spruce trees I saw seven dark bulky shapes, the bull with his pale antlers clearly identifiable. Using the screen of trees as cover I forced my

Prior to winter Blue Jay scavenged for meat and fat. Game Department helicopters would fly low in the hope of flushing the massed birds off an abandoned game animal carcass. Alaskan game laws required all edible meat was to be recovered for human consumption.

tired legs to carry me forward. I'm totally focused on my quarry, that's how I almost bumped into a small bull.

Shit! With nose high and antlers thrown back the young bull raced to my left and even as I watched I saw the big bull and his cows take flight, running in the same direction as the smaller bull. Desperate now I started to run. My first few steps were a real struggle, but as I gathered speed I didn't sink as deeply into the quagmire.

Hope sprung strong within me. I veered to run on an intercept course. Ahead, a gap in the trees. As the cows passed my front I stood firm, dry-firing at each to judge my timing and swing. The bull. I led and squeezed.

As I hastily reloaded I heard the "thwack" of a solid hit and saw the bull stumble. But he was up again and again I was running. I seemed to be closing. Through yet another screen of trees I saw the cows dashing off, but the bull struggling to stay with them. Once more I was running, fighting the clinging mud. Once more I stopped and planted my feet. As the bull passed through a gap in some trees I triggered two rapid shots, one a hit, one a miss. Now the bull turned and was stumbling towards me.

Slamming yet another round into the breech I charged directly towards the bull, demanding that my body give me that last burst of adrenalin to conclude this incredible encounter. The bull saw me and stopped. I missed my next hasty shot. It was impossible to hold the rifle steady. I let it swing in sympathy with my pounding pulse and hammering heart, patterned the rhythm and squeezed. It's over…

Suddenly Bob was beside me.

"Came to back you up", he gasped.

The pair of us stood there, knee-deep in swamp mud, giving our hearts respite from the punishment we'd inflicted on them. Side by side we fought our way across the last of the swamp to finally reach the downed bull, his pale giant antlers rising ghost-like from a patch of low brush.

Deeply grateful for the outcome of the day I closed my eyes, but my ears started ringing and I felt slightly faint. Eventually my heart slowed and my pulse returned to near normal.

By now it was pitch dark. Somehow the three of us managed to gut the Moose, prop open the chest cavity, with three or four robust sticks – to allow cooling overnight – knowing that we'd have to be back on the swamp soon after daylight to take care of the trophy and all the meat.

It was close to midnight when we finally arrived back at camp. After each horse had been given a double ration of oats we consumed the last of Bob's stew and with a final cup of coffee in our hands retired to our respective sleeping bags. It was a day I'll never forget.

NOTES:

Moose are the largest species of deer in the world. A large bull Moose may measure up to 2.4m at the shoulder and weighing as much as 550kg. Despite their great size an adult bull is able to move virtually soundlessly through dense cover. With nose held high and antlers acting rather like the bow of a ship many a hunter has been amazed at their silent departure from danger. This characteristic is not unlike the behaviour of our Sambar deer.

While known to not have very good eyesight Moose rely largely on their hearing. Look at the size of their ears the next time you have a chance, they are real sound-gatherers.

With exceptionally long legs many observers consider the Moose to be a rather gorky ungainly deer, but when they run their gait is not unlike that of a well-trained high-stepping show pony. Obviously they've developed this high-stepping after thousands of generations of living in swamps.

Moose are unique in the deer world in that they have a system

Bob Hart, left, the author right, with his trophy bull Moose. With an outside spread of 64 inches and carrying a total of thirty-one points this trophy scored 218²/₈ and placed #50 in the Boone & Crockett Record Book.

218¼ points. My trophy was entered into the Boone & Crockett Book of World Records and placed fiftieth in the Alaskan Moose category.

Client Walter Schubert poses with the author's B & C trophy Moose.

of muscles in their nose that allows them to close their nostrils off completely while feeding underwater. During the summer period, while growing their massive antlers, bull Moose will seek to feed on water hibiscus in shallow lakes. This food source is highly nutritious, contributing to the massive antler growth of Alaskan bull Moose.

My trophy bull stood 78 inches (2m) at the shoulder with a depth of chest at one metre and length of leg the same. We had no way of weighing the body of the bull, but we did weigh the antlers, (with skull cap), at 27.3kg.

Outside spread of the antlers was 64 inches (say 1.64m) and after a required period of sixty days drying out the Boone & Crockett Score was

Walk The Man Down

…that never in his life had he guided a client who could climb as well as he could, or travel as fast, or as far in a day. He then lifted his head and looked directly across the campfire at Bob and I…

Lashing rain kettle-drumming on the tent roof woke us long before daylight. The threatening storm of the past few days had finally arrived. Snuggling deeper into my Fairydown Twenty Below I must have quickly dropped back into a deep sleep.

"Wakey, wakey," (rough hands shake me) "Come on Kiwi hunters, today's the day you both get your Dall rams…"

"Go to hell Chuck de Freest, it's raining cats and dogs, only idiots would climb a mountain to hunt sheep in these conditions. You're mad…"

"A day like this is perfect for hunting sheep, they can't see you stalking them."

"And how the hell are we going to see them if they can't see us?"

Chuck then explained that we would use the curtains of lashing rain to hide us while climbing the mountain, all the while hoping the storm would pass over once we were as high as the sheep, to then use the terrain to our best advantage. Bob and I knew that Dall sheep always seemed to locate themselves,

during the day, where they had a grandstand view of all the country below them. So, if we could get to the same altitude as the sheep, advantage could maybe swing in our favour. But I knew we'd be wet as shags long before we returned to camp!

An hour later, after an extra hearty breakfast, we stepped from the shelter of camp into the lashing rain. Parka hoods were pulled tight, rifles upside down in the hope of the barrels staying dry, scopes covered with plastic bags, our pikaus bulky with extra ammo, additional warm clothes, cheese sandwiches for lunch, all secured in plastic bags. We'd left our cameras in camp, concerned that they'd get wet and ruined.

It was within the first few minutes of departing camp, the cold rain stinging and chilling my face, that I recalled Chuck's boast at the campfire the previous evening. Bob agreed with me, that Chuck knew, when he made his boastful statement, that he'd be guiding us the following day, and that undoubtedly he'd offered up a rather obvious challenge.

Chuck was just twenty-two years of age, had largely guided elderly clients who wouldn't be anywhere as fit as Bob and I after our years of experience of hunting in New Zealand, plus the many months we'd spent in the Alaskan boondocks.

We thought it might take our minds off the atrocious weather if we accepted Chuck's challenge, something to occupy our minds, a sort of distraction. So we made a "Plan". We'd allow Chuck to lead our party, always staying right on his heels, to push the pace, but never overtaking. But, at that distant point, somewhere later into the day, when we finally turned for home, Bob and I would alternatively take the lead forcing the pace for each other, hoping to drop Chuck further and further behind.

With their snow-white coats Dall rams were easily spotted in their grey rock habitat from many miles distance. (NOTE - This is a photo of a painting in the author's trophy room)

There was absolutely no malice in our plan; Kiwi pride was at stake.

For the first hour we trudged up Caribou Creek, trying, as much as possible, to stay within the shelter of the Spruce forest, but finally giving up for we were getting soaking wet fighting our way through the underbrush. At the end of that hour we were saturated from the knees down and water was beginning to lazily trickle its way down the back of our necks. I was better off than Bob or Chuck for I'd taken the precaution of wrapping a small cotton towel around my neck in the manner of a scarf.

An hour and a half after leaving camp we finally arrived at Sheep Creek. Here we found a broad gravel creek bed offering easy travel. Having changed direction the rain was now driving at our left shoulder, not into our faces, and as we progressed on the easy travel gravel of the creek we enjoyed a measure of shelter from the storm the further we advanced up Sheep Creek. We could see nothing of our surroundings.

Ahead we could hear the muted sounds of white water tumbling over boulders. At a large rock, sheltering us from the still lashing rain, Chuck called a halt and outlined the plan for the day. He told us that a few days prior Johnny Luster had flown with Don Deering and located a group of legal trophy rams away up in the head basins of Sheep Creek. To Johnny it was obvious that his more elderly clients would never get to where the rams were located; Chuck was to guide the two Kiwi hunters in the hope of success. At best guess our objective was some twelve kilometres from where we stood. It was going to be a long day.

Chuck explained that we needed to immediately climb out of the creek, to avoid a deep narrow gorge about a kilometre ahead. He understood there was a good leading ridge that would access us to the largely open face of the mountain, above the gorge; that we'd know we were on the right track when we encountered a series of deep "gutters" cutting the otherwise open mountain slope. We would have to cross each of these "gutters" always seeking to gain height to finally locate a series of three mountain top basins. The rams would (hopefully) be located in one of these three.

It must have been early afternoon when the rain suddenly ceased, the wind dropped, the curtain of cloud lifted, and we got to see where we were for the first time that day. Chuck's 'blind flying' had been spot-on for ahead we could see what could be the rim of a basin. Taking a breather, to mainly take in our surroundings, we saw that across on the opposite side of the valley were towering cliffs, and even with the naked eye you could see those tell-tale white spots, Dall sheep. By now we were away above the last of varieties of low brush and squaw berry patches; underfoot we had fine gravel offering easier climbing conditions. Caribou Creek appeared as a slim ribbon of silver a very long way away.

Within a few minutes we were close to the rim of the first basin, so carefully scanned all the slopes above to ensure we had no rams in view. Well aware of the excellent eyesight of Dall sheep we stayed as close to the ground as we could, belly crawling to where we hoped we'd get a clear view. Before us was a basin devoid of any game…!

Taking only time enough to carefully scan all surrounding ridges, still climbing hard to gain further height, we made a beeline for a high rocky ridge that we hoped would provide an elevated view into the second basin. We'd paid little attention to the lower part of the basin for we knew there was no game to be seen. It was the disappearance of the sun, a cold clamminess of the air around us that caused us to pause in our climb. Like some nebulous long tentacled creature from science fiction thick tendrils of fog were fingering their way up the mountain towards us. Even as we watched it increased in speed and we knew we had a race on our hands if we were to get a look into the second basin.

Without exchanging a single word the three of us raced for the rocky ridge above, praying that we might sight rams before the

Typical Caribou Creek hunting country late in the hunting season, winter is close at hand.

fog dropped its forbidding curtain. We lost the race. Standing, panting hard, we stood on the ridge as thick swirling fog rapidly engulfed us, completely blotting out the landscape. Chilled we quickly donned additional woollen pullovers, struggled, once again, into our wet parkas. Dejectedly we broke open our cheese sandwiches for there was nothing else we could do!!

Glumly we huddled in a shallow hollow, seeking to gain whatever shelter was on offer. Munching our cheese sandwiches we tried to figure out a best next course of action? It would be equally as dangerous to go back as to go forward. It was while attacking my second cheese sandwich that I felt a small wellspring of hope nudge my dejection. I awoke to the fact that the fog was not a solid mass, but instead a series of fingers moving and reforming and in so doing opening clear ground between tendrils. Even as I watched the fog drifted and swirled and there below us was a clear view of sections of the lower slopes of the basin.

Encouraged by this phenomenon we eased across the ridge into the second basin where we immediately saw that it held a series of wide and flat benches. With each swirling of the fog, and the sudden offering of yet another view of the basin, we'd drop to the ground, our binoculars busy. Nothing.

We were high towards the upper most rim of this basin when the action started. And we were caught unawares. Without giving us the slightest warning the whole mass of fog suddenly lifted, leaving us fully exposed and without anywhere to hide!

Quickly dropping to the ground and staying as low as we could we watched, amazed, at this rapid weather change. Like a giant theatre curtain the fog rapidly lifted and there just 150m below was the first character in the drama of the day – a Dall ram.

He was feeding away from us, our binoculars told us he wasn't large enough to be taken as a trophy.

NOTE – Alaskan Game Law (at that time) dictated that a ram's horns must be a minimum of threequarter curl to be taken as a trophy. This ram was clearly not yet legal.

Our attention wasn't held for long on this solitary ram, for far below, on the very lowest rim of the basin, the fog had rolled back to expose eight Dall rams resting beside a tiny stream, in the shelter of a large boulder. Even as we watched one ram detached from the group, walked to the rock and began rubbing the tips of his horns.

All who hunt sheep know that when the horns on an aged ram grow to a length where the tips of the horns obstruct his side vision, the ram will diligently rub those offending tips to restore his full unimpeded side-vision. This is known as brooming.

Any dejection we were feeling rapidly evaporated, like the fog, but how were we to get close enough for a shot with the immature ram between our hoped-for quarry and us? We knew, for sure, that if the solitary ram took flight the other eight would see him and likewise depart at speed. At 230m to our left was a small hillock. If we could get to the offside of this we could just have a chance of closing in on the group of rams. The grasses around us weren't even long enough to hide a rabbit, let alone three adult men!

It was Chuck who whispered the suggestion that if we were to double over and move on hands and knees we might be lucky and be mistaken for bears. There was no other solution to our quandary, so we set off across the slope, playing at being "The Three Bears". We'd covered less than twenty-five metres when the solitary ram sighted us, took flight and raced down the basin towards the group of eight. They, seeing him in flight, also hit the panic button and within less than two minutes the entire basin was devoid of Dall rams. The last we'd seen of the group was them racing over the far skyline rim of the basin.

With the flight of the rams Chuck gave up on the hunt. His opinion was it was now too late to go chasing after the rams for we had a long way to go to get back to camp. Even if we did continue the chase it would be many hours after dark that we'd finally get back to camp.

(Here I digress. Bob and I had discovered that none of the American hunters we'd associated with in Johnny Luster's camp liked to be out in the field after dark. Time after time we'd seen parties returning to camp during that magic Hunter's Hour, the hour before nightfall. We never did ask any of them if they were afraid of the dark (we couldn't), we guessed they were not so afraid of the dark, but what might be out there in the darkness! Surprisingly, here was Chuck displaying a similar trait, he wanted to be "home before dark!")

With Bob and I both standing there, trying to figure what our next best course of action might be, Chuck turned and started on his way back towards camp. Bob was thinking the same as me. We'd climbed a bloody long way during the day. If we turned back now we'd have to climb the mountain again another day. Certainly the eight rams had taken flight, but only after sighting their fleeing comrade. We were certain they hadn't sighted us. I recalled days hunting Tahr when we'd spooked mobs only to re-connect with them a couple of hours later in an adjoining gully or basin. Would a group of Dall rams behave in a like manner? Would we find the rams in the third and last basin secure and happily resting on some lofty crag?

"Chuck, let's stay with them, our luck may change," I called to our departing guide.

"But it's too late."

"Let's get the rams and then worry about the time," this from Bob.

"You Kiwis are terrors for punishment."

"Come on Guide, guide", I said with a laugh, for I could see Chuck was much more interested on retreating than advancing, but his pride forbade him from labouring the issue.

The third basin was nothing like the two we'd passed through. A landscape of snow and ice greeted our first tentative searching. The centre of the basin was a massive glacier of tumbled tortured pale blue ice. On the far side forbidding snow peaks taunted us with their snowy serrated smiles. Below, an undulating snowfield began at a snow-smothered ridge. And, on that ridge, not 275m away, were the rams. Our hunch had paid off.

The failing light told us nightfall wasn't too far off. By using the depressions between snow hummocks, we ploughed our way through deep snow to easily reduce the range to about 180m. We could get no closer for the ground fell away sharply, we'd be in full view if we advanced any further.

Not all the rams were in view for the ledge where they stood evidently sloped away on the far side. Also, they were slightly above us. The combination of these factors made for more difficult shooting. But, we were committed to this position so had to make the best of it. We'd run out of choices. Unable to find a really good shooting position I eased to my right where I flopped down on the snow. Wriggling to further settle my body into the snow I discovered I was really comfortable. Bedding my elbows into the snow and then sighting through the scope I felt confident (for the first time that day) that I would be securing my trophy Dall ram. Then, before I could quietly close the bolt of the Husqvarna two things happened simultaneously. It started to rain, and the rams lay down!

This is where Dall rams roam. They may be very easy to see, due to their white coats, but their excellent eyesight, plus physically demanding terrain ensures a challenging hunt.

Within a short second I had only the top half of the back of a ram's back for a target, seen as a blur through driving rain and droplets of water on the scope lens. Concentrating, but entirely uncertain of the outcome I touched off the 180-gr Norma round. A small geyser of snow erupted below the bedded ram. Even before the first echo had slammed back at us from the bluff behind the rams, they were up and disappeared. Shouting to Bob to follow me I charged down the slope about fifty metres, somehow knowing, instinctively, that I was taking the right action. And there they were.

Majestically, in single-file, the rams paraded across the snow face above at a trot. Flinging myself once more down onto the moulding snow I shouted to Bob to start shooting. Work the bolt, swing to lead, touch the trigger. In slow motion the leading ram falters and tumbles from the cliff face, followed by a cascade of powder snow.

Bob has not yet fired a shot so I rapidly reload and set myself for a follow-up shot should he wound his ram. By now the remaining rams are in full flight, climbing the cliff face in great lunging bounds. From my grandstand position I see Bob's first shot plough an eruption of snow immediately above the shoulder of the leading ram. He'd not allowed for the steep uphill shot. I call his shot, reminding him to hold low.

Reacting to Bob's shot each ram takes a different escape route. One dashes into the bluff, climbing fast in great lunging bounds. And that's how Bob tumbled him. At fully 350m and in mid-bound, Bob's second shot pealed that ram off the bluff. And it was still raining.

Within a very short half hour, taking advantage of the last of the daylight, we caped the two rams, and boned out all edible meat. The load of meat was shared three ways, our horns and capes lashed finally to our pikaus well away from blood staining the pure white capes. Struggling to get the straps of our pikaus over our wet parkas we finally turned and began the long trek back to camp.

Side-by-side Bob and I struck off. Chuck, with no one to pace him, slowly fell behind and was lost in the darkness. At the point where Sheep Creek joined Caribou we stopped and waited for Chuck. Forty-five minutes passed before he finally materialised out of the darkness. It had stopped raining. Not a word about the obvious challenge was said, but we did allow Chuck all the time he needed to regain his breath and have a rest.

Cold and stiffening from the long wait for Chuck Bob and I were slow to get back up to speed, but tramping side-by-side, forcing each other's pace, we started to warm and increase our speed. The small aggregate gravel bordering the creek offered excellent underfoot conditions so we were soon smoking along. Wet from the waist down we didn't bother about finding a shallow crossing in the creek we just charged through for we couldn't get any wetter. Behind us Chuck was once again lost in the gloom.

Finally the high dark bluff across the creek from camp came into view in the darkness; we knew we were just ten minutes from camp. Here we stopped and waited for Chuck. Even though we well-knew we'd chill while standing there in the depth of an Alaskan late fall night we had no wish to humiliate Chuck in front of the whole camp. If later he told people that we could have been back in camp a full hour ahead of him that was his to tell. We had proved our point and won the "race".

At last Chuck appeared out of the gloom. We gave him a soft whistle.

"You Kiwi guys waited for me?" he sounded genuinely surprised.

"Sure. Can't return to camp without our Guide."

"Thanks for waiting. Thanks a lot."

The day Bob Hart and the author set out to hunt Dall ram driving rain prompted the hunters to leave their cameras safe and dry in camp, so no photos of their eventual trophies. This photo is of the author's trophy Dall ram in his trophy room.

We dined like kings in hunting camp. Here Walt Schubert and Bob Hart are preparing our usual breakfast, a large Moose steak each, with a couple of eggs plus a stack of pancakes. We seldom ate lunch!

The sincerity in Chuck's voice was heart-warming, for I was sure that throughout his solo trek back to camp in the dark, he was living in advance the scene when he walked into camp far behind his "clients."

Together the three of us finally walked in to camp sixteen and a half hours after leaving it. We were bone-weary, wet to the skin and extremely hungry, but once again we'd returned to camp with trophies.

Next day, while the three of us took care of our ram capes Chuck made a point of sincerely thanking us once again. And that was the end of the story. Except…

A couple of months later Bob and I finally found a barber in Anchorage and had our first haircut in about five months. As always happens in a barbershop, conversation flowed. After a while the barber asked if we were the two Kiwi hunters who'd spent the hunting season working in Johnny Luster's camp? After being told that indeed we were those persons the barber confided that a couple of weeks earlier Chuck had dropped in for a haircut. Conversation had flowed (as usual) and Chuck had told the barber about the two Kiwi hunters.

"Don't ever go climbing with them," he had warned.

"They are a cross between a Mule and a Mountain Goat…"

NOTE;

Dall sheep are the northern most of four species of wild sheep native to North America. Being pure white they are extraordinarily easy to see on the mountain, showing up readily against the natural colours of the habitat, except when the landscape is smothered in snow. Mostly found within the state of Alaska they are often identified as Alaskan Dall.

A full mature ram will stand up to 46 inches (1.2m) at the shoulder and are about 200lb (90 to 92kg) in weight, a body-weight similar to an adult bull Tahr, but the Tahr is shorter at the shoulder, 40–42 inches (102-107cm). Ram horns longer than 40 inches (1m+) are exceptional. A ram with 40 inch horns is akin to we Kiwi hunters seeking a 14 inch bull Tahr, Top Shelf stuff. Longest length of horn ever measured is 48⅝ inches. The horn bases on a mature Dall ram (at 13 to 14 inches) are somewhat slimmer than the horns of a Rocky Mountain Big Horn.

Bob and I didn't enjoy eating the meat of our Dall rams for we found the fat to have its own rather distinct flavour, leaving an unpleasant residue on the roof of our mouths.

Our experience of hunting Dall was limited solely to the chapter you've just read. But hunting them is not at all unlike hunting Tahr, easier perhaps for Dall are so easy to see on a mountain. After that the same stalking skills would apply. Dall are gregarious, like Tahr, so find a mob and look for a trophy ram.

We found that hunting where Game Laws applied was a new and challenging experience. We quickly learned to seriously assess a likely trophy before firing a shot for in most cases only one male of a species was allowed during any season AND sometimes strict minimums (for antler or horn length) applied. Make a mistake and it could be costly in time (inside) and wallet. Always the Game Department was about in their helicopters.

SECTION FIVE

– USA
(Lower Forty-eight)

Desert Racers

No Way Back

King of the Desert

Second Time Lucky....?

Hide & Seek

M. BAILEY

DESERT RACERS

Having now been shot at twice the buck was in full flight.
Settling the crosshairs briefly on his shoulder I began my swing, counting off what I judged to be six body lengths before I touched the trigger.

What a dramatic change of scenery we were experiencing. Having departed Alaska here we were sitting in a vehicle with the vast desert expanse of the Shirley Basin, south-east Wyoming, before us. First impressions were of how vast and desolate this colourless landscape was; how could any animal live, survive, in such a habitat? The only vegetation we could see was sage brush and spiny cactus.

At 6000ft above sea level we were quickly aware of how dry the atmosphere was. We were immediately also aware of the pervading smell of sage brush, (a smell that would remain on our clothing for weeks after the hunt was over). It wasn't long before we were also aware of a slight grittiness in our eyes, dryness in mouth and nostrils. Our host, Lloyd, explained that the desert was seriously alkaline and we'd likely suffer discomfort due to the combination of altitude, low humidity and the ever present alkaline.

Our host also kindly offered us a small history lesson. Early pioneers travelling the Oregon Trail crossed the Shirley Basin.

Each wagon needed to carry with them enough water to last their party seven days, for they would travel 160 kilometres before finally arriving at the Sweetwater River to replenish their supply. Throughout their navigation of the Basin they would aim their wagon train at Split Rock, the only visible distinctive landmark for hundreds of miles in any direction.

The history lesson was interrupted when Lloyd whispered – "Antelope."

He was pointing at a plume of pale yellow-white dust created by some speeding object. I can only guess it was at least two kilometres away, for the shimmering heat haze made distance judgement impossible. To the naked eye the plume of fast rising dust looked more like the smoke from a fast moving train, but my 7 x 35s allowed me to distinguish seven tan and white antelope racing one behind the other. Following their leader they seemingly flew along the distant ridge, their feet – due to the heat haze – appearing not to touch the ground. The rising dust marked their progress otherwise we may never have sighted them.

Something had set this small herd to flight? Lloyd volunteered that we had perhaps caused the antelope alarm, for our vehicle was in full view atop the ridge. If that was the case, if we had indeed caused the small group to take flight, how were we to get within rifle range of these sharp-eyed desert runners? I was alarmed by the fact that the antelope hadn't just stood and stared at us, as other game most likely would have done at such a distance, but had taken instant flight. That afternoon we learned that hunting Pronghorned antelope wasn't going to be easy.

At our next vantage point we left the vehicle hidden behind

Pronghorned antelope country, Shirley Basin, southern Wyoming.

a low ridge and after sneaking to the crest dropped down and crawled, stopping when we had a view, each screening ourselves behind sparse sage brush bushes. Lloyd (once again) was the first to sight a group of about twenty antelope far out and close to the most distant point of the shallow basin we had under observation. With the body colouring of the antelope combining with the extreme heat haze, counting the actual number of animals was difficult. After watching the group for a short period we were aware they were interested in something out of our sight and far to our left. Lloyd suspected that another hunting party could be what the antelope were studying, so suggested we simply wait and see… Bob and I were only too happy to "wait and see"

for we were not enjoying the heat, alkaline and low humidity after our bodies had begun adjusting to the onset of an Alaskan winter. We were suffering…!

A muffled salvo of shots from the direction of the northern rim of the basin brought an explosion of action, and dust, from the herd of antelope. Trailing their now telltale plume of dust the herd raced down the far rim and lo and behold, directly towards us! Before Bob and I could get a grip on what was happening the antelope were racing across our front, at an unbelievable speed, to crest our ridge, splash through the river behind us, and disappear over the far bank. It was only after the mob had disappeared that Lloyd informed us that the one buck in the group was not of trophy proportion. If there'd been a trophy buck in the group I doubt that neither Bob nor I could have got a killing shot away within the split second or two offered.

That evening, before retiring for the night, and after a lukewarm shower, consuming many a can of American beer, and a great barbequed steak dinner, we had a sort of "de-brief". Lloyd made the comment that the antelope hunting season was almost over and likely all the big buck had been shot on those sections of the desert easily accessed by four-wheel-drive. He planned, that on the morrow, we'd hunt the rougher country to the north of the basin on foot. Bob and I had no objection to hunting on foot in rough country for we were as fit as buck rats from our months in Alaska. The strategy for the next day was agreed.

The first suggestion of the new dawn found us way out in the desert awaiting sufficient light for game spotting. The idea was to be nice and early to get a good look around before the heat haze arrived. Those very first few minutes of light, after sunrise, showed us a very different landscape to that which we'd experienced the day before. We were in a series of rough red rock hills broken by shallow canyons and brushy arroyos. Rocks of every conceivable combination of shape and size reminded me of a space odyssey film set. But, what was there for antelope to eat? According to Lloyd there were a series of shallow basins adjoining the rock "playground"; the antelope fed on nutritious short desert grasses during the night, seeking shelter amid the rocks during the day. This was especially so after continued hunting pressure out on the desert.

Within just a few minutes of sunrise we had a small group of five does and one buck in our binoculars. Lloyd informed Bob and I the buck was of good trophy class. The antelope were about 800m away so Lloyd decided that we'd race up to the group in the vehicle and once close to them he would apply the brakes, we would both bail out and both shoot…! We were his guests so we did what we were told. Bouncing furiously over rough ground the vehicle finally got close to the now fleeing still accelerating group of antelope. I glanced down at the speedo – 75 mph and climbing…!

Before I had time to sort out what was actually happening there were the fleeing antelope right beside the vehicle. With a "Now", Lloyd slammed on the brakes, the vehicle bucked to a stop, Bob and I piled out, working our rifle bolts as we did so, flopping onto the ground, seeking a target in our scopes. All we could see was a massive billowing of choking fine alkaline dust. By the time we could actually see those racing antelope they were about 275 metres away, getting closer to 300m with every

flashing stride. We both threw a couple of shots after them, knowing we hadn't a hope scratching the buck.

We had another "de-brief". It was mutually agreed that chasing after those fleet desert runners, capable of accelerating to about 75mph, was a waste of time (and ammo), that henceforth we'd fall back on good old fashioned Kiwi-style stalking.

So, about an hour later, I sighted a group of nine antelope including a nice buck. Leaving the vehicle we set off on foot, the agreement being that whomever got the first chance at a shot was to take it. The antelope were feeding on a slight rise in the centre of a three kilometre wide basin. We were on the east rim, slightly higher than the antelope. Numerous dry watercourses scarred the basin wall, allowing us easy and concealed access to shallow arroyos on the floor of the basin. From here it was a matter of moving forward from one concealment to another, always remaining hidden from the ever-alert antelope.

With no trees or brush to hide behind (as we'd had in Alaska), we had no choice but to move from one rock to the next, sometimes having to slither on our bellies in the acrid alkaline dust, avoiding cacti as we progressed, (slowly). Yes, progress was slow. But finally we estimated we were about 360m from our objective. But here we were stumped, for the ground at our front fell away and there were no bushes for concealment! With our black Stetsons stuffed down our shirts we cautiously watched, from behind convenient concealing rocks, as the master buck chased a young buck away from his harem.

In a soft whisper Lloyd asked us if we were comfortable to take a shot at this range. Neither of us spoke, we just gave Lloyd the universal thumbs-down sign. Directly below was a narrow one metre deep gully that cut to our left and gave access to what appeared to be dead ground. If we could reach the ground immediately below our current position, without disturbing the antelope, we would be able to climb almost to the nearest animal without being seen. With the choice of taking a long-range chancy shot, or attempting the gully, we crossed our fingers, and with care to be as quiet as possible, slid down the narrow gully, never once raising our heads to determine if we'd been seen or not?

My guess had been correct. In the bottom of the draw we were completely out of sight of the antelope, unless one walked to the rim and looked down. The gentle wind drift prompted us to move about thirty metres to our right. We didn't want a lightly wafting breeze to screw up the stalk at this late stage.

The canyon wall in front of us was about double our height, so ever so gently closing the bolt of the Husqvarna, (I watched Bob as he closed the bolt on his Parker Hale); with a nod to each other we eased up the slope. The sand was firm underfoot; it was easy, quiet climbing. A little to my right a small rock outcrop broke the edge of the ridge, I eased towards it, hoping it would break my outline as I crossed the ridge. Arriving I glanced to my left to see Bob already exposed on the ridge. Two quick steps brought me to my vantage point. There was the herd in full flight. Had they heard us making our final climb, or had they seen Bob as he crossed the ridgeline?

Bob was ahead of me. Even as I threw up my rifle I heard the whiplash crack of his rifle shatter the desert silence. I saw a small geyser of dust erupt behind the fleeing buck. Now it was my turn. Having been shot at the buck was now racing at full speed. Swinging the crosshairs onto his shoulder I counted five imaginary body lengths ahead of him as I swung the rifle to lead and fired. Frantically working the bolt I heard Lloyd shout – "Right in line with the shoulder but a whisker high…."

Having now been shot at twice the buck was in full flight. Settling the crosshairs briefly on his shoulder I began my swing, counting off what I judged to be six body lengths before I touched the trigger. Before I could even lower the 30-06 to crank in another shell the buck faltered in mid-stride, cartwheeled and collapsed in a cloud of dust.

Lloyd was shouting.

The remains of an old Pony Express way station close to Split Rock an important landmark on the historic pioneer Oregon Trail crossing the Shirley Basin.

Photo of the author with his Pronghorn trophy, a pre-historic animal living in modern times. Note the flat and sparsely vegetated antelope habitat.

"What a shot! Sonavabitch, what a shot!"

Bob was also shouting, congratulations. I was the only silent member of our party for I was truly stunned by my amazing fluke shot. No doubt a fluke. We paced the distance; it was 238 of my longest strides…

What a handsome trophy a Pronghorned antelope buck is. The neck and back is tan with crescents of white below the throat and across the brisket. The face is most aristocratic with white under the chin and along either side of the jaw. From the nose to behind the horns is a deep chocolate shade. They have a very large caudal patch.

Bob was having trouble with his Parker Hale; it didn't like the change of conditions from wet and cold Alaska to the dry low humidity of Pronghorn country. We'd re-sighted the rifle a couple of times, to discover it would change the point of impact with the changing temperatures we experienced during each day. The afternoon of the day when I'd shot my buck Bob took my rifle, and with Lloyd as his guide collected his own trophy Pronghorned buck later into the afternoon.

Our trophies were almost a pigeon-pair with horn length of mine at 13½ inches, Bob's at 13¼ inches The only noticeable difference was my buck had lovely white ivory tips to each horn.

NOTES:

The Pronghorn is unique for it is in fact a pre-historic mammal living in our modern times. Authoritative experts consider the Pronghorn could date back one hundred to two hundred million years. No other ungulate on earth today is a kin to this extraordinary animal. Although they are commonly spoken of as Pronghorned antelope they are not zoologically members of the antelope family.

They are the fastest animals in North America, having been "clocked" at speeds in excess of 75 miles per hour. A fully mature buck will stand 32 to 40 inches at the shoulder (.82m to 1m) and 100 to 125lb (45.5kg to 57kg), so slightly taller at the shoulder and twenty-five percent heavier than a mature buck Chamois. The longest set of horns recorded in the Boone & Crockett Record Book are from a buck shot in 1899, 20 inches. The best recorded in the SCI Record Book is from a 1977 trophy – 18½ inches.

It seems that everything about this animal is unique; their eyes are about the same size as those of a horse and are set high in the side of

The author's Pronghorned antelope trophy, horn length 13½ inches, note the rare ivory tips on both horns.

Three horn features again make the Pronghorn different to all other antelope. The horns divide (hence their name), the horns are compounded hair and are cast annually.

Hunting Pronghorns was a great experience for Bob and I. They offered a fine stalking challenge, which we enjoyed to accept. They amazed us with their speed, ability to see danger at great distance, the beauty of their grace of movement. And they make a wonderful mount in a trophy room.

their head. This provides the Pronghorn with 360-degree vision and it is generally accepted they are able to detect a moving object as far off as three miles. No one really knows but it is possible their eyesight is akin to x8 binoculars.

The brittle hair on the coat of the Pronghorn contains numerous pithy air cells; designed to protect them from the often searing heat of the desert. The caudal patch is also unique for when alarmed a Pronghorn raises this patch. It seems that almost by some sort of telepathy all other Pronghorn within sight immediately raise the caudal patch, thus rapidly spreading alarm far and wide. Pronghorn also give off an alarm scent that can be detected by other Pronghorn up to a kilometre away.

No Way Back!

It wasn't going to be easy. I was standing on a steep soft sand slope.
The range was too far for accurate off-hand shooting.
The steep uphill angle and poor light had to be considered.

I sat perfectly still, only my eyes moving as they roved from the pieces of apple close to my boots to the crack in the warped and bleached boards of the old verandah. After cutting up the apple and placing it at my feet I had sat like a statue for about fifteen minutes. Finally a tiny questing nose appeared, a nose sifting and testing the various smells, tantalised by the aroma of fresh-cut apple. Hardly breathing I watched as hunger overcame caution and she scurried forward to sit close to my boot. Now perched on her hind legs she leaned forward to grasp a piece of apple in her tiny forepaws. However, before lifting it to her mouth she turned to eye me with miniature disdain, at the same time poised for instant flight.

I remained motionless for this was the very first time in my life that I'd seen a chipmunk at close range. My previous past experience being that of – now you see me, now you don't – for they moved as fast as lightning.

Keeping a watchful and suspicious eye on me the chipmunk began to eat, gnawing at the succulent apple with the same jaw action as a rabbit or guinea pig. My attention was riveted on this wonderful little animal so I didn't see the others arrive. Mentally I counted. I had seven chipmunks at my feet.

I was reclining, relaxed, in an old armchair on the verandah of the "Lone Wolf", my legs outstretched. The previous day we'd been partially sizzled and dehydrated in alkaline Pronghorn country. Today, here I was in the shade of tall and green cottonwood trees, surrounded by a lush alpine meadow. Everything was green. My metabolism was having some difficulty in adjusting to too many environment changes over the past week or so.

Arriving back from the Shirley Basin we'd overnighted at Lloyd Tillett's ranch house, a short night for we'd risen long before dawn, to travel for four slow hours to our destination, "Lone Wolf". Built early in the 1900s, as a Dude Ranch, this two-storey log cabin, with shingle roof, nestled grey and faded within the shade of giant cottonwoods planted at the time of building the cabin. While the basin where the cabin sat was green and lush the mid-slopes were clothed in dark pine forest rising to canyon rims slashed regularly by raw-red canyons. It was the stuff of western movies.

Although the day had dawned fine and clear the weather had slowly deteriorated during our drive from Lloyd's ranch house. By mid-afternoon we were experiencing gusty and swirling winds that seemed to be building in intensity with the progression of the day. Clearly the Mule deer would be feeding in sheltered nocks away from the annoying wind, they'd be hard to find!

After travelling for about half an hour in the Land Rover Lloyd pulled to a stop, all three of us very aware of the wind

It was within this inaccessible canyon that the author shot his fine Mule deer buck.

buffeting the vehicle. Climbing from the vehicle Lloyd took one last critical look at the sky and then announced his plan. Above us to the north was a high "V"-shaped canyon seeming to tower maybe sixty metres above the talis slope. Sheer vertical walls of pale limestone-like rock enclosed the canyon. Clearly, in some distant past era a mighty upheaval had formed this escarpment much like the unscaleable walls of a medieval castle. The skyline was a continuous serration of sharp weather-smoothed pinnacle rocks.

Between the canyon walls and us was a generally open gentle slope, with scattered varieties of low brush, including the inevitable sage brush. Mentally I guessed we had an easy thirty-minute climb before reaching the canyon wall. Bob and I were loading our magazines and making sure we had all we needed in our pikaus when Lloyd slowly drawled… "I'm a third generation Tillett to live on this range. My grandmother arrived here as a five-year old girl in a Prairie Schooner. As far as I know no one has ever entered this canyon. Cattle have never been able to access it so we've never bothered to have a look at it. With the wind the problem it is today, I figure it's our best chance of maybe finding a trophy Muley buck or two hiding in this inaccessible secluded sheltered safety.

Lloyd led us to a sharp-backed ridge that rose above the talis slope and appeared to offer the only easy access to gaining the canyon's skyline rim, an easy climb to warm us. We saw no deer. It was when we were about thirty metres from the canyon wall when a Bobcat exploded from some low brush ahead of us. Before we could bring rifles to our shoulders the Bobcat had disappeared amid the skyline rocks. Giving me no time to collect my thoughts he suddenly appeared again, streaking between the giant's teeth-like serrations of the skyline. Reflex took over – aim… lead… fire. Dust erupted, a ricochet whined. A miss. Chambering another round and bringing the Husqvarna to my shoulder I was in time to see him again, fifteen or twenty metres further on, still racing between the serrated rocks. I had a split second longer this time for the gap in the rocks was wider. The Husqvarna dropped him in his tracks.

While Lloyd and I climbed towards my most unexpected trophy cat Bob sought a more direct route to the skyline. I was in the act of picking up the Bobcat when there was a shout from

Mule deer were regularly sighted in canyon country such as shown in this photo. When alarmed they'd make directly for large tracts of thorn bush.

Bob! Both Lloyd and I spun, expecting further action, but there was Bob, sharply visible on the skyline, holding aloft another Bobcat. I'd not missed with my first shot after all. It didn't take the three of us long to skin both cats for (possible) future full body mounts.

With both skins in my pikau, warm against my back, we began our search for a route into the canyon. From the rim we could see much of the landscape ahead. Pine forest predominated, but there were numerous small clearings of grass and brush – perfect deer habitat. Our first searching without the aid of binoculars we saw no deer, but more careful study with our glasses soon had us identifying small groups of deer, grey ghosts within the

deep shadows of the conifers, Periodically the landscape was interrupted by rocky outcrops, wonderful observation points from which to glass.

Working our way along the rim rocks we were rather fortunate for we happened upon a clearly defined deer trail. Following it we were led under a large overhanging rock to a narrow cleft where the trail ended abruptly at a two-metre drop! Deer prints in the sand below showed us that deer jumped down. We did the same. But, on looking back at the face of the rock wall there wasn't a handhold or foothold to aid us climbing back. It was immediately patently obvious that we'd never exit the canyon by the route we'd entered it.

Up on the rim of the canyon the ever-increasing wind had howled and sighed around us, here within the canyon the air was still. By now it was about mid-afternoon, the deer should be moving about and feeding before dark. Slowly we moved forward, always stopping after every few steps to glass ahead. The sky above was heavy and oppressive, perhaps a storm was gathering, the blanketing dark grey cloud reducing visibility, especially within the deep shadows. But, despite this we saw deer. Ghosting silently within the shade and shelter of the pine forest we saw small groups of female with young, no bucks.

From another rock outcrop we had a small 2 x 2 Muley buck immediately below, he was totally unaware we were watching him. We watched as he soundlessly melted into a windfall of weathered trunks and branches, his grey coat blending so effectively we actually lost sight of him.

Diligently we searched, for where there was a small buck there may be his grandfather? Methodically, moving ever so

It isn't until you have first-hand experience that you learn just how fast a Chipmunk can move. The obvious challenge it to gain a photo such as this.

slowly, we worked our way further in to the canyon. At about 275m from the head the canyon branched left and right. It was while we were deciding which branch to follow that Bob picked up a very good cast Elk antler. Lloyd figured we'd take the left branch; it would be more sheltered from the wind. Bob decided to not climb this last nasty steep pitch; he'd await our return to the junction.

Scattered along the ridge we were climbing were a few large conifers that deprived us of a clear uninterrupted view of much of the surrounding landscape. I don't know what prompted me to stop and look back. Habit? Instinct? Who knows? The strangest fact of all is that I didn't stop to sweep and search our back-trail. Instead I looked directly at a small clearing within the thick pine forest, stark against the canyon wall. There in the gloomy shadows stood two Muley bucks. At a range of about 230 metres I could see the uppermost buck carried only small antlers, but the second buck, standing partially hidden by a fallen tree, carried antlers clearly of real trophy proportions.

"Shoot," was the only word Lloyd uttered.

It wasn't going to be easy. I was standing on a steep soft sandy slope. The range was too far for accurate off-hand shooting. The steep uphill angle and poor light had to be considered. But, I didn't have time to consider. Even as I was desperately, hastily, evaluating my situation both bucks melted into the deep gloom of the forest shadows.

I glanced at Lloyd and I know the disappointment on his face mirrored my own.

"You didn't have much time. Look!"

Even as Lloyd spoke I looked once again at the clearing. There, merging with the deep shadows was another buck. And he was the biggest of them all. My Nickel scope gathered light from the surrounding gloom for me. As the buck paused in mid-stride I swept the crosshairs onto his shoulder, triggering a shot as I did so. Did I miss? A crash of smashing branches signalled the passage of the fleeing buck. Ghost-grey he flashed through the scattered timber, showing himself only briefly as he raced to my left. With finger tightened on the trigger I followed his flight through my scope. Each time he appeared in the slightest of openings I jerked the crosshairs to the left, hammering the trigger. I couldn't tell whether I was scoring or not, but I'd hastily re-load to follow him once more in the scope. Three times I

Lloyd Tillett and the author with his fine Muley buck trophy. With eight points per side and beam length of 36 inches and spread of 31½ inches the final B & C Score placed it just outside the minimum Score for entry into the Boone & Crockett Book. That fact in itself declares the trophy to be of high quality.

sent the 180-gr Normas on their way, still not knowing if I was scoring hits? Without pause the buck was still crashing to my left, firm in his line of flight.

I'd left the "Lone Wolf" with seven rounds of ammo,

The Lone Wolf, away back in the Pryor Mountains in north-east Wyoming, was originally built, in the 1930s, as a dude ranch. We used the cabin as our base hunting camp, later as accommodation while assisting with a major cattle muster.

considering that sufficient for one trophy Muley buck. But, I'd used two on the Bobcats. With just one round seated ahead of the firing pin the buck was still plunging away. But, excitement leapt in my chest. I saw the buck was no longer running strongly; instead he was lunging and sliding downhill. Through the scope I watched as he tried to gain his feet. He stood, paused. I triggered my last shot. With my now useless rifle in my hands I watched as the buck tumbled over and over to come to rest far below.

Whooping to Bob, Lloyd and I raced and skied down the fine sandy slope. Bob arrived at the buck a second or two ahead of us.

"You've shot a bloody Elk," was his gasping explosive remark.

With nightfall very close at hand we gutted the buck, having decided to return in the sunlight of the next day to get good photos and recover the meat. We desperately needed to find a way out of the canyon before full darkness fell.

It is a well-considered rule for all outdoors folks – never follow a creek bed, always stay on the ridges. We followed the creek bed, for the glistening water was the only clear guide we had once darkness fell. That's how we fell into the trap that all who follow the creek beds eventually fall into, a waterfall.

Long after dark we finally found ourselves back at the Land Rover, soaked to the skin. We'd been forced to exit the canyon by climbing down the side of the waterfall, the rocks slick and slippery and wet, wet, wet.

NOTES:

A mature Mule deer buck will stand about 40-42 inches (102-107cm) at the shoulder and weigh anywhere between 200-250lb (90-114kg), so very much the same shoulder height and bodyweight of a big Rusa stag. Both deer with the rounded bulky body confirmation.

My Muley buck was a true trophy. Carrying seven points aside, two of which were outer tynes, the beam length was 36 inches (91.5cm) and outside spread 31½ inches (80cm) Due to the outer tynes the antlers were classified as "non-typical" for Boone & Crockett. The trophy failed by just 14 points to meet the minimum for entry in the Boone & Crockett Book for "non-typical" Mule deer.

King Of The Desert

If a wily old Muley buck was nightly feeding on the only patch of green grass in thousands of hectares of desert, where would he be hiding during the day?

For seven long days we hunted for a trophy Muley buck for Bob, without success. Up each morning, long before daylight, we rode horses; used the Land Rover, to place us in likely locations. We hunted the tall timber, the side canyons, the large gullies choked with thorn brush. Sometimes Lloyd and I acted as "beater" driving a canyon, with the wind at our backs, Bob on a suitable high point giving him a commanding view. Sometimes Lloyd and I threw stones or rattled cans full of stones in the hope of moving a buck from cover. Sometimes we rolled large boulders from canyon rims – "High Country Huntaways!"

Each day we saw dozens of deer. One morning we must have flushed forty-odd deer from one thorn brush-choked canyon, but there wasn't a shootable buck amongst them? Virtually every day we flushed bucks of modest trophy proportions, but we three were determined that Bob should have a chance at a buck at least equal to, or bigger, than mine. Tension was high for with the setting of the sun each day we were one day closer to the closing of the deer-hunting season. Tension was high also for we were hunting intensely, the pressure on Lloyd and I to find a buck for Bob, the pressure on Bob to maybe make a killing shot with only a split second warning.

During our pre-dawn breakfast, just two days before the season closed, Lloyd held a sort of "council of war". Obviously he'd been thinking and maybe hadn't slept so well. He began by suggesting a complete change of scenery. Apparently, away out on the desert, not too far from his ranch house, there lived a very large Muley buck, a buck that had outsmarted all local deer hunters for three or four seasons. Lloyd wasn't shy about remarking that the buck would likely also outsmart two Kiwi hunters, but it was worth a try.

So it was that a couple of hours later Lloyd rolled the Land Rover to a stop. Around us, in every direction, all Bob and I could see was flat featureless desert. There was the odd stunted mesquite, jack pine and cacti, plus the expected sage brush. I remember asking myself how deer could live and thrive in such an unkindly environment, especially a master trophy buck?

Lloyd must have read my thoughts, or seen the expressions on our faces for he explained that back in the distant canyons there were places where moisture up-welled and sustained great deer fodder. Pointing to the north he suggested we headed for the somewhat distant Pryor Mountains until we reached the foothill canyons. His last words were: "Work all the side canyons and draws, pay close attention to any that look too narrow to even hide a rabbit, let alone a deer. I'll pick you up after dark where the track crosses Crooked Creek Canyon."

With that he started the engine, turned and drove away – trailing the expected plume of dust. Silence. Neither of us was optimistic, the mountains had seemed like ideal deer country.

What a sight! A fine Muley buck, but not yet old enough to have antlers of Top Shelf size and quality.

The barren landscape surrounding us looked more like the surface of the moon, more like a place to hunt lizards, not trophy Muley bucks. But, Lloyd knew that somewhere in those tens of thousands of hectares of "moon-scape" was maybe a trophy buck for Bob? We started walking towards the distant mountains.

Within just a few minutes we came upon deer sign, our spirits lifted. Within the next ten minutes we had crossed the tracks of three different four-wheel-drives. Our spirits slumped! On this flat desert, which appeared as if a four-wheel-drive could drive over the lot of it, where was a Muley buck to hide?

It was clearly obvious we'd not find a trophy buck anywhere near wheel tracks, so if he was still alive he must be living somewhere it was impossible to drive a four-wheel-drive, and, difficult for hunters on foot. We had learned that many American deer hunters would hunt country only over which they could drive. So, we sat and searched, seeking a location we judged to be too tough for the locals to explore! And we found it.

Far off, close to the side canyons of the foothills of the Pryor Mountains, rose a tall rugged weather-scared mesa, slashed and chopped by a jumble of canyons. Fans of erosion marked the base of each canyon with wedges of bright red. The ragged crest showed no sign of any form of vegetation. It was the last place any sane deer hunter would look for a trophy buck. If we hunted it were we sane or insane? Would this be the daily hiding place of the "King of the Desert"?

Our spirits lifted a little; at least we had an objective for the day. We trudged on, for the mesa was quite a distance away. From time to time we'd stop and sit, working our glasses for we had no desire to "jump" a prospective trophy and Bob not get a shot. We were both extremely fit and could move fast over the flat ground so finally the mesa wasn't too far off.

"Hey, look at this!" a whisper from Bob.

"What is it?"

"A buck, and right out in the open!"

There was a Muley buck standing fully in the open with seemingly not a care in the world? He was too far distant, and the daily heat haze was starting to generate, so although it was clear to us he was indeed a buck we couldn't assess his antlers. He was standing on one of the many red earth fans scarring the base of the mesa. Our spirits lifted another notch. We needed to get closer.

Close to our left was a shallow gully. I suggested that I should stay where I was and Bob should make a solo effort, starting at the gully, to close in on the buck and determine if it was to be his trophy. My plan was to hold the buck's attention, should he become nervous, in the hope of buying time for Bob to get within shooting range. Once Bob was safely hidden within the gully I settled my binoculars on the buck and then ever so slowly raised my hat at arms-length above my head. Holding the hat perfectly still for a minute or two I then very very slowly moved it left to right, left to right. I had the buck's riveted attention. I held his attention for twenty minutes or more.

Finally I was able to see Bob, he was behind a large boulder, just thirty-five metres from the buck. As I watched with my glasses he gave the thumbs-down signal and I knew the antlers weren't of trophy class. Not wishing to alarm the buck I carefully followed Bob's line of approach to finally be resting beside him behind the rock. Amazingly the buck was still standing; his attention still on my previous location, but the sound of my camera shutter sent him racing up the red earth fan to disappear into one of the countless canyons on the face of the mesa.

For most of that afternoon I was Bob's gundog, scrambling into canyons, barking as I went, throwing stones into every shadowed gutter and cleft, rolling large boulders into the unseen depths of the deeper canyons. I walked into the wider canyons, watchful for both deer and rattlesnakes! Always Bob was stationed at a vantage point commanding a view of any likely escape route. For over three hours we methodically searched every square metre of every side canyon we approached. The only deer we "jumped" was the very same small buck we'd seen earlier.

Another hour and a half of searching brought us to the side of the mesa overlooking our start point where Lloyd had dropped us off. We were on the very top of the mesa, our first opportunity to get a really elevated view of this section of desert. Nightfall was less than an hour away, somehow within the next forty or fifty minutes Bob needed to have his crosshairs on the shoulder of a trophy buck! For the umpteenth time I settled my back against a convenient rock and began my usual sweeping search of the ground far below. You know the feeling… a sort of subtle warmth spreads from your guts?

Far below, and some distance from the mesa, a green stain

This photo shows the desert landscape where Bob Hart and the author finally successfully hunted Bob's Trophy Muley buck.

showed in stark contrast amid the washed pastel shades of the desert. Only from such an elevated position as high on the top of the mesa would this low green vegetation be so obvious. Surely this would be the place where a trophy buck would feed during the hours of darkness.

If a wily old Muley buck was nightly feeding on the only patch of green grass in thousands of hectares of desert, where was he hiding during the day?

Encouraged by sighting the green vegetation we continued for below us were a series of narrow deep canyons, all pointing directly at the green patch out in the desert. Twenty minutes of soundless stalking produced no buck, by now we were about ninety metres above the desert. Placing each foot with care we began our final descent. Bob is a few paces behind me, both rifles loaded and ready. Every few steps we stopped, not wishing to be dropped into reacting, we wanted the initial advantage.

Still no deer. Now we were only about fifty metres to the floor of the desert.

From a cleft at my feet, narrow enough for me to easily jump across, came the rattle of stones. Before I could react the small Muley buck, the same one we'd seen twice previously, exploded from the shadows to race out onto the desert. But, stones are still rattling within the narrow canyon. I spin, and there virtually at my feet is a set of massive heavy sweeping antlers bobbing down the cleft following the path of the escaped smaller buck. I yell to Bob, but he's seen only the smaller buck.

"Too small."

"No. Behind him!"

"Where did he come from?"

"T'hell with where he came from. Drop him!"

The racing buck had turned left from his daytime haven and was lunging for the rim of the nearest ridgeline, only thirty metres from safety. The explosion of Bob's Parker Hale was followed by an eruption of sand under the belly of the buck. A miss!

Now, as Bob reloads I know it's going to be a very close call! The buck has about ten metres to go and he'll crest the rim. Gone! Not wishing to kill or wound Bob's trophy buck, but help if I can, I lay my sights on the end of his nose, swing left and squeeze. An explosion under his nose peppers his face with gravel and small stones. For just a split second the buck pauses on the skyline. Bob's rifle barks again. He has him.

Bob's excitement is boundless. After the pressure of the last eight days the emotions he has contained overflow. We slap each other on the back and dance a mad "victory dance" before we race across to where the buck has fallen. Bob's trophy was the granddaddy of them all. With wide heavy beamed antlers, seven points on one side, five on the other, Bob has the better trophy Muley buck. He earned it.

Reaching out to take my hand in a firm handshake he spoke – "Thanks Gary."

It was long after dark that we finally located Lloyd and the Land Rover; he'd left the parking lights on. He didn't need to ask if we'd been successful, our smiles gave us away. One look at the trophy Bob lifted into the headlights was sufficient for Lloyd to firmly state:

"Bob, you've got the 'King of the Desert.'"

At last! After seven days of hard hunting Bob Hart took this outstanding Muley trophy. With thick beams, seven points on one side and five on the other Bob's trophy was in every way superior to the author's.

NOTES:

Of all the deer species I've butchered and eaten the Mule deer has the most meat on the ribs. Often we had roast deer ribs for each rib held as much as two inches (5cm) of succulent flesh.

Bob and I enjoyed hunting these deer. Yes, we had no end of disappointment until we secured Bob's wonderful trophy, but hunting is not all about success, it is also about enjoying new country, new species and most of all new people. We found Lloyd Tillett to be as fine a companion as anyone could wish for. His knowledge of the game, the country where we hunted, the local history, all sustained our interest throughout our time with he and his family.

You've figured out where the Mule deer got its name?

FOOTNOTE

Bob Hart and I were with Lloyd Tillett, on our way to visit the Museum of Western Art & History at Cody, Wyoming, the day US President J. F. Kennedy was shot. Within just a few hours many a Wyoming male was thinking of forming vigilante groups to go down to Texas and "deal" with the SOB who'd shot their President. Jack Ruby did the job for them.

SECOND TIME LUCKY…..?

He was walking directly towards where we were hiding. If he continued on the same line he'd walk right up to us. Here at last, without doubt, was a Boone & Crockett bull Elk.

This story begins at a slot machine in the MGM Grand Casino in Reno Nevada.

We'd had a highly successful SCI convention; my back pocket was bulging with deposit cheques. Ian Davidson, our chairman of directors, my team member for that convention, suggested we should celebrate by enjoying a steak dinner at one of the more swanky restaurants in the casino. A bottle of fine red wine much enhanced our enjoyment of the meal. Were we flushed with success, or was it the wine, I don't recall, but we both agreed that as we'd had a lucky convention maybe we could continue our luck and have a small "flutter" on the slot machines.

When I presented my $US50 bill to a change lady, seeking twenty-five cent coins, she remarked on my unfamiliar accent. I was the very first New Zealander she'd ever met. My courage no doubt bolstered by the red wine at dinner I asked her if she could place me at a slot machine that was primed to pay out. Taking my elbow she walked me to a single machine at the end of an island of machines, directing me to stay there until it paid. She offered the information that the previous evening a punter

had sunk over three thousand dollars into this machine, it was bursting to pay.

I discovered that to win the maximum payout I needed to feed three of my coins into the machine at a time, I followed the instructions. It didn't take long for my plastic cup of twenty-five cent coins to diminish rapidly. I was actually in the act of trying to discover just how few coins I had left in the payout tray on the machine when all manner of coloured light began flashing and numerous bells ringing.

Before I could fully comprehend what was happening two expensive-suit gentlemen were standing close to me. I'd won $US7,300. Time was taken up with the signing of papers, one of which was a Tax Form. I learned that our NZ Government had a tax accord with the State of Nevada; I was to lose thirty percent of my winnings!

I arrived back in New Zealand with just over $US5000 in bank notes well hidden in my western boots. In those days the exchange rate was very much in favour of the New Zealand dollar and UDC was offering 18.5% on medium to long-term investments, so I deposited my winnings. Out of sight, out of mind.

But, each year I'd attended SCI annual conventions I'd always been drawn to the 'White Mountain Apache Reservation' booth where they displayed supreme sets of trophy Elk antlers, the results of their previous seasons hunting. It seemed that at each convention the "White Mountain" booth was within view of our "Lilybank" booth. I became acquainted with Phil Stago, the outfitter for White Mountain Elk hunts.

That's how I discovered there was a five-year waiting list, for of all the places in the United States where a hunter might take a trophy Elk that would qualify for inclusion in the Boone & Crockett book White Mountain was first choice of all serious trophy Elk hunters. I signed up, my name at the bottom of a very long list. Meanwhile, the interest on my "Elk Fund" was accumulating.

You've guessed it. My name finally came up. Phil Stago telephoned from Arizona. Did I want one of their remaining openings for later that year? Did I ever…

Located in the north-east of the state of Arizona White Mountain contains the largest natural Ponderosa forest in the United States. It is also an Indian reservation where the Apache have their own Game Department; Council of Members administrates all functions within the reserve. In recent times the Indians have begun harvesting mature trees and to facilitate this commercial activity hundreds of kilometres of high quality roads now criss-cross the forest. Obviously these roads facilitate excellent access to all corners of the vast forest, a forest supporting two separate hunting camps, each servicing eight hunting clients, tons of room for everyone.

I found myself at Maverick Camp, along with seven other hopeful trophy Elk hunters, all from the United States. This was the very first time in my life that I'd been in an American hunting camp, so was fascinated by everything that took place. The first evening in camp, with everyone getting settled in, we enjoyed a supper of steak and lobster. If the hunting was as good as the food, we were in for a real treat.

All talk around the table that evening was about trophy Elk with my fellow Elk hunters, without exception, stating that they

Before the hunt all eight clients in camp declared they'd not kill a bull Elk unless it was clearly of B & C class. At the end of the seven day hunt eight bulls had been shot, just the one bull – this one – qualified for Boone & Crockett.

would be highly selective, that they'd not make a kill until a B & C bull was in their sights. The guide assigned to me was Jeff.

On Day One we were all woken at 3.30am, away from camp long before daylight. Jeff drove us to our assigned block where he parked on a high point; we listened for bugling bulls. Once a number of bulls had been marked we would set off to have a close look at all we could. Jeff used a cow call, which without fail drew bulls to our location. We were hunting in the forest but often we would come across clearings, locally known as senicas. I was daily intrigued by our pre-dawn sorties along forest roads for the frosted tips of the new growth on the trees edging the road glowed as if fluorescent.

Determined that a lack of physical fitness wouldn't hinder my once-in-a-lifetime hunt I had spent many hours a week building my fitness to a point where I could Indian trot for hours on end without fatigue. Jeff soon discovered I was perhaps fitter than he was, (he was fifteen years my junior), so he and I covered a lot of country. That first morning we must have gained close contact with a dozen or more bulls, some looking to be in the 340-350 class, but the minimum for Boone & Crockett was 375, so why kill a bull under that magic mark the first day of a seven-day hunt at White Mountain?

Back in camp about noon, lunch followed by a siesta, I soon discovered that Jeff and I were seeing a lot more bulls than my fellow hunters, for no doubt my fitness was much to our advantage. My fellow hunters were somewhat critical of the fact that I was wearing my usual shorts! I was told more than once that the Elk would see my (brown) legs and run off: these same critics wearing blue jeans, blue and very noisy when forcing through underbrush.

Every day Jeff succeeded in bringing us into close contact of bugling bulls, the cow call like a magic magnet. Often we were within ten or fifteen metres of these giant magnificent deer, often Jeff would give me the thumbs-down signal and we would retreat without alarming close-by Elk. Often we would return to Maverick Camp, around midday, having seen a dozen or more bulls, up close, but none in the 375 plus class. A couple of times I'd given Jeff the index finger trigger movement, but always he counselled patience, wait for the obvious B & C bull.

By the evening of Day Five, still two more hunting days ahead, all my fellow hunters had made a kill and only one of the bulls shot measured better than the magic 375. Each of the hunters I spoke with confided that they'd seen better bulls than what they had killed, that they knew when they squeezed their trigger that their sights were not on a B & C bull. Despite this they had made a kill, not wanting to go home empty handed. The rapid erosion of trophy standard in just five days fascinated me; six immature future B & C bull Elk had been killed solely to satisfy a human frailty, the male ego. They none of them wanted to go home and report they'd failed to make a kill.

After having spent the morning of Day Six covering areas we'd previously hunted, without sighting the desired class of bull, Jeff had a word with Phil during lunch. That afternoon we'd hunt one of the low country blocks previously hunted by one of the guides whose client had made a kill.

Virtually all our time during the first five and a half days of my hunt had been spent high within the Ponderosa forest and the associated senicas. It was wonderful stalking country for there was always the trunks of majestic Ponderosas to use as cover, always allowing us to get really close to study any bull of promise.

That afternoon we had a real change of scenery. I am guessing we drove for well over an hour, always downhill, until suddenly we were no longer in forest, we were in arid almost desert-like landscape, not unlike where I'd hunted Pronghorned antelope those many years before in Wyoming. It was dry and dusty with dry water courses and vast open areas, impossible to stalk across. Here and there were small stands of what I think may have been cottonwoods. Jeff informed me that out here in the desert water was important, we'd hunt close to a series of ponds where Elk would drink.

Leaving the vehicle hidden in a shallow depression we worked our way up a dry watercourse to a low hillock. Ahead was open terrain, denying any chance of advancing without being seen. The hillock had a couple of scraggy looking bushes growing atop it, so settling down, using these to screen us, we began to glass a vast landscape stretching out on either side and away ahead to the fringe of the forest.

It was well over an hour of inactivity before we saw our first bull Elk. He was walking directly towards where we were hiding. If he continued on the same line he'd walk right up to us. Here at last, without doubt, was a Boone & Crockett bull Elk.

When you see a big one, of anything, you know it instantly. I knew he was a real trophy for I'd heard that sharp intake of breath as Jeff focused his glasses. The bull must have come from the forest high above and we'd not noticed him until he was about 400m or more away. Walking down a shallow ridge we had a clear front-on view of the antlers. With head held low, in that typical Elk carry of a massive rack of antlers, we had plenty of time to determine an undoubted trophy, for with every shambling step that bull was taking he was drawing closer and closer to us.

It was just a matter of how close we'd let him get before I settled the sights of the Husqvarna on his brisket and squeezed. I was shooting my own handloads, a special Elk load a past Lilybank client had recommended – a 190-gr Hornady projectile, Magnum primers with 51gr of 4064 powder. I closed the bolt.

Off to our right, at about 150m distance, was a small stand of trees about the size of two tennis courts. They looked like cottonwoods: they weren't conifers. As the trophy bull reached this small copse he suddenly veered to his left and within a second or two had disappeared from view.

We sat. We waited. Suddenly a bull Elk burst from the trees and started racing across our front.

"Take him," shouted Jeff.

"Is it the same one?" an urgent question from me, for a tiny alarm bell was ringing in the back of my head, something wasn't right?

"Take him, take him, before he gets away."

By now the bull had passed us and with every racing step was increasing the range. Behind the shoulder on a bull Elk is a dark patch of hair. I settled the crosshairs on that patch, swung left and squeezed. The bull stumbling a couple of steps before rolling into a shallow depression, out of sight excepting for the top tynes. Something didn't look right?

We've talked about "ground shrinkage" before? I was gutted, so much so that all my energy was taken up with trying to swallow the giant lump in my throat, desperate to breathe, for at our feet half hidden in a shallow pond, was a small bull Elk. Not the B & C bull we'd watched walking towards us. Jeff had made an enormous mistake and very quickly acknowledged it. I could see his utter disappointment matched my own.

We never saw the B & C bull again. He must have run off while we were engrossed in the small bull he'd chased out of the

A pair of promising <u>future</u> trophies.

stand of trees.

Jeff was doing his very best to console me. I could see that he was totally devastated with the turn of events, so did my best to minimise his distress. I didn't take any photos.

We loaded the bull onto the vehicle and headed for Maverick Camp. Unbeknown to me Jeff must have radioed Phil, for at a junction in the road, away back up there in the Ponderosa forest, there was Phil waiting for us. Phil immediately, without questioning, acknowledged a most unhappy mistake had been made. I was to not count this bull as my trophy; Jeff and I would continue to hunt the following day, Day Seven, the final day of my hunt.

Are you expecting a happy ending? The following morning I woke at 4.40am, no one had woken me at the usual 3.30am. Camp was silent and sleeping. I found Jeff struggling into his hunting clothes; no one had woken him either. We discovered the cookhouse was locked, so no chance of coffee or breakfast. Knowing that we were right behind the eight ball we raced out of camp, but despite Jeff doing all he could to rescue the situation all we saw that morning was one excellent bull Elk racing through the forest away from us, with a dozen or more cows following him.

That afternoon we returned to the desert in the (faint) hope of once again seeing the B & C bull. We'd departed camp following a violent electrical storm. Heavy rain chased by lashing winds was what we encountered upon arriving at our planned destination. We saw not a solitary Elk that afternoon. Hunt over.

Words fail me, these many years later, when I try to give some indication of how deep my disappointment was when I crawled into my sleeping bag for the last time at Maverick Camp. I'd been patient throughout the hunt, turning down very good bulls, always in the hope of taking a B & C trophy. It was the seeing of the majestic bull, plus the anticipation of success turning so dramatically wrong, that was the awfully bitter pill to swallow.

SECOND TIME …?

Beginning when Sue and I moved to Lilybank we each year sent out a newsletter with our Christmas cards. You'll all understand my disappointment, after my White Mountain Elk hunt, featured in one paragraph of our newsletter that year. Minford and Judy Beard had hunted a couple of times with us and our family had developed a close deep friendship with this wonderful couple who lived on "Three Springs Ranch" away off in the north-western corner of Colorado.

Judy (now deceased) was a wonderful letter-writer, my Christmas newsletter prompting her to write a long letter in response. Her letter-in-reply contained a paragraph captioned "For the Information of Gary". "Three Springs" had recently entered into a "Ranchers for Wildlife" contract with Rob Raley a professional hunting guide. This contract allowed him to guide hunting parties on "Three Springs" for both Elk and Mule deer, but in return for this privilege he was to manage the game resource, undertake predator control and protect the ranch from poachers. Judy went on to report that Rob was annually allowed just five Elk Permits by the State of Colorado Game Department, would Gary like his name on one of these five? Judy also wrote that "Three Springs" had never produced a B & C trophy bull Elk, and I needed to know this before committing to an Elk hunt on the ranch.

Sue and I talked it over at length. I'd hunted at "White Mountain" in the certain knowledge that my chances of a B & C trophy there were high, but being in the B & C book wasn't the be-all and end-all of Elk hunting. Had my expectations at "White Mountain" been too high? A fine trophy and a fine hunt were first and foremost, not hunting for a placing in some Record Book. It was agreed, yes, Gary would be delighted to have his name on one of the Elk permits for the upcoming season.

Judy and Minford met us at the Grand Junction Airport and drove us the four hours to "Three Springs". I had a couple of days before the hunt was scheduled to start so sorted my gear and made sure the Husqvarna was "on the button" I was shooting my 190gr Elk loads.

Sue and I had visited Judy and Minford on two previous occasions, so have a reasonable knowledge of the layout of the property. The ranch house was about 6500ft (2000m) altitude and the Karren Place, base hunting camp, some twenty kilometres distance but at almost 10,000ft (3075m) altitude. So when Rob collected me from the ranch house I had some reasonable knowledge of where we'd be hunting.

The landscape of "Three Springs" is dramatically different to "White Mountain", for there was no extensive areas of forest. Here we would be hunting largely open terrain, in fact a high dry alpine plateau. Vegetation was low and stunted, plenty of sage brush, some areas where the brush was about waist high and intermittent stands of trees about six or seven metres high. For much of the time the landscape could be mistaken for parts of our Mackenzie Basin.

Within an hour of arriving at the Karren Place Rob had us off and away, looking for Elk. To begin with we drove and glassed, seeing Elk and Mule deer constantly. But late into the afternoon, about an hour before dark, we parked the truck and walked in to Luxon Creek. On all sides there appeared to be a vast flat plain that stretched to far distant horizons. My first thought was how difficult it would be to stalk an animal standing away out there. Here was terrain like where I'd hunted Pronghorned antelope.

Then, suddenly, we were standing on the rim of a vast deep canyon system. I would guess the far rim to be four or five kilometres away, the depth maybe five hundred metres. I was standing on the rim of a canyon smaller but with very much the same landscape features as the Grand Canyon. The walls of the canyon were sculptured by millenniums of wind and water erosion. The setting sun highlighted the different colours of layer upon layer of rock strata. As we seated ourselves on a shallow bench, offering a good view of much of the canyon, Rob informed me that many of the coloured layers of rock forming the canyon wall contained seashells and experts were able to determine that this landscape had been under the ocean seven different times.

We began glassing, watching many Elk and Mule deer slowly working their way towards the creek in the floor of the canyon, a slim skein of silver from our high vantage point. But by this late hour much of the canyon was in deep shadow for the sun was now low in the sky. Rob suggested that maybe we should be at this same viewing point somewhat earlier on the morrow.

Next morning we were well away from the Karren Place long before daylight, driving and searching. I would guess that during

Entrance to the 'Karren Place' hunting camp for the author's Elk hunt on Three Springs Ranch north-west Colorado.

that morning we sighted somewhere between one hundred and fifty and two hundred Elk of which twenty to thirty were bulls, only two appeared to be trophy class. Rob's strategy was to drive to a high point and glass, but most of the Elk we glassed were a kilometre, or more, away.

We were back in camp for lunch about noon, the plan being to head back to Luxon Creek about 2pm.

Our sortie into Luxon Creek was somewhat delayed for we got "pinned down" by a small group of cow Elk being escorted by a non-trophy bull. However, they finally moved on and we were able to take up our canyon observations from the exact same vantage point as the day before.

If you've ever hunted Elk you'll know just how easy they are to see in open ground when the sun is at a low angle, their pale cream coat is almost like a beacon. Rob had his x30 spotting scope in action; he invited me to, "Have a look at this…."

Away to our left and far down the canyon a small steep ridge rose from the canyon floor. Rob's spotting scope showed me the ridge appeared to be covered with some form of reasonably thick brush. It wasn't until the bull stepped fully into the open that I spotted him, amazed that despite his light body colouring I had failed to spot him when he was standing stationary in the brush. Mind you, the Elk was maybe three kilometres away, so I beg forgiveness.

All afternoon we watched that bull, for I could sense Rob was very interested. Throughout the afternoon the bull wandered slowly closer, sometimes in view, sometimes unseen for a period of time, but always he was working up-canyon. When he had covered about half the distance, from where we'd first sighted him, he slowly began to climb, following a more or less razor-backed ridge that terminated on the-far rim of the canyon. It was when the bull finally crested out, skylined against a clear blue sky, that Rob quietly informed me that we'd get a closer look at that bull in a couple of days time…!

Rob obviously noted the questioning look on my face. He explained. He was sure he knew where the bull was headed. The rut hadn't really started, but he knew of a high basin where the cows gathered and the bulls were drawn to this gathering of cows. We should hold off for a couple of days.

I had a great couple of days, sort of R&R. Each day started well before daylight, we saw plenty of Elk, Mule deer, the odd coyote, and away out on the flats small groups of Pronghorn

Frequent sightings of many Elk offered wonderful photo opportunities such as these three immature bulls.

antelope. Always Rob was on the lookout for a very large bull. He took me to where I could see dinosaur bones and from time to time would take me on a "walkabout" to see rings of stones where Indians had once pitched their teepees. He was an excellent guide for he had a great knowledge of local history, plants and animals.

R&R is great, but always in the back of my mind was – "When

will I get a chance at a trophy bull?" Those two and a half days dragged for I'd had two bad experiences with Elk in my life, the "Dwarf Bull" in Fiordland and the "Mistake Bull" at White Mountain. Yes, it wasn't until we were seated having lunch that Rob finally announced we'd go take a closer look at the "Canyon Bull".

After driving for well over an hour we had arrived at the foot of a series of long gentle ridges that Rob informed me rose to meet the rim of the canyon where we'd last seen the bull. We were now on the opposite side. Nestled just below the canyon rim, and at the very top of the ridges in view, was a shallow basin where cows traditionally gathered at the onset of the rut.

Big country is deceptive, it took us over two hours to climb until we were close to the canyon rim. By now we were aware of bull Elk bugling somewhere above and ahead. The only cover we had was small depressions in the ground, so we were meticulously careful to stay down and out of sight. I allowed Rob to work ahead of me, awaiting his signals before I moved forward a short distance at a time. All this time the sound of bugling bulls was louder and getting much closer.

With simple hand actions Rob signalled for me to close the bolt on the Husqvarna. He then waved me forward. We were flat on our stomachs on the very edge of the basin. The sound of many bulls bugling was continuous. Whispering into my ear he told me that at his signal I was to stand and move forward quickly. He would direct me to the best of the bulls.

Three quick steps and there before me was a shallow basin and a jamboree of Elk. Bulls were bugling and chasing each other, cows and calves were milling around creating a continual melee. To my immediate left was a large bull, apparently stunned and stationary at our appearing so suddenly.

Rob quickly pointed at this bull, whispering "Take him."

From deep in my sub-conscious came the question.

I whispered – "Is it the right one?"

"Yes".

It wasn't an easy off-hand shot for the lower half of the bull's body was hidden; he was standing in a shallow depression. Despite this it was a one shot kill.

Rob was over the moon for he immediately declared my trophy to be the best bull he'd ever got for a client. He also expressed his admiration for the knockdown power of the 190-gr Hornady projectile.

Once we'd taken plenty of photos Rob radioed his wrangler who somehow managed to drive the four-wheel-drive pick-up all the way up to where we stood beside the trophy. That's when I witnessed the most ingenious use of a portable Honda winch to load the bull on to the pick up. We returned triumphantly to camp where the Elk carcass was hung to cool overnight.

Yes, I'd been second time lucky.

NOTES:

A fully mature bull Elk is a large deer. He will stand as tall as five feet (1.54m) at the shoulder, a body length of as much as 10ft (3.1m) and weigh up to 1000lb (455kg).

In ancient times Elk were a plains animal, their range being virtually the entire continent of North America, excepting for the Far North and Deep South. Today they are largely found where they can hide, tall timber or high basins.

With a beam length of 51¼ inches this classic 6 x 6 Elk scored 343⅜ Boone & Crockett, so 31⅛ points below minimum entry for the Record Book. The author had turned down larger trophy bulls at White Mountain, but today values his Colorado Three Springs Ranch hunt for the wonderful folks associated with his eventual Elk hunting success.

Out of curiosity we did B & C Score my 'Three Springs' trophy. With a longest beam of 52¼ inches we arrived at a Score of 343½, so 31½ points below the B & C minimum. Without a doubt I'd turned down larger trophies at "White Mountain" but that was a different place, a different time, different criteria.

Today I am proud of my Elk trophy for it reminds me, daily, of "Three Springs Ranch" and Judy and Minford Beard, (both now deceased), two very special people dear to the hearts of every member of our family.

If you've ever wondered just how big a mature bull Elk is just hang one up and stand back….!!

HIDE AND SEEK!

For four hours I'd stealthily eased my way downhill in the oak forest, aware that it hadn't rained for three years, the dry leaves on the forest floor crunchy as potato chips. I'd seen not a single deer! Where were they hiding?

This story also began at a Safari Club International annual convention at Reno, Nevada, United States of America. Sue and I were standing in our Lilybank Safari Lodge booth when Lucia Morgan appeared, excitedly holding aloft a small piece of paper. Lucia and her husband Bill had hunted with us a couple of years prior and we'd formed a great friendship with them. But, what was exciting Lucia?

A condition attached to anyone securing a booth at an SCI convention is a requirement to make a substantial donation to provide funds for SCI to do their many good works. We had donated a hunt for a high scoring Gold Medal Red stag. The convention organisers had decided that our donated hunt would be a one hundred ticket raffle, to be drawn at the annual ladies luncheon. Lucia's excitement was that she'd bought the very last ticket in the raffle. There and then she informed us that she was going to be the winner.

Everyone who buys a raffle ticket, or Lotto ticket, says (or hopes) they'll be the winner, so Sue and I didn't pay a great deal

of attention to Lucia's statement. A couple of hours later there was Lucia, once again racing towards our booth, to excitedly inform us that she'd won the Lilybank Raffle. She and Bill would be hunting with us once more.

So it was that a couple of months later Lucia and Bill arrived at Lilybank for Lucia's hunt. It wasn't an easy hunt. I had a particular stag in mind for Lucia, but after three days of diligently hunting we'd not sighted that stag? A wise professional guide assesses his successes, but more importantly he should also assess his failures. I figured that the reason why we were not seeing the stag I sought was because he was going into hiding with the first suggestion of dawn in the eastern sky.

We were away out on the hill long before daylight the next morning. I knew the general area where I might find the stag so we'd stumbled through the dark (no torches), to finally take up a position where we'd have an excellent view with the first brightening of the sky in the east. Yes, there he was, highlighted by the very first rays of the rising sun. But, even at that extremely early hour the stag was on his way to his secret, and no doubt secluded, daily hiding place. He was about 400m away and moving further from us. We had to make a fast forced march around a small knoll, to bring us out onto a ridge almost opposite the departing stag.

When Lucia was comfortable, in a sitting position, I gave the stag a whistle. He paused, luckily almost broadside on, and just the one shot from Lucia's rifle concluded the hunt. Bill, meanwhile, had recorded it all on his video camera.

We all know about and have experienced "ground shrinkage". As we walked up to the downed stag we three experienced the

The California habitat of the Blacktail deer is very similar to some areas of North Island hill country. This photo is of part of the ranch east of San Francisco where the author hunted.

very opposite, for with every step we took closer to Lucia's trophy the bigger those antlers appeared to be.

Months later, after the required sixty days for drying, Lucia's trophy stag was officially measured by an SCI Master Measurer, it was the new Number One for South Pacific Red stag. Yes, a lady hunter was #1.

Another landscape photo of Blacktail country east of San Francisco. Any deer sighted in the open soon made a dash for cover and there was plenty of that!

Prior to attending the SCI convention the following year Lucia and Bill insisted that Sue and I stay with them on their 4000 acre ranch in the hills thirty miles east of San Francisco, and while we were there Lucia explained her wish to reciprocate. Gary was invited to visit with them during the next hunting season to hunt for a trophy Blacktail buck on their ranch.

Lucia and Bill collected Sue and I from the San Francisco airport. After getting settled and a late lunch Bill invited me to bring my rifle and take a tour of the ranch. Off we went in his farm 4 x 4. The property reminded me of North Island hill country for it was a continual series of ridges and gullies. Bill explained that about two thirds of the property was forested with various species of oak, blue oak, California black oak, live oak, with some digger pines. The low brush was mostly the familiar manzanita with some coyote brush and chamille. The only grass appeared to be at the lowest altitude, close to the house. I discovered that Bill had been busy with bulldozer and grader for he had an extensive series of farm tracks criss-crossing the whole property, both within the forest and along the brush covered ridges.

As the afternoon progressed we began seeing deer, all females with young. But upon cresting a small rise, there, across a gully at about 250m, was a buck. Bill urged me to try a shot. I was able to rest on the bonnet of the 4 x 4, but as I was settling the buck broke into a slow trot down the ridge towards the safety of the forest. Swinging to lead I squeezed off a hopeful shot, and, down went the buck.

It wasn't until we had walked across to the buck that I saw he was a youngster, with two points per side. It was just on dark when we arrived back at the house, the buck in the back of the four-wheel-drive.

Upon seeing the buck Lucia "exploded", berating Bill for allowing Gary to kill a "baby" not a real trophy. Poor Bill. I walked away for Lucia's anger was very evident.

It was after our evening meal that Lucia told me that she and Bill had to go to work the following day, Monday, but if I was happy to get up a couple of hours before daylight she would drive me to the highest point on the ranch (2,300 ft) where she'd drop me off and I could spend my day working my way downhill back to the house, looking for a real trophy buck as I went.

True to her word Lucia woke me in darkness, and she drove me to the highest point of the ranch. Wishing me luck she headed away, not wanting to be late for work. I found myself in

This is the author's Blacktail buck trophy, the biggest buck ever shot on the ranch. This particular set of antlers have never been scored for either SCI or B & C, but many a visitor to Gary's trophy room have suggested it would qualify for B & C.

moderately open forest, the trees not all that tall, no underbrush to obstruct my view. Testing the situation I thought I could clearly see, with the aid of my binoculars, up to fifty metres ahead. However, the sun hadn't yet risen so I sat and waited in the forest gloom. The pre-dawn day was cool and silent.

Certain that my slightest mistake would deny me of a shot at a buck, and knowing that I needed to see a buck first, so I could assess antler, I moved ever so slowly, stopping often, glassing the forest ahead and either side. Time after time I'd move downhill just a few paces to sit with my back against a tree trunk, search with my glasses, listen for any sound of movement. The hours ticked slowly by.

For four hours I'd stealthily ease my way downhill through the oak forest, aware that it hadn't rained for three years, the dry leaves on the forest floor crunchy like potato chips. I'd seen not a single deer! Where were they hiding?

Yet another hour of super careful stalking in the forest brought no sighting of deer, brought me to a creek, the only running water on the ranch. The bed of the creek was rather open, affording a clear view both up-and-downstream. The noonday sun, shining through the forest canopy, was dappling the sand either side of the softly whispering creek. Five hours of nervous careful stalking and I was in need of relaxation. A convenient fallen log offered a cosy back rest. Relax Gary.

And then it happened. I'd maybe been sitting there for ten minutes when I heard what I instinctively knew was an antler striking against a tree limb or branch. Before I could register and react a Blacktail buck exploded from a narrow deep gutter almost at my feet, (exactly the same scenario as Bob Hart's Muley buck those many years before in Wyoming). The buck had many an escape route to take, but his mistake was to splash once in the creek then race up an open sandy spur. He was running dead straight away from me, so all I had to do was place the crosshairs between his ears and touch the trigger.

The gutter that buck was hiding in was so narrow I was able to stand with a foot either side. Obviously he had heard me approach and sit, and then with the ticking off of the minutes had finally lost his nerve and sought to escape. Had I not sat down beside his hidey hole I'd never have known he was there; such is the (sometimes) luck of the hunter.

That evening there was much celebration for Bill was certain my trophy was the best they'd ever taken off the ranch. Lucia was happy, (Bill was now forgiven) for my trophy was equal in every way to her Lilybank Red stag. Reciprocation was complete. I learned the name of the creek was Millar Creek, and the bend in the creek where the buck had hidden was Deer Camp. Rather an appropriate name don't you think?

NOTES:

I've never had my eight-point trophy Blacktail buck officially scored, but here are some measurements. Outside spread – 22½ inches. Beam length – 18 inches. Back tynes – 11 inches. It is a fine trophy taken under unusual, unique, circumstances.

Blacktail deer habitat is mostly the Pacific Coast of the United States and Canada. They are also found on coastal Alaska and offshore Alaskan islands where they are known as Sitka deer. A mature buck will stand about 38 inches (97cm)) at the shoulder and weigh 150lb+ (68kg +), so about the size of a medium sized Fallow buck. Classified as a "small deer" they are largely forest dwelling browsers.

SECTION SIX

– South Africa

Preamble
Kiwi in Bok Country
Harvest in the Oats
Canyon Challenge
A Walkabout With Hazards
Trackers Extraordinaire
Stretching the Barrel
Last Days at Madikwe
Quickly, Quickly
In the Land of the Ancient Bushmen
I Didn't Know Trophy Hunting in
South Africa was a Spectator Sport!
Seeking Houdini

Preamble

It is an undeniable fact that had my father not left me an inheritance, somewhat larger than I'd anticipated; I'd have never experienced a safari in South Africa. It was my wife Sue, who urged me to do something really special, something that all my life had been an impossible dream, in memory of my father's gift. So, we two planned a safari in South Africa.

We were exceptionally fortunate that through our connections with international hunting, via our many attendances at international hunting conventions, we knew the person whom we could unreservedly entrust with the planning for our once-in-a lifetime safari – Beverley Wunderlich of J/B Adventures & Safaris.

While Beverley worked on the details of the hunting safari, Sue and I frequented our local library, reading every book that would further inform us about South Africa, for we both felt the more we could learn the more we would enjoy our seven-week safari. The history of that country is absorbing.

Aware that Sue is a non-hunter, and wishing that we could both see as much of South Africa as possible, within our timeframe, I provided Beverley with a Wish List of antelope species found at a number of widely dispersed and different locations, to ensure that along with the hunting we also would (hopefully) see much of that vast country. We would eventually hunt out of six different lodges or camps and travel almost the full length of the country.

Our itinerary provide for ten days in South Africa ahead of Day One of the hunting safari for we knew of the need to become acclimatised and overcome the effects of long distance jet travel. For those ten days we were "tourists", beginning in Cape Town with day trips to the Cape of Good Hope, Stellenbosch the wine region, and on a perfect day the cable car trip to the top of Table Mountain. Next a six-day conducted tour took us through the Cape Province, the Transkei, and KwaZulu Natal Province, travelling the Garden Route, to finally arrive at Durban.

Our professional hunter (PH for short), Darren Baker and his wife-to-be Mia collected Sue and I from our hotel in Durban after lunch one Sunday afternoon, our destination the city of Hilton where Coenraad Vermaak Safaris had their base.

I now invite you to join Sue and I on our once-in-a-lifetime South African hunting safari.

KIWI IN BOK COUNTRY

All he wanted to talk about was the All Blacks and the Webb Ellis Trophy.

Standing there, and looking around me, I could easily have been mistaken, thinking I was somewhere in the North Island hill country, for the sharp ridges and many spurs were totally familiar. The homestead was not unlike the lovely expansive homes I'd seen as a child when living in Hawkes Bay. The skyline, in all directions, was densely bush-clad hills, the bush spilling down to the grass paddocks. In the paddocks close to the house were all the usual expected domestic farm animals. As I absorbed the scenery Darren explained the forest was a mix of yellow wood, forest elder and cape beech. From a distance it appeared to have a tight canopy.

It was only after we'd been invited into the house for a cup of coffee that I knew I wasn't in New Zealand, for Darren introduced me to Ginger McKenzie, the property owner; that delightful South African accent. We'd arrived at Boston House Farm about 2pm to hunt Bushbuck. Ginger suggested we were too early; the bucks would still be back in the forest. Why not come in and have a coffee, killing some time. I think he had an ulterior motive, for very soon after we were seated at the kitchen table, coffee mugs in hand, he broached the subject. All

This Cape (Cape of Good Hope) style house, with thickly thatched roof and plastered white washed walls, was Base Camp at the beginning of our South African hunt with Coenraad Vermaak Safaris. We saw many homes of this same style.

he wanted to talk about was the All Blacks and the Webb Ellis Trophy.

I'll not traverse in detail that conversation/discussion, for this is a hunting story, but in summary our host, plus Darren Barker my PH, had only one wish, that the Poms didn't win the Cup. They were happy for the All Blacks, the Wallabies or the Boks to win, but please, please, not the Poms. When pressed (by me) they admitted the All Blacks should do it this time around.

Yes, we were hunting Bushbuck. Together the farmer and Darren explained that Bushbuck were creatures of habit, feeding

Author with his Bushbuck trophy SCI Gold Medal.

early morning and late afternoon on the grass paddocks edging the forest. Here was I with the preconceived idea that hunting in South Africa was based out of tent camps on the Veldt, but today there I was in a location not at all unlike hunting Fallow buck at Lake Wakatipu!

I guess it was about 4pm when Darren and I finally returned to his Toyota, which he moved to a position where we could sit comfortably within and keep a series of large gullies, running up to the forest margin, in view. Maybe it was half an hour before Darren drew my attention to the very first Bushbuck I'd ever seen. In pointing out the distant buck I sensed a measure of excitement in his voice, but being the professional that he is he wasn't about to lift my hopes too high. First we had to stalk the buck and secondly I needed not to miss.

As we watched the Bushbuck started feeding further and further from the forest edge, slowly working his way down a sharp-backed ridge. Below the buck was a series of tight little gullies that my x10 glasses revealed to be chocked with various species of dense brush.

After moving the Toyota to the left, and out of view of the feeding buck, we started our approach. First we were within the forest, but as we reduced the distance so the forest changed to this nasty thick, noisy, brush. The lay of the land was forcing us to work our way firstly under the buck's position, then uphill. I've never liked stalking uphill for the turn of any hill means a shortened view ahead. If we were to reduce the range to a reasonable distance we had no choice but to work our way across the face of the hill, then up a narrow steep gully, always fighting the thick brush. Our approach was much complicated by the fact that we had a swirling wind that at any time could waft our scent uphill.

With the buck about 150m away we suddenly ran out of cover! Ahead was open pasture, not a single bush or rock for cover to stalk closer. Darren asked me if I was comfortable with the distance. I was. But, as I eased into a half crouched position I could see that to have a clear view of the buck I'd have to stand and shoot off-hand. Here I was on the very first day of my extensive South African safari and my first shot would have to be off-hand. The choice was mine.

I'll not draw out your agony. I made a clean one-shot kill, the shot through both shoulders. After we'd got all the usual photos and gutted the carcass we were able to easily carry it to Darren's Toyota to return to camp at Hilton, about a forty-five minute drive. After the cape had been taken care of Darren SCI Scored the horns. With 14⅜ inch horns my first South African trophy qualified for an SCI Gold Medal.

How about that? A Kiwi in Bok Country had opened his score with Gold. Was it a good omen?

NOTES:

As my Bushbuck trophy was my sole experience with the species I'm not in a position ot offer up buckets full of advice. All I can do is repeat what I've stated above, it is like hunting Fallow buck along the bush edges at Wakatipu.

A fully mature Fallow buck and Bushbuck both have the same shoulder height – 36 inches (91cm), but whereas a big Fallow buck will weigh out at close to 200lb (90kg) a fully mature Bushbuck will tip the scales only to 140lb (63kg).

Harvest In The Oats

Where just a second or two before there'd been no game in sight, we now had fifty or more pairs of eyes watching us...

Away from Coenraad's Hilton lodge long before daylight, today with Darren's two Zulu trackers in the back – Nkosnati and Thorge. Once again we'd be hunting farming property not too distant from the township. I was still sort of out of step with myself, not having yet got my head around the fact that not all game in South Africa was away out there somewhere on the veldt.

The first two or three hours of the day drew a blank for us. We were hunting Common Reedbuck in an area that had recently been burned, and not a head of game did we see. Darren finally "pulled the pin", we headed back to Hilton, had a cuppa, collected Sue, who'd decided not to make the super early morning start, and off we went again, this time to a different farm.

But, once again we didn't see a single head of game. We were slowly driving and searching reed beds on either side of a moderately small river. We flushed no end of all manner of waterfowl, including crane and stork, but not a single four-legged animal did we see. All morning we drove slowly, searched diligently, saw nothing.

By now Darren was starting to get puzzled and concerned why an area that had produced all manner of great Common Reedbuck trophies on earlier hunts that season was now devoid of game.

I guess it must have been close to noon when he finally drove away from the river and up onto a small knoll above the river. I could see farmland stretching in every direction, the river meandering through many a field. Immediately at our front was a very large field of oats, obviously irrigated by a centre pivot. Apparently uncertain what he could do to rectify the situation Darren switched off the engine and turned to look at me, a perplexed look on his face.

While facing Darren I had the full extent of the irrigated field of oats in view behind his head and shoulders. Where just a second or two before there'd been no game in sight, we now had fifty or more pairs of eyes watching us.

"Look behind you, I whispered."

Instantly it was clear that every local Common Reedbuck, male and female, had collectively decided that the best place to hide during the day was in the waist high irrigated oat crop. But we were not out of the woods (oats) yet, for most of the Reedbuck in sight were (maybe) 500m away. Moving as slowly and cautiously as he could Darren reversed the Toyota back down the slope of the knoll and following the river – out of sight of the Reedbuck – he detoured to once again bring the alerted Reedbuck into sight. The range was now about 300m. We could get no closer. I've said it before, I say it again – when you see a really big male you know he is Mr Big. Out there in that oat field was a buck with horns standing far far higher above his head than any of the other bucks.

Author with his Common Reedbuck. With a horn length of 15¼ inches this trophy placed high in the Gold Medal listing of the SCI Record Book.

Sue and I were now seated on the back of the hunting car, so I had an unobstructed view ahead. My daypack was on the seat beside me so slowly I brought it forward and placed it on the crossbar in front of me, a fore-end rest. I had to sort of settle myself down in a rather bent position, but with a final wriggle I had me a rock-solid rest.

With the crack of the rifle all but one Common Reedbuck raced away to splash across the river and disappear – quickly – over a near horizon.

Darren sent his trackers off to find the downed buck, and it wasn't easy to find in that oat crop. Can you understand how I wasn't yet sort of getting my head together about hunting in South Africa? I had just harvested, what to me was a rather exotic species of game, in an oat crop!

Darren must have had an arrangement with the farmer that the carcass was to be left in his killing shed, so we took photos and removed the cape there and then, before returning to Hilton and a somewhat late lunch.

It was at the dinner table that night that Darren informed Sue and I that we'd be heading for Emanweni (place of many cliffs) the following day, about a four-hour drive. Our camp cook would be Darren's fiancée Mia. If Emanweni translated to "place of many cliffs" we clearly wouldn't be hunting away out on the more or less flat veldt!!

NOTES:
Once again I'd made a one shot kill and with a horn length of 15¼ inches, my trophy placed at #28 in the SCI Record Book, my second Gold Medal trophy. I'd made a golden harvest in an oat crop!

A landscape shot of the type of terrain where the author hunted Reedbuck west of Durban in KwaZulu Natal province.

The Common Reedbuck stands about 36 inches (91cm) at the shoulder and weighs 145 to 170lb (66 to 77kg) so stands about the same height at the shoulder as a Fallow buck, but is slightly lighter in bodyweight.

CANYON CHALLENGE

There was no doubt this was a one-shot deal. One step in any direction and the bull would disappear into the dense forest. But the crosshairs were waving about…!

We arrived at Emanweni about noon to a complete change of scenery. While based at Hilton we'd hunted various farming properties, at Emanweni there was no sign of farmland in any direction, we were finally in what appeared to be wilderness. But, still no vast flat veldt! In every direction all we could see was range after range of heavily forested hills, with all manner of interlocking ridges and spurs. If you didn't know you were in South Africa's KwaZulu Natal province you could be forgiven for thinking you were in some of the roughest North Island forest country like the Waioweka Gorge.

Closer inspection with my binoculars revealed grassed areas, all liberally dotted with thorn bushes, here and there olearia and the distinctive euphorbia. Standing beside me Darren provided the information that the river I could see in the distant northeast was the Tagela, a river famous in South African history. (Our travel agent had informed us that if we were hunting south of this river we'd not need to take malaria medication.)

Base Camp at Emanweni was also different. Set on top of the highest hill in the immediate area the lodge comprised

This was our 'hunting camp' at Emanweni.

whitewashed, rough cast, concrete block rondels with beautifully and intricately thatched roofs, the lashing of the thatch visible, along with natural timber beams, as the ceiling in each guest house. While Mia and Darren worked on lunch preparations Sue and I got settled in. We were both beginning to feel, indeed, we were finally on safari in Africa.

This feeling quickly compounded when Darren took us for a drive later that afternoon, for within the span of a couple of hours we saw Giraffe, many Zebra, Impala, Wildebeest, Kudu, Nyala, Baboons, and various species of Duiker. Darren spent the most time studying two distant Nyala bulls, but he made no comment. Yes, we were definitely on safari in Africa. I do confess the excitement level was rising.

At this early stage of our safari I'd not got to know Darren very well, for he was a sort of self-contained and reserved person, but I could sense an air of urgency when he woke me some two hours before daylight the next morning. It was still dark when the four of us departed the safari car – Darren, me, and the two Zulu trackers.

In the half-light of the pre-dawn I could see we were parked on a narrow grassed spur with dense forest chocking the slopes on all sides. I'd little time to "stand and stare" for with a nod in the direction of the nearest forest, and the universal pressing of his index finger to his lips, (for silence), he eased his way, very quietly, into the darkness of the forest. The two Zulu trackers followed me. They made not a sound.

After only about ten minutes of trying my best to be as silent as the two trackers on my heals, we arrived at a sort of rock ledge, which seemed to slope deeper into the gorge. Darren obviously knew the ledge was there and that it would provide a more silent descent. In such a circumstance measuring time is not something we attempt, so I can only guess that we progressed ever so slowly along this ledge for (shall I say) ten minutes. Throughout this slow descent Darren would stop and use his binoculars, searching the opposite face of the gorge whenever an opening in the vegetation allowed. We were in deep silent shadow for the sun hadn't yet touched the ridge tops. I had no idea what Darren was searching for, I just left my glasses down my shirt front, I was busy at being quiet as a mouse.

When Darren arrived at a small opening, providing an

The Nyala was standing in a very small clearing in the bush across the other side of the valley. It was a 'one-shot' chance.

almost unobstructed view of the opposite face of the canyon he indicated that we should stop and be seated. Once settled he got busy with his binoculars, and after just a minute or so pointed at the binoculars down my shirt front and then slowly pointed across the gorge.

For some seconds I didn't see anything? We were still in deep shadow, so poor light and lack of contrast conditions. Darren had pointed at a very small clearing well above our position, so I focused and re-focused my 10 x 40 Leitz glasses on that general area. That's when I saw an ear move. How perfect the camouflage was. Slowly I was able to discern the general outline of an animal, a set of rather tall horns, and with real difficulty the face with the horizontal small white marking between the eyes.

Darren whispered – "Nyala. We'll wait for the light to improve."

How cool was this PH? Wait for the light to improve! So, I sat there pretending to be a statue, the Nyala bull across the canyon was also as still as a statue. The light did improve; the earliest rays of the sun began to light the ridge high about the Nyala.

Finally Darren turned to me and whispered –"Can you get a good shot?"

Moving as slowly as I could, hoping that the Nyala wouldn't see

Darren and Jonty. Darren wrote to the author about his dog an extract is included.

Jonty was a Jack Russell and named after Jonty Rhodes, the cricketer because of his lively or energetic character. He was my best friend and always offered unconditional love and loyalty. He was a soul mate on safari. He had an incredibly strong nose and found many wounded animals, speeding up the tracking process hugely. He found many thousands of dollars worth in what would be lost trophies for clients. Like a bird dog on point he was amazing to watch following a wounded animal's trail. Much of the time there would be no blood at all ... just the scent. He had a heart bigger than a Lion's and even found me wounded Buffalo on several occasions.

Jonty even stood his ground to a pride of Lions once and even chased an Elephant out of camp on another occasion ... that was quite hilarious actually until the Elephant decided to chase the dog ... and where does the dog run ...straight back to me. I can tell many stories of his short life. It was very sad one day when biliary , a tick born disease killed him.

any movement, I brought the Husqvarna to my shoulder hoping to rest my elbows on my knees to provide a steady shooting platform. But the ledge on which we were seated prevented me from using my knees to support my elbows. When I did get the crosshairs on the Nyala I had about a foot of air between knees and elbows…!

Holding my breath, and willing the rifle to be still I tried a second time. No go. I knew from my experience of indoor rifle shooting that to score a 10.1 everything had to be right, otherwise a poor shot was always the result.

There was no doubt this was a one-shot deal. One step in any direction and the bull would disappear into the dense forest. But the crosshairs were waving about, no matter how hard I tried. Bullet placement was going to be extraordinarily important with this 300m shot.

"Relax" – just the one word from Darren.

A nod to Thorge, who silently headed back up the ridge we'd come down. Silence. The Nyala bull still as motionless as a statue.

I didn't hear Thorge arrive back, he was not there one second, there the next. He was carrying Darren's shooting sticks. I'd never before shot with such fore end support, but with Darren's help I finally had the crosshairs rock steady on the Nyala. He was facing to my right, but not full broadside. Remembering that I was shooting uphill I could see that if I held on the front edge of the roll of his right shoulder blade I should do fatal damage to

the heart/lung area.

With the multiple echoes from the shot bouncing back and forth within the confines of the canyon the Nyala simply dropped from view. We couldn't see him. Darren was sure he

The author's Nyala trophy where it ended up after plunging from a cliff, spoiling the skin and ruining any chance of a full life-size body mount. Horn length 27⅜ inches, another SCI Gold Medal.

Often Sue didn't join the party on hunts starting pre-dawn. Instead she'd watch a nearby waterhole sighting countless variety of game, such as these female Kudu with young at foot.

hadn't run off, confirmed by slight nods from Nkosnati and Thorge. Silence once again. A short time later we became aware of the bull thrashing, but hidden from us by a few low bushes. As we watched the thrashing animal came to the edge of the narrow shelf he'd been standing on, to then free-fall thirty or forty metres to land with a thud well below our position and out of sight.

Thorge and Nkosnati easily found my trophy in the very bottom of the gorge. It was when we moved the bull for a better photography position that Darren confirmed to me he'd been aware that one of the Nyala bulls we'd seen the previous evening was a real Top Shelf trophy. He'd not said anything for it's wise not to build up the hopes of a client too much, but that was why he'd got me out of bed extra early that morning. Did I mention it was 7am when the Nyala tumbled off the ledge?

In planning for our trip to Africa I had studied all the different species I hoped to secure trophies of; I'd even made simple "Flash Cards" of my chosen species, so I'd not be a total idiot when it came to recognition in the field. I had also decided that if I was lucky and shot a Nyala, that would be the one trophy I'd have full body life-size mounted.

Sadly, we discovered that in tumbling from the cliff the skin of the Nyala was extensively damaged, no chance of a full body mount. We removed the cape. The two trackers then gutted the carcass, cut it in half, and carried a half each back up to the safari car.

NOTES:

It was while we were enjoying a late lunch that Darren explained a certain habit peculiar to Nyala. It was well known that Nyala will seek the warmth of the early morning sun, after a cold night, sometimes standing in the sun for two or three hours, before seeking a hiding place for the balance of the day. That was why Darren was so (casually) happy to wait for an improvement of light, wait for Thorge to go back to the safari car for the shooting sticks. If only he'd told me, while we were deep in the cold shadows of the canyon, I would have   been so much more relaxed.

A mature Nyala bull may be as tall as 42 inches (1.1m) at the shoulder and weigh up to 310lb (say 140kg), so close to the same shoulder height as a Red stag, but considerably lighter in body weight. An aged male carries exquisite body markings, not unlike that of the Bongo.

With horns 27⅜ inches long my Nyala was yet another SCI Gold Medal trophy. Three trophies so far, three one-shot kills, three Gold Medals. We all know it couldn't last. Don't we?

A Walkabout With Hazards

...and told me we were in Rhino country.
If we were to encounter Rhino I was to climb a tree.
There were no trees to climb...!

After my success with Nyala we hunted a further day at Emanweni, but saw nothing of trophy quality of the species on my Wish List. That evening at dinner Darren informed Sue and I we'd be heading for our next hunt destination early the next morning.

We were on the road about 8am a nine-hour road trip which would see us skirt around Johannesburg, pass through Gauteng, cross the Val River to finally climb the Van Reenan Pass 3300ft (1016m) to find ourselves – at last on the High veldt. Yes, in every direction, as far as the hazy horizons, the land was flat and largely featureless, not unlike the Prairie Provinces of Canada.

When we finally reached our destination – Madikwe (translates to a gift from God) – we knew for sure we were 'on safari' in Africa for our new home was a traditional tented camp, (with all mod cons I might add). The camp was set up in a loose cluster with three traditional safari tents for clients and nearby a dining and cook tent, and surrounded by what we'd become very used to, acacia thorn bushes. Just 60m from our tent was a waterhole, visited daily by many species of game, including

"He told me that should we unexpectedly come upon a Rhino I was to climb the nearest tree. There were no trees to climb!"

Elephant. We even had hot running water in our tent; water heated by a boiler and piped direct to our ensuite. We learned that one of the camp boys rose before daylight every morning to ensure we had hot water available all day. Absolute luxury.

Before dinner that evening, after we'd settled ourselves into this unexpected luxury, Darren arrived at our tent with

181

instructions to not leave our tent after dark unless I was carrying the .375, and to always check thoroughly the area close to our tent with my torch before heading for the mess tent? "Watch out for eyes," was his warning.

He then informed us that the hunting party the previous week had had more excitement than they wanted when a very large angry dominant male Lion had chased a young male Lion through camp. It happened that the hunting party comprised two couples with children, so the level of fright and re-action was extreme. Darren was not the PH for this particular party, but completed his account by telling us the family party insisted they be taken to a somewhat distant tourist lodge, despite it being the early hours of the morning. No doubt parents were concerned for their children and unhappy to have only the thin canvas wall of a tent between themselves and an angry Lion.

For the next two days I didn't burn any powder. We were out and about pre-daylight every day; either scouting in the safari car, walking into locations not visible from the vehicle, even sitting for hours in a blind overlooking a waterhole. Sad to report the landscape was uninspiring for it was thorn bush after thorn bush in every direction and much of it had been burned, no doubt a game habitat practice to encourage better spring growth. We also came across many areas where it looked like a tornado had uprooted many trees. No, Elephants were responsible. No wonder the Game Authorities in Africa needed to undertake control of Elephant numbers. I'll not list all the many species of game we sighted during those two busy days, but in checking my diary I am able to report we sighted – 12 Elephant, three Lion, nine Rhino and one Leopard. Yes, four of the Big Five.

Game was really plentiful but largely we just weren't seeing trophy quality males of the species I was seeking. I discovered the smaller species of antelope were extremely alert and were in flight instantaneously upon us unexpectedly encountering them. Most early mornings Sue didn't join the hunt for she thoroughly enjoyed sitting out on the "porch" of our tent and watching the waterhole with her binoculars. At luncheon we would compare notes and often she'd seen more game, and more variety of game, than Darren and I. After lunch, and a siesta, we'd once more set off scouting for game, Sue always joining us for the afternoon outing

It was Day Nine of the safari when Darren woke me extra early and we'd travelled for about an hour in darkness before the sky began to lighten. As we enjoyed the warmth of the Toyota heater Darren explained that we were heading for a remote location, where there were no four-wheel-drive tracks, in the hope of finding some Kudu. On the back of the safari car were Thorge and Nkosnati, both buried deep in heavy ex-Army great coats.

As soon as the light improved I could see why there were no four-wheel-drive tracks. We were driving along a well-formed track, but on either side was extremely dense thorn forest, the bush perhaps three times as tall as me. It looked impenetrable to man and beast! Darren explained we were about to encounter two or three of the of the larger species of thorn bush in South Africa, knob thorn tree, corkwood tree and Chinese lantern. He went on to explain, as he slowed the vehicle, that the knob thorn

It was in thick brush like this that we hunted Kudu. The thorns were about three inches long the bushes twice the height of a man. Giant Matagouri!

(locally known as the "Wait a Bit Bush") had barbed thorns which were difficult to withdraw from clothing or flesh, and that the Chinese lantern thorns were so tough they regularly punctured tyres on safari cars. I was somewhat amazed when Darren rolled to a stop, on the side of the track to announce – "We walk from here."

I lifted the Sako .375 from the gun rack, pulled off the lightweight dust cover; loaded the magazine.

The thorn forest wasn't impenetrable. Even as Darren took his first steps into the tangle of wiry branches and vicious long thorns, (let's say 7-8cm long) I could see he'd begun to follow some sort of trail, no doubt a game trail, for who else would be penetrating and traversing such an unpleasant and scratchy location?

I soon realised that by weaving back and forth and following many connecting game trails we would be able to advance, but at a slow pace, for constantly we were forced to "go walkabout" when trying to retain our general direction. No trail led directly in Darren's desired direction so we found ourselves sometimes almost doubling back; just to get ahead a little further. It was terribly slow travel, not at all enhanced by the fact that the three-inch long thorns on every bush delighted in snagging clothing, or scratching whatever unfortunate piece of exposed human flesh they encountered.

The closeness of the thorn forest prevented any chance of seeing more than three or four metres ahead, so the chance of surprising (say) Kudu was NIL, yes in capital letters. We must have been struggling our way through the thorn forest, for that is what it was, for well over a couple of hours, when we finally stumbled onto a small clearing, Darren stopped, turned and told me we were in Rhino country. If we were to encounter Rhino I was to climb a tree. There were no trees to climb! In the two hours since we'd departed the safari car we'd seen not a tree, only thorn forest. I know my level of adrenalin jumped a dozen notches and stayed there!

It was well after 11am when at last the thorn forest began to thin and off to our left I could see a low thorn-free ridge. Darren pointed to the ridge; we climbed to its crest, now we were in grassland. Yes, below the ridge and extending for many hundreds of metres were an extensive flat area covered in a sparse grass, the odd thorn bush dispersed here and there. No game that I could see.

The first I knew something was up was Darren tugging at my sleeve and whispering – "down." Indicating that I should use my binoculars he pointed to one of the tall acacia out on the grass flat. I'd always been told the name for Kudu was 'Ghost of the Veldt' and that day I realised just how apt the name was. Even with my x10 glasses fine focused I could just make out the outline of a Kudu bull standing motionless in the shade of the tall thorn bush. He hadn't seen us.

The stalk began, for the bull was perhaps four hundred metres away, too far for me with the .375. Using the odd dense thorn bush for cover, and weaving a zigzag course, always keeping thorn bushes between ourselves and the Kudu, we closed the range to about one hundred and fifty metres. We were just about to move forward to yet another thorn bush when Darren spoke quite loudly - "Quickly, Quickly."

He was pointing. The Kudu bull had taken a couple of steps from the shade of the thorn bush and clearly was on the verge of flight. Once again I heard "Quickly, quickly," this time with breathless urgency.

Whether it was shooting an unfamiliar rifle, or Darren's quickly quickly, but I didn't take that last instant pause to steady the crosshairs before I squeezed the trigger. We all heard the solid strike of a good hit, but after a couple of stumbles the Kudu dashed off, running away from us, to disappear into the thick thorn forest.

Without a word being spoken Nkosnati and Thorge trotted off to disappear into the thorn forest at the very point where the Kudu had crashed into the thorns. Darren and I must have stood there for well over half an hour before Thorge suddenly appeared. He was gently indicating that we should join him.

With Thorge leading, me following him, Darren last in line, we slowly advanced within the tall thorn forest, Thorge clearly following a trail, a trail invisible to me. Suddenly, there was Nkosnati. With a slight nod of his head he indicated to a point five metres to his right. Facing away from us, his nose almost touching the ground, was the Kudu bull. This time I took care to line the crosshairs up on the very last rib on the left side before touching the trigger.

A Kudu trophy was my Number One priority trophy for my South African safari and there before me was that trophy. I knew I'd never have seen it again if it hadn't been for the super human tracking skills of our two Zulu trackers. I thanked them. They seemed embarrassed with my praise of their skills.

Then we experienced a bit of a hiccup! After taking plenty of photos Darren asked the boys if they had a knife, he'd overlooked putting his on his belt that morning. No, neither of the trackers had carried their knives that morning.

"Gary, have you got your knife in your day pack today?" from Darren.

"No Darren. I left mine back at camp. I knew you, Nkosnati and Thorge always carried knives so I could see no point in me

The author with his Kudu trophy. A Kudu trophy was Number One on his South African safari trophies Wish List. It was on this hunt the author once again experienced the extraordinary tracking skills of PH Darren's Zulu trackers.

Just 80 metres from our accommodation tent, at Madikwe, was a water-hole. Sue was able to sit quietly in the shade of the tent's 'verandah' and during a morning of 'game watching' see a greater variety of game species than the hunting party.

carrying mine…!"

So, while Darren and I sat by the carcass the two trackers returned to the vehicle where they discovered no knives. They then had driven to a Game Department Station, borrowed a skinning knife and finally found their way back through the thorn forest to Darren and I and the Kudu. Let's say a two-hour excursion.

That was yet another day we were very late back in camp for lunch, but I had my Kudu. There'd been no shortage of game for on our return trip we saw – Elephant, Kudu, Waterbuck, Eland, Tsessebe, Hartebeest, Wildebeest, Giraffe, Mongoose and a species of squirrel.

Yes, we'd had a bit of a "walkabout" to finally secure my prized Kudu trophy, but we'd not made contact with the local hazard – Rhino.

NOTES:

It is probable that the reason why we didn't see many Kudu during our cruises in game country was their ability to hide. Combining their coat colourings with the dappled shadow of trees and tall thorn brush created a camouflage that was remarkable. We had the same experience with Zebra. Much of the country we hunted was red earth country. Zebra would roll in the dry red dust and then stand in dapple shadow. Time and again Sue and I would more or less take a "double take" unaware, at first that we were looking at Zebra in the deep shadows.

A mature bull Kudu is not a small animal. Standing up to 60 inches (1.54m) at the shoulder and weigh up to 650lb (290kg) they are virtually the same height at the shoulder and weight of a bull Elk. (USA Elk not NZ Wapiti.) I'm sure you understand why my PH insisted on the .375. Any Kudu trophy carrying horns of better than 60 inches in length is considered outstanding. Horn length on my trophy was 53½ inch horns, a SCI Silver Medal.

TRACKERS EXTRAORDINAIRE

Nkosnati and Thorge had been tracking the Eland for more than three hours when suddenly, from our left, a mob of Zebra and Wildebeest raced across our front, across the spoor the two trackers were so meticulously following.

During a couple of our early morning starts from camp we had unexpectedly encountered Eland within twenty minutes of setting out for the day. On both occasions the Eland had crossed the four-wheel-drive track ahead of us and disappeared into the usual jungle of tall dense thorn bushes. Darren was of the opinion the Eland were returning from a feeding area, heading for the place they'd bed down for the day.

In an effort to maybe intercept the Eland Darren dragged me out of my warm bed at 5.30am one frosty morning and we were on the roads by 6.30am. It was still dark. After parking the safari car a few hundred metres from where we'd previously sighted the Eland we started a quiet approach on foot. I was carrying the Sako .375. Darren was carrying his .375 also. For the very first time, during my safari, Nkosnati and Thorge were ahead of Darren and I. It took me a second or two to realise they were looking for fresh tracks, tracks of Eland that may have very recently crossed the road.

Maybe ten minutes after departing the vehicle the two trackers had a quiet word with Darren, while pointing at the ground. Darren signalled that I should quietly load the .375 and then indicated with a hand gesture that we should move to our right. We were easing through a really dense thorn forest that had recently been subjected to a fierce fire, for there wasn't a touch of green anywhere, just the blackened stark branches of the vegetation. The thorn bushes, should I call them trees (?), were maybe 10m to 15m tall, so we were walking within a forest with a burned thorn canopy. Underfoot the soil appeared to be very like the harsh scoria we are all familiar with in our volcanic regions of the North Island. It was slightly "crunchy" underfoot, so we were placing our feet with care with each step we took. The sun had not yet risen. We were in that pre-dawn poor light time of the new day.

Most unexpectedly we found ourselves looking down an avenue of clear ground, about ten to fifteen metres wide and well over one hundred and fifty metres long, very like a tree-lined gravel driveway leading to a house. Then it happened.

One instant the "driveway" was clear. In the next instant a very large bull Eland was standing broadside to us, at about 125m, and looking directly in our direction. It was one of those occasions where the bull had to take just one step forwards and he'd have been out of sight. I remember bringing the .375 to my shoulder, I recall it all happened so fast Darren didn't even have time to give me his usual "Quickly, quickly". I squeezed (or did I jerk) off a shot. I think I looked down as I reloaded, I looked up and the "driveway" was clear….!

Darren and the two trackers jointly agreed they'd clearly heard the strike of my bullet. I hadn't… Nkosnati and Thorge

There was a point during the marathon tracking of the wounded Eland that we had to play like being lizards while a small group of Elephant ambled by!

moved slowly forward. I saw Nkosnati drop to his knee and touch something on the ground with his forefinger. No words were required when he moved quietly to Darren and showed him the fresh blood on his finger. Out there, somewhere in the burned-over thorn forest, was a wounded bull Eland.

And so those Zulu started tracking. They were meticulous and slow. Darren and I kept a good ten to fifteen metres behind, moving slowly forward only after the trackers had advanced.

Always we were watching ahead, but it very soon became clear we were in for a long day, for after about an hour we'd not located a dead bull Eland. My shot had not been fatal. I made no attempt to get close to Nkosnati and Thorge for I had no wish to step on a vital spoor print or drop of blood.

After two hours we were still very slowly following the two trackers. Darren wasn't saying much at all, he mostly was watching out ahead of the trackers in the hope of sighting the wounded Eland. Me, well my mind was really working on me. I was devastated that maybe we'd never find the bull. My stomach was beginning to churn, my nerves winding tighter and tighter as the time ticked by. In my entire career as a professional hunting guide I'd had only the one client wound and lose a trophy, a Red stag. Was I going to join his "club"? It was the possible waste of a fine trophy that fully occupied my mind; I had nothing else to do but think.

Nkosnati and Thorge had been tracking the Eland for more than three hours when suddenly, from our left, a mob of Zebra and Wildebeest raced across our front, across the spoor the two trackers were so meticulously following. Seeing the ground, churned by the fifteen or twenty racing animals, my heart and hope struck rock bottom. And stayed there.

Amazing as it may sound this intrusion into their tracking didn't visibly appear to bother the two trackers at all. After crossing the churned area of scoria-like soil they set about casting wider and wider until, yes, I could clearly see that they were back on the tracks of the bull Eland.

When we'd been on the tracks for well over four hours we had a rather disturbing interruption that had all four of us flat on the ground, doing our best to be lizards, me praying. Off to our right a small herd of Elephant were slowly mooching their way through the burned thorn forest. Yes, we were still in the burned area. No, they didn't see us.

I can tell you that it was almost exactly 1pm when Darren sighted a group of nine Eland bedding down beside an extra dense stand of burned–over thorn trees. If I'd fired at the Eland close to 7am, the two trackers had been on the trail of the Eland

When my trophy bull Eland was finally dead on the ground I had experienced 'My Longest Day' of hunting in my life. My nerves and knees were raw.....!

for five hours.

Now began an excruciating approach. Nkosnati and Thorge had been brilliant in locating the Eland, their work was done. Placidly they squatted down behind a screen of brush. Darren handed me a small hand-held radio, with whispered instructions on how to do it, then began an ever so slow belly-crawl towards the resting Eland herd. He would attempt to locate the wounded animal.

After covering about half the distance to the Eland, say 80m,

Darren settled himself behind a scraggy looking low bush and started glassing the Eland. I was also working my binoculars for as they say "hope springs eternal", maybe I would yet secure a trophy Eland. It was all up to Darren and me now after the two trackers had demonstrated such extraordinary skills.

A soft crackle on the tiny radio - "Gary, crawl up to me, take it slowly, don't let them see you…."

I'll not give you a metre-by-metre account of that crawl, maybe the most important in my life. But I will tell you that by the time I was beside Darren, the Eland still unaware we were close-by, I had shredded most of the skin off my knees through slithering and crawling across that harsh scoria-like soil. Yes, I was wearing my usual hunting shorts.

Whispering virtually into my left ear Darren patiently drew my attention to the wounded bull Eland. My (hasty) shot had hit the bull in the "no man's land" area of below the spine but above the lungs. He whispered that he and I would both take prone positions and both shoot, and keep on shooting until there was no risk of the Eland escaping. And that's what we did.

Relief washed over me like a hot shower on a cold day. Such relief. Until I was standing beside my trophy I hadn't realised just how tight my nerves were wound. I could see Darren was also experiencing a sense of relief. It had been a rough day for him as well, even though he was a PH and no doubt had suffered similar experiences on previous safaris.

After Nkosnati and Thorge had helped us with photos

Darren sent them back to bring up the safari car. Somehow they managed to work their way through the burned-over mess of thorns to arrive at the kill. I stood intrigued and amazed as Darren and the two Zulu expertly used the front mounted winch with the aid of a pulley about the vehicle cab to load the whole Eland onto the back of the safari car.

It was somewhat after 3pm when we finally arrived back in camp for a very late lunch.

NOTES:

Of the many trophies I have hunted during my adult life I shall always remember in detail that day when those two Zulu trackers expertly followed the spoor of the wounded Eland bull, to ensure my hunt ended successfully. To them it was all in a day's work, whereas to me it is one of the most amazing demonstrations of a human skill I've ever witnessed. I hope such skill is not lost in future generations.

The Eland is the largest of all the species of antelope in Africa and belongs to the spiral horn family. A fully mature adult bull may weigh as much as 1,600lb (say 730kg) and will have a shoulder height of 72 inches (1.85m). (Turn to the photo of me with my trophy and you'll see that the depth of chest is about the same as from my waist to the ground – 1m.)

With a horn length of 35 inches my trophy was high in the SCI Gold Medal class.

Thanks to Darren, Nkosnati and Thorge for they brought the day to a happy and satisfying conclusion.

At last! Author with his trophy Eland. With 35 inch horns yet another Gold Medal trophy.

Stretching The Barrel

Instantly I saw why he was anxious, for off to our right, racing directly towards the distant Gemsbok, was a Zebra.

I'm sure you recall my previously mentioning that during our first two days of hunting at Madikwe not a shot was fired. That's not to say we weren't hunting, obviously we were. On two early morning occasions Darren had us sneak in to dense tall thorn thickets, trying to get a shot at a bull Gemsbok. Each time we made a sneak it took what seemed like ages to work our way through impossibly dense growth, all the time sharply aware that a wrong movement or sound would ruin our stalk.

On one occasion, with much patience, and very slow movements, we managed to place ourselves within about fifteen metres of a group of six or eight Gemsbok. That tells you clearly just how dense the vegetation was. But the situation was impossible, for Darren dared not speak, and whatever hand signals he made had to be tiny and mostly not understood by me. The major problem was that this was my very first close encounter with Gemsbok and in the thickness of the thorn grove I couldn't clearly differentiate between male and female, for both sexes carry horns! On the two occasions that we had these close encounters the group finally woke up to our intrusion and with much snorting, and crashing, rapidly disappeared.

One afternoon Darren decided on a change of tactics. Mia and Sue were invited to join us; we'd be seeing some new and different country. With Sue, Mia and I up on the open back of the Toyota, the two trackers seated behind us, Darren driving, we set off through the now familiar thorn thicket landscape. After about an hour we crested a low hill and there ahead was a vast almost tree-less savannah of short brown winter grasses. This new landscape stretched as far as a distant range of hazy low hills to our south, while to the west, Darren informed us, was the border with Botswana.

Within just a few minutes we encountered game – Zebra, Wildebeest, Red Hartebeest, a couple of Giraffe that allowed us very close for excellent photos. (Sue fell in love with Giraffe). We even almost drove over a small snake that was lazily crossing the four-wheel-drive track. Sue didn't like that.

There are times when hunting that we get a "feeling" that today is the day. You've experienced it? I had "the feeling" that afternoon. I guess we'd slowly driven the edge of the savannah for about half an hour when unexpectedly Darren very slowly reduced speed and allowed the Toyota to roll gently to a stop. His attention was on a solitary Gemsbok far out on the plain. After studying the somewhat distant animal for a minute or two through his glasses he turned to me and asked if I was comfortable with a long shot?

I didn't get a chance to ask how far off the Gemsbok was for Darren was anxiously muttering – "Quickly, quickly, quickly quickly…"

Instantly I saw why he was anxious, for off to our right, racing

The Gemsbok was away out in the middle of a flat like this when the opportunity for a shot was diminishing with every fleeting second.

directly towards the distant Gemsbok, was a Zebra. We all could see that it would only be a matter of seconds before the Zebra alerted the Gemsbok, and goodbye Gemsbok.

My daypack was beside me so after placing it on top of the roof of the Toyota I loaded and settled behind the Husqvarna. Even in the x4 scope the Gemsbok looked rather small, but there certainly wasn't time for discussions about range and bullet drop. I needed to place those crosshairs where I judged they needed to

Wife Sue was with the author when he pulled off a 'pressure' shot to secure his Silver Medal Gemsbok. Yes, with horns measuring 37⅜ inches only a Silver.......

How far was the Gemsbok from the safari car? Shall we say something like 350m, or more? (In those days PH's in South Africa didn't carry range finders, and, we'd not have had time to use one that afternoon.) Where did the Hornady 150gr projectile strike? Exactly in the centre of the shoulder, ten inches (25.5cm) below the line of the back.

After we'd taken plenty of photos of me with my trophy, Darren took a great shot of Sue and I with the trophy. Nkosnati and Thorge loaded the Gemsbok into the back of the safari car. Sue agreed with me, the Gemsbok would be the one trophy from our South African safari that we'd have full life-size mounted.

NOTES:
Today the full mounted Gemsbok is the first of my trophies you'll see when you walk through our front door. All who see it agree the body markings are exquisite.

A fully-grown male will stand as high as 48 inches (1.23m) at the shoulder and weigh up to 465lb (210 kg), almost the exact same measurements as for a mature Red stag.

My trophy had 37⅜ inch horns, a SCI Silver Medal trophy.

be, for off to my right, out of the corner of my eye, there was the Zebra still racing on a collision course with the Gemsbok.

Mentally crossing my fingers I let the crosshairs drift upwards until I figured I was holding about one-quarter of the depth of the shoulder below the line of the back. I touched the trigger.

With the report of the rifle two things happened instantaneously, the Gemsbok dropped to the ground, his legs just folded, the Zebra made a sharp dust generating right turn to smoke his way into the far distance of the savannah.

Last Days At Madikwe

...to date Sue had not had a close encounter with Elephant. He turned his head and asked – "Is thirty metres close enough?"

Throughout our safari at Madikwe we'd seen very few Waterbuck. My reading, prior to departing home, had informed me that these antelope were most often found along rivers, hence their name, as yet I'd not seen a river at Madikwe? One afternoon, shortly after lunch, a Game Department Toyota arrived in camp. The driver was a game ranger by the name of Shadrack. Darren introduced us.

It transpired that Shadrack's job was to constantly track and monitor groups of Rhino, no doubt to discourage poaching of their horns. He knew every secret corner of the local area, so Darren was sure that with his help we'd find a trophy Waterbuck. Like many species of game the Waterbuck is known to remain in hiding until the sun is close to the horizon, so we sat in the shade until Darren gave the word to move. Sue and Mia joined us for their regular late afternoon safari.

With Darren driving and Shadrack his co-pilot, Sue, Mia, Thorge and I were up in our usual positions on the back of the safari car. That afternoon we took a different route to any we'd previously travelled, more a south-easterly direction. That was

the afternoon we saw the devastation wrought by Elephants, many trees up-rooted from the ground, as if a local violent tornado had savaged the forest. Shadrack informed us the trees were libombo cluster leaf trees, also known as silver leaf, a very tough hard heavy tree that Elephant habitually pushed over as a test of strength. We were astonished to learn that after pushing the trees over the Elephant seldom fed on the leaves.

After well over an hour of travel, seeing different species of game all the way, we could finally see that ahead was a change in vegetation, it was green – the river. Darren parked the Toyota under the shade of some tall green trees; the two girls remained in the vehicle with Thorge to watch over their safety. We boys went for a wander and there on the sandy edges of the quietly flowing river were so many prints of so many different cloven-hoofed animals it was simply impossible to not step on the spoor. Darren and Shadrack were quietly identifying different spoor, I was listening only when I heard, repeatedly, the word Waterbuck.

Darren and Shadrack had a quiet conference there beside the river; it was decided to return to the vehicle and very slowly cruise the bank of the river, in the hope of intercepting Waterbuck as they came to the river to drink. I guess we'd only been cruising for about fifteen minutes when Shadrack signalled Darren to stop. Yes, we'd intercepted a nice Waterbuck on his way to the river. But, the buck was standing deep in a dense acacia thicket, at about 150m, watching us, alert, but as yet not running back into cover. It was tricky for I really didn't want to try and punch a 150gr projectile through the web of thorn bush branches.

The Waterbuck was on our left side, the side where both Shadrack and I were seated. Darren slowly began to back the vehicle with Shadrack talking him back until there was an open avenue for me to try a shot. Even before the Toyota had stopped its slow backing everyone in the vehicle heard the "quickly, quickly". Everyone in the vehicle also heard the strike of the bullet, but the buck didn't go down. Instead he started to slowly walk parallel to the vehicle. Once again, with Shadrack talking to him, Darren attempted to manoeuvre the vehicle to a position offering me a second shot. After three or four abortive attempts I had a brief clear line, and this time the Waterbuck dropped. This time I don't think I heard "quickly, quickly."

On the ground at our feet was my last Madikwe trophy.

When it came to measuring the horns we discovered one had about two inches broken off, so that affected the SCI Score – however with Darren and Shadrack's combined effort I had an SCI Bronze Medal trophy Waterbuck with the longest horn at 28¼ inches.

Next morning we slept in until 7am. Mia cooked us a full breakfast, we spent the balance of the morning packing our gear, for at daylight the following day Mia and Nkosnati would head for Hilton, while Darren and Thorge would take Sue and I south to complete our safari down in the Cape Province.

As previously mentioned Sue would not rise early each morning, happy to sleep a little longer then much enjoy her mornings watching the animals coming and going at the waterhole close to camp. Of the Big Five I'd seen all but Buffalo, whereas Sue had seen only Lion.

We were mildly surprised when after lunch Shadrack arrived

"Sue, is this close enough to an Elephant for you……..?"

in camp. He would be "guiding" Darren in an effort for Sue to see some more of the Big Five. We would leave the CV Safaris

At Madikwe water was in short supply. Whenever we made a silent approach on a waterhole we saw many heads of game. At dawn one morning we alarmed a young Leopard obviously waiting for a chance of an easy breakfast.

white safari car in camp; we'd travel in Shadrack's green Game Department Toyota, Darren the driver, Shadrack tour guide and game spotter. Sue had fallen in love with Giraffe, so each time we came upon them I was instructed to get a few more photos. Got many splendid shots.

I was in the act of explaining to Shadrack that Sue hadn't had

a close encounter with Elephant, when he turned his head and looking at her, asking if thirty metres was close enough? We'd been busy looking out the left side of the vehicle, but following Shadrack's pointing figure, there, not thirty metres from the right of the vehicle, stood a bull Elephant. It must have been the fact that we were in the familiar green Game Department vehicle,

for after one casual glance the Elephant continued to quietly feed. What a sight. I do suspect thirty metres was a bit too close for Sue, but she was determined to not show her nervousness. I noticed Darren had kept the vehicle in gear, the motor running.

That night we had a male Lion roaring close to camp for much of the night. We were being farewelled by Madikwe?

NOTES:

An adult male Waterbuck is about the same size and weight as a Sambar stag. Shoulder height for the male Waterbuck is 53 inches (1.36m), a Sambar stag 48 inches (1.23m). Weight-wise they are virtually the same, both ranging from about 475lb (say 216kg) to 600lb (say 273kg). Both have rounded chunky bodies.

The most conspicuous feature of the Waterbuck is the wide white circle of hair on the rump, around the tail.

The last trophy at Madikwe, a Bronze Medal Waterbuck with 28²/₈ inch horns.

Quickly, Quickly!

…I might suggest that a translation for quickly, quickly could be: "For f..k sake squeeze the bloody trigger…"

After thirty odd years of experience as a professional hunting guide, and after having guided some hundreds of American clients, I feel I am qualified to make some generalisations. American trophy hunters are mostly excellent rifle shots, but are terribly slow at settling and getting their first shot away. It is excruciatingly frustrating to climb a mountain all day, finally to be in position for that first critical shot, to then wait for what seems likes ages before your client squeezes the trigger.

My "modus operandi" was to quietly tell my client to make sure he was settled, to take his time and make that first shot count, while in my head I'm screaming at him to squeeze the trigger. My attitude was that I needed to do everything to defuse the situation, to not pressure or "spook" the client into a hasty shot, for a miss would mean having to climb another mountain another day. In many cases the animal my client and I were targeting was unaware of our presence, so the ticking clock didn't create a pressure situation.

Darren's situation was different for I very quickly learned that the game in Africa were alert and primed for flight at the slightest suggestion of danger, and the smaller the species of antelope the more quickly they hit top gear then over-drive and were gone. They none of them "stood and stared"… Translated in to colloquial South African English I might suggest that "quickly, quickly" could be – "… for f..k sake squeeze the bloody trigger….."

No doubt Darren's experience of guiding American clients was the same as mine, their slowness to settle and shoot. I never asked Darren if he was aware of his habitual "quickly, quickly", but I suspect it may be possible he was unaware of him speaking these words almost every time I was about to shoot.

I confess that initially the "quickly, quickly," was a little disconcerting, subconsciously causing me to (maybe) hurry my shot, but after a few days I put it from my mind, tyring my best to succeed with a one-shot kill. (In a later Chapter you'll read the story of the day when Darren didn't mutter "quickly, quickly"…)

Given the propensity for the smaller species of African antelope to race for thick cover, never taking a second glance back at danger, it was an absolute that a hunter had to be quick – regardless of Darren's "quickly, quickly"… Getting a shot at some of those racing shadows, as they dashed for, or through the dense thorn thickets, became a constant daily challenge. Powder was wasted.

Let me tell you about a few of them: -

STEENBOK – Shoulder height – 23 inches (.59m) Weight – up to 32lb (14.5kg)

We were driving slowly through dense thorn thickets, as usual, when Nkosnati pointed to a fleeing Steenbok. I had a split second to load, aim and fire as the ram raced across a small

Steenbok, like most of the small species in Africa just don't stand around when alerted.

This Steenbok appeared and disappeared so fast Darren didn't even have time for his usual 'Quickly, quickly.' With 5⅛ inch horns this trophy placed about 12th in the Record Book. Gold Medal.

Impala are common throughout Africa.   After many abortive attempts (missed shots) the author finally scored on a Silver Medal trophy with 23 inch horns.

opening in the brush to disappear from sight! Nkosnati jumped from the vehicle and within a minute or so appeared with the Steenbok. It all happened so fast Darren didn't have time for a quickly, quickly…

With a horn length of 5⅛ inches my trophy was a very high placing SCI Gold Medal, placing about #12 in the SCI Record Book at that time.

IMPALA - Shoulder height - 38 inches (.96m) Weight - 160lb (72kg)

I suffered a real "jinx" with Impala. Time and again we'd jump a ram, he'd be racing off, "quickly, quickly", I'd try a running shot, I'd miss. Impala are numerous and common over much of South Africa, but I wasn't connecting at all. Also, what Impala we saw were prone to dashing for cover instantly. It was only after about my fourth or fifth miss that Darren informed me that they'd had a busy season on Impala and that prior to my hunt fifteen trophies had been shot by clients. I suggested that maybe we should lower our trophy expectations to a lesser horn length; many of the small family groups we'd seen (daily) contained what were obviously immature rams.

"Quickly, quickly" was my signal. There was an Impala racing into the thorn thickets. This one stopped, deep in cover, but I could see the back third of his body. Risking the possibility that the flight of my 150gr Hornady might be deflected by striking branches of thorn bushes, I lined up in the last rib, hoping to take out the offside shoulder. It seems I was the only one in the team to see the Impala drop in his tracks. Darren called a miss. Thorge was sent to investigate, I went with him. Yes, we finally had settled my "jinx"…

The horns measured 23 inches (.59m) so qualified as a SCI Silver Medal.

Val Rhebok are hunted in a manner similar to hunting Chamois, but Rhebok have amazing eye-sight and once running always disappeared over a distant horizon, never looking back.

VAL RHEBOK - Shoulder height – 30 inches (.77m) Weight up to 50lb (22.5kg)

Our destination after departing Madikwe was Stornberg, a daylong nine hundred-kilometre trip, always-travelling south. Mia and Nkosnati had headed for Hilton, where the bride-to-be would be attending to wedding preparations, we four Darren, Thorge, Sue and I were the hunting team for the final few days of my twenty-one day safari.

Val Rhebok live in real mountains, rising to 6,500 (1660m), we were back hunting farmland, but fences few and far between. As we'd driven south the weather had deteriorated, with nasty rain squalls driven by almost gale force winds. The next day the conditions were very much the same, so Sue elected to stay in camp – a lovely well-appointed bungalow.

Let me set the scene. Val Rhebok are a misty pale grey colour, so blended into the grey rock to the point of virtually being invisible. Add to this a buffeting wind, rain squalls, leaden grey skies, thick mountain mist, plus really poor light, and I hope you'll forgive me for having no end of trouble actually seeing the animals Darren attempted to point out to me. For two days he did his best to get me a shot at a trophy male, but not once did I actually have the sights on a potential trophy. In all my hunting experience I'd never experienced such spooky animals. It seemed that no matter how far we were from a small group the minute Darren stopped the vehicle the Rhebok were racing for a distant horizon, sometimes four or five kilometres away, and never stopping until they'd disappeared over that rain shrouded misty skyline.

On a couple of occasions we left the vehicle on the reverse side of a set of hills, to maybe climb and ambush some Rhebok on the opposite side. This also failed for instead of climbing to the top of the ridge and then carefully looking over from the crest, Darren tried to sidle the hill. This didn't work for when a hunter sidles a series of ridges the ground immediately under his feet is unsighted, while any game on the opposite face sights the hunter immediately he is skylined. Twice we "jumped" small groups of Rhebok below us on a side hill, but never did I get half a chance at those misty grey mountain racers.

Each day our first stopping point was a series of ridges where on a previous safari Darren had seen, but failed to secure for his client, a very good trophy Rhebok. Each morning we failed to sight this elusive buck, so would hunt other locations, to finally return just before dusk in the hope of sighting what Darren had reported was an outstanding trophy.

On the third evening, after three days of nil success in Rhebok, we did sight a male high on the very face we'd searched diligently previously. Darren quickly informed me that it wasn't the exceptional trophy he'd hope to locate for me, but recommended I should take a shot. It was a 200m+ steep uphill shot. My first shot was a hit, but it must have been more a graze than fatal for the ram continued to climb away. I got in a couple of shots at about 300m+ and the animal was down. I was amazed at how quickly Thorge climbed to the downed animal to carry it back to us on the valley floor.

With a horn length of just 7¼ inches my trophy qualified only for an SCI Bronze Medal, but at least I had a trophy. What is a trophy anyway? Is it the length of the horns or the experience of securing it?

GRYSBOK – Shoulder height – 18 inches (.46m) Weight – 29lb (13.1kg)

Another change of scene. We were based out of a lovely hunting lodge with the name of Nxakwe Bush Camp, in the East Cape Province, near a town with the name of Queenstown, inland from East London.

Darren had informed me that as the Grysbok was a totally nocturnal species of antelope South African Game Laws allowed for them to be hunted by spotlighting, apparently the only species legally allowed to be taken with the aid of a light. We'd departed Nxakwe about 4pm and after a drive of about two and a half hours arrived at a farm not too far from Grahamstown.

I couldn't believe the multitude of game we saw in the spotlight that night on that farm. Wherever Thorge shone the light there were numerous tiny antelope species Sue and I'd not previously seen. That farm was literally crawling with a wide variety of small game. I freely confess I had no idea what we were seeing, relying entirely on Darren and Thorge to call the shot. Odd as it may sound Darren was constantly working his binoculars for it was illegal to kill a female Grysbok. It was his

Searching for Val Rhebok. PH Darren Baker front right.

responsibility to check for horns before telling me to shoot, the fact that a top shelf trophy male may have horns only as long as 2½ to 3½ inches, therefore shorter than the length of the ears, made the identification of a trophy male, even in x10 glasses, a constant challenge for Darren. More disconcerting (for me) was my observation that few of those tiny antelope held in the light. They may have paused for a fleeting instant, and then they were running.

"Quickly, quickly" muffled, for he still had his binoculars to his eyes. Thirty metres ahead of the vehicle a small antelope paused for a split second then dashed across about a six-metre gap between bushes. I can honestly say I don't recall even getting the Grysbok in the scope, I just swung and fired as I would a shotgun. The antelope disappeared.

Miraculously I'd hit my target. When Thorge lifted the antelope into the headlights there was a great deal of excited discussion between Darren and Thorge. It seems I had just shot the biggest Grysbok Darren and Thorge had ever seen. No credit at all to me.

With a horn length of 4¼ inches my trophy was a very high placing SCI Gold Medal trophy, a new #5 in the SCI Record Book.

Grysbok are fully nocturnal and so are the only species of small antelope allowed to be hunted at night with a spotlight. They seldom stand in the light so only running shots are offered!

FOOTNOTE:
There you have it. The smallest species of game I shot during my safari was actually my biggest African trophy – a #5.

In The Land Of The Ancient Bushmen

We were in a perfect position. The Springbok, standing broadside, was unaware of us.

Translated *de ja vu* means having the feeling that this has all happened before. That's the feeling I had when we crested a ridge in CV Safaris safari car, to overlook a vast shallow basin, seeking Springbok. Within seconds every Springbok within that basin had disappeared, just like bait fish in the ocean when a large predatory fish appears.

We'd spent most of the day unsuccessfully hunting Val Rhebok in the nearby mountains; Darren felt a change of scene might lift morale a little for those Rhebok had surely given us a run around since daybreak. Now, here we were on the plains, and the Springbok were beating us to the draw as well. I've said it before, I say it again, the smaller antelope in South Africa run and never look back when alarmed, both Val Rhebok and Springbok not pausing in flight until safely over a far horizon.

For an hour or more we slowly cruised country very similar to the Mackenzie Basin landscape south of Tekapo, vast, featureless, sparse vegetation, the horizon distant in every direction. Each time Darren eased the white Toyota to the top of a low ridge, first one, then a dozen, then all Springbok were racing each other to their nearest horizons.

It was about our fourth or fifth such result at our intrusion into Springbok country that I, as gently as I could, remarked to Darren that I wouldn't mind if we had a bit of a walkabout. Darren seemed happy with such a diversion, so leaving Sue in the vehicle, with Thorge for company and protector, Darren and I set off for a walk.

We worked our way around the foot of a long low ridge that curved to our left, so with every few steps we took a new section of the terrain ahead was open to our view. It was a perfect stalking situation. As would be expected it was Darren who was the first to see the Springbok buck. A touch on my shoulder, he studying with his glasses, me quietly loading the Husqvarna.

By now I'd been on safari with Darren as my PH for over two weeks and I'd finally realised that if I listened carefully to his "quickly, quickly", I'd have a pretty good idea of the quality of trophy by the levels of excitement in his voice. When he gave me the "quickly, quickly" while studying the solitary Springbok buck I had a clear idea his "Excitement Meter" was registering on "High".

We were in a perfect situation. The Springbok, standing broadside, was unaware of us, two steps ahead was a small boulder, which, when I sat behind it, gave me a perfect fore-end rest for the 30-06.

I whispered to Darren – "How far?"

"Three hundred plus."

My rifle was sighted to be dead-on at 275m so lifting the rifle to place the crosshairs two thirds up from the line of the brisket I touch off. Yes! A one-shot kill.

It wasn't long before we heard the Toyota approaching, Thorge

205

Springbok habitat.   Like the Val Rhebok the Springbok raced to parts distant immediately they were disturbed, alarmed.

at the wheel. Photos and handshakes, and then, out of character, Darren pulled a tape measure from his pocket! A quick measure of horn length – 13¼ inches - and circumference of bases and he delightedly announced we had an SCI Gold Medal trophy. Was I starting to gain a more subtle understanding of "quickly, quickly"?

During our eleven-hour drive from Madikwe to Stornberg many topics were discussed, one of which was the ancient bushmen of the Kalahari. Sue and I had both read many books about South Africa, including much about the bushmen. We were aware that the area where I'd be hunting Val Rhebok and Springbok was historically country the bushmen had travelled over, so naturally, I had asked Darren if any bushmen cave drawings or artefacts could be seen in the area. Darren's response had been taciturn and rather non-committal, such that I wasn't sure whether I touched on a forbidden subject.

With my Springbok trophy safely in the back of the Toyota we finally arrived back on the secondary country road we'd accessed the Springbok country. I was aware that Darren would turn right to finally reach the main highway back to our accommodation. I said nothing when he turned left, for I simply thought we were returning to the Stornberg Lodge via a different route.

But, after driving for perhaps twenty minutes Darren turned the vehicle left off the road to arrive at a padlocked gate. The gate was unlocked and re-locked behind us. Another locked gate. Still Darren had made no explanation; Sue and I asked no questions. When he pulled up to a stop he indicated we should depart the vehicles and bring our cameras.

These ancient bushmen rock drawings of Springbok are probably thousands of years old. The author and his wife Sue were enthralled to be standing where those famous little people once lived and thrived.

We walked along a small creek until rounding a bend and there ahead was a rock outcrop, let's say twenty feet above our heads, with a very robust wire-netting fence, bristling with barbed-wire, encircling the outcrop and the creek bed beside it. Darren had a key to unlock a steel-framed netting-clad door.

Sue and I had sensed something special was happening, that Darren had not offered an explanation about this mysterious side-trip. Upon walking through the unlocked doorway we suddenly understood where we were.

We were within a small cave and on the walls were exquisite, realistic bushmen cave paintings. We had no difficulty at all in

Springbok down. With horns measuring 13¼ inches here was another SCI Gold Medal trophy.

the rock face of the cave, some across the priceless bushmen paintings. It was this senseless vandalism that had prompted the landowner to build the netting and barbed-wire fence, allowing only a few trustworthy people to now visit this priceless historic treasure. Had we not asked Darren he'd have never told us of the cave and the wonderful treasure it hid. Clearly we had joined the privileged few.

NOTES:

A mature Springbok buck is about the size of an adult female Fallow deer, standing between 30-35 inches at the shoulder (75-90cm) and weighing from 70 to 100lb (32–45kg).

recognising Springbok and Eland. Sue and I were dumbstruck, realising that we were standing on the very earth that thousands of years before the ancient bushmen had stood, had sheltered in this cave while hunting the area for the very same Springbok we'd hunted. We both experienced the feeling of being in a sacred place, rather like standing in an ancient church.

Darren explained that we were on private property, that the landowners were very cautious about allowing anyone to know the cave paintings were in the cave. That is when Darren drew our attention to various initials that had been scratched onto

I Didn't Know Trophy Hunting In South Africa Was A Spectator Sport!

Instead of the usual "quickly, quickly" I was non-plussed for a second when I heard him say, "take your time."

For the final leg of our twenty-one day South African safari our accommodation was Nxakwe Bush Camp, about four hours' drive nor-west of the city of East London. We were now in Cape Province. At dinner that night Sue and I were introduced to Juan a game warden who would accompany us each day we hunted.

Juan explained that in Cape Province all trophy hunting was very strictly controlled and that each farming property that was party to safari operators hunting their land, size and number limits applied. That night I learned that Darren and I would be seeking one specific Bontebok, one specific Red Lechwe.

Tentatively I had booked to take a second Kudu, thinking that those found in the Cape Province were a different species to those we'd hunted at Madikwe. Darren explained that there was no difference, they were the same species, so I passed on taking a second trophy. We did spend a morning looking over a number of local Kudu, but nothing we saw surpassed my Madikwe bull.

Are cell phones an asset or a nuisance? Throughout our safari Darren hadn't used a cell phone, no doubt not wishing to intrude on the hunting, but also maybe due to no coverage. That wasn't

the case down at Cape Province. Late into our first morning at the Cape Darren received a call from the farmer where we'd be hunting for my Bontebok. After completing the call Darren explained that the farmer where "my" Bontebok was had located the buck and had suggested – "we come and get him".

At the gate to the property were three four-wheel-drive vehicles. Standing about, in a loose group, I counted five very large Boer farmers, each one big enough and strong enough to lock a Springbok scrum. Sue and I remained in the vehicle; Darren had a conversation with the group.

Upon returning to our vehicle Darren informed me that the "word had got out" that a Kiwi hunter was to take the Bontebok and they'd come to witness the action. I do confess I had no idea trophy hunting in South Africa was a spectator sport!!

So it was that a convoy of four vehicles, ours first, proceeded up a farm track, in the floor of a shallow valley, to a point where Darren rolled to a stop, causing the "convoy" to follow suit. The farmer explained that just over the ridge to our right was where the Bontebok was bedded down on an open grass knoll about 275 to 300m away.

Darren very carefully worked his way up the shallow ridge to return with a report confirming the Bontebok was certainly there and unaware, but felt that he should drive the safari car slowly onto the ridge to give me a clear line of sight over the medium height thorn brush smothering the ridge. I just hoped that the Bontebok didn't light out for a distant horizon like his smaller cousin species did.

Sue and I were seated up on the back of the safari car. I had my day pack settled in place, the rifle loaded, as Darren crept

Thorge and Game Ranger Juan busy getting Gary's Bontebok ready for photographs.

The Bontebok has a dramatically marked skin best shown off in a trophy room by a full life-size body mount. Horn length 14⅜ inches SCI Silver Medal.

the vehicle forward. There was the Bontebok still bedded down, but now looking in our direction. Darren came around to stand close by me, and that is where he broke the pattern.

For instead of the usual – "quickly, quickly" I was nonplussed for a second when I heard him softly say - "take your time."

I didn't have time to do a "double-take" at this departure from the usual for the Bontebok stood up, alert. I simply took a split second longer to make sure the crosshairs were steady high on the shoulder, then touched the trigger. The Bontebok dropped dead on the spot.

That is when a loud round of applause erupted. I looked to my left. There on the ridge were five smiling Boer farmers, all clapping their hands. They'd caused the Bontebok to rise to his feet; they'd caused him to be at the point of racing away. They could have screwed up my hunt.

Have you ever stood close to a very large Boer farmer? It's intimidating. I can now fully understand how a new young All Black back feels when first he is close to such a behemoth. But, they were great guys. Like the farmer away north, inland from

Durban, where I shot my Bushbuck, these guys were deeply interested in the All Black's chances of winning the Rugby World Cup. Also, like their fellow northern countrymen they didn't care who won the Cup, just so long as it wasn't the Poms.

NOTES:

The average adult male Bontebok is about the same weight 160-180lb (73-82kg) as a mature Sika stag but is taller at the shoulder, the Sika being at about 36 inches (.92m) while the Bontebok is around 40 inches (1.03m)

Bontebok are one of the more colourful of the African species, so much so I was very tempted to have my trophy life-size mounted. If you get a chance to take a trophy do carefully consider a full body mount.

The name Bontebok was given this species by the early Dutch settlers in South Africa in reference to its many-coloured coat.

With a horn length of 14⅜ inches my trophy was Silver Medal, missing out on Gold by just 1⅛ points.

Seeking Houdini

I knew as the rifle discharged that, due to my flimsy rest, my shot was off to the left.

The usual pre-dawn start saw us up and away from Nxakwe Bush Camp – (more like a five star hotel) – long before daylight for Juan, our game ranger, wanted us to be 'on top of the Red Lechwe' with the breaking of the dawn. Juan was confident that after keeping an eye out for the Lechwe, ahead of our arrival at Nxakwe, we'd have no trouble securing the trophy.

But, we'd been driving towards the hunting area only about fifteen minutes when we ran into super thick pea-soup fog! At best visibility was a short fifty metres. All morning we persevered, stopping constantly to search the fog on either side of the road. Nothing.

Late morning the fog lifted a little, so Juan suggested we take a walk. That's how we almost walked onto the Red Lechwe bedded down on an open area. I am guessing that we had him in sight for two or three seconds before he disappeared into the thick fog. I didn't have time to load my rifle; it happened too fast for Darren to mutter his usual "quickly, quickly".

Back to Nxakwe for lunch, a siesta, out on the road again by mid-afternoon. Day Twenty of my twenty-one day safari. The fog had lifted; we had a perfectly calm sunny afternoon, although the air was cold. I learned a lot about Red Lechwe, one in particular, that afternoon. For more than an hour we had cruised backcountry gravel roads constantly searching the farmlands on either side. I am guessing it would have been after 4pm when there was the Lechwe, feeding in the middle of a large grassed area, not a tree or thorn bush in sight.

We drove slowly past until we were out of sight, then Darren turned the vehicle to return so Juan could have a last look before I took a shot. The Lechwe had taken scant notice of us driving by; no doubt having seen many farm vehicles drive past him every day of his life. We rolled to a stop, Juan verified that indeed this was to be my trophy, the Lechwe lifted his head, one quick glance in our direction and away he went, to disappear over a shallow rise on the far side of the large paddock. Clearly that Lechwe didn't mind a vehicle rolling on down the road, but a vehicle stopping immediately activated his "Alarm Button."

Both Juan and Darren were confident that after giving the Lechwe a few minutes to settle down we'd make a quiet approach, crest the low ridge the animal had disappeared over, and…

We very slowly and quietly eased up to the crest, one slow step at a time, to finally have a view of a vast flat featureless plain that stretched forever to a distant horizon. We all searched for many a long minute but not a single Red Lechwe did we see. The plain appeared flat, without any form of gullies or copse of trees or brush and yet that Lechwe had escaped and disappeared as effectively as Houdini would have done.

It was a less confident Juan that returned to Nxakwe with us at dusk that night for he, like me, had discovered that afternoon that Lechwe didn't like vehicles that stopped on the road.

This landscape is where we hunted 'Houdini' the (often) disappearing Red Lechwe.

We had about four hours sleep that night for we'd travelled to successfully hunt my Grysbok, a total of five to six hours travel, getting to bed about 2am. Yet Darren had me out of bed long before daylight for we were at Day Twenty-one of my twenty-one day hunt.

A change of tactics. We'd cruise the roads until the Red Lechwe was sighted. We'd not stop, but roll on by, drop me and Darren off while still moving, we'd make a stalk until in range. And that's what we did. Yes, we sighted the Lechwe, as usual, away out in the middle of a large pasture. Juan slowed the vehicle; we dropped out on the off side and rolled into the roadside ditch. No water. Juan drove slowly on down the road.

The only hitch to our plan was the fact that other than the ditch we had no cover, whatsoever, that we could use to our advantage to get closer. The Lechwe was well over 400m away and I wasn't going to stretch my barrel to maybe wound and lose a trophy, for we'd quickly learned that this fellow had Houdini genes and wounded he'd be even more skilled at disappearing and hiding.

He must have seen us lifting our heads to ascertain our chances of making some sort of stalk to close the range, for even before we'd moved from the ditch he was up and running. As we'd done the day before we eased on foot across that pasture to the crest of the ridge the buck had disappeared over. Yes, you've guessed it; Houdini had once again disappeared from the landscape.

Juan and Darren were determined they'd not be outsmarted by this lone Red Lechwe, so for the next couple of hours we searched the pastures where the Lechwe may have run to and hide. Noon came and went. One o'clock. By about 2pm we were all in need of food, for along with lack of sleep we'd had a very early quick light breakfast. Bacon and eggs were awaiting our return to camp. Darren and Juan agreed, we'd head for camp and a very late breakfast.

We were on the main highway, gathering speed on a long up-hill gradient, when some instinct prompted Juan to look back into a long shallow valley on our left, a valley we'd not had an opportunity to overlook during the morning. Juan asked Darren to slowly pull off to our left. Binoculars. Yes, in the very centre of a forty to fifty hectare open flat, surrounded by trees and the usual thorn thickets, was "my" Red Lechwe. What truly amazed me is the fact that the Lechwe would have been well over three kilometres away, yet Juan had picked him up with the naked eye.

We turned, drove back, out of sight of the Lechwe, to a point we judged to be more or less opposite his location. Juan and Thorge stayed in the vehicle, Darren and I began our stalk, likely to be somewhere in the region of one to one and a half kilometres, most of it out of sight of our quarry. To start with it was easy for we were fully out of sight of the Lechwe. We had to climb over, or crawl under farm fences, so each time we did so we made sure we made as little noise as possible for the day was deathly still.

We were going nicely until we suddenly discovered ourselves confronted by a railway line cutting across our line of approach. More fences to climb over or wriggle under, use the line embankment to crawl and crawl and crawl, always reducing the range. Crawling until we were close to a thicket comprising tall trees and underbrush. Flat as lizards drinking we slithered across the railway lines to at last feel reasonably safe within the copse of trees. Moving ever so carefully now we discovered that while standing we could see the Red Lechwe, still bedded down in the middle of the pasture, but when we sat he was out of sight.

That was when we also realised that we had no more cover. I'd have to take a shot from here or not at all, take a standing shot. Darren was guessing the range at three hundred-plus metres. My PH had done a masterful job in getting us this close to the Lechwe that was still totally unaware of our presence. It was now my task to make sure his effort as my PH was duly rewarded.

Moving very slowly I rose to my feet, seeking a spindly sapling as a rifle rest, knowing that shooting at this distance, at a sitting target, was always a gamble. But, Lady Luck smiled on me right then for a pair of Steenbok started racing around the pasture, running too close to the Lechwe. He stood up, broadside.

I knew as the rifle discharged that, due to my flimsy rest, my shot was off to the left. Quickly I reloaded and changed rests to a more robust sapling. As so often happened on open ground surrounded by trees, the echoes of my shot prevented the Lechwe from determining our location. He stood, uncertain. My second shot ended my Coenraad Vermaak South African safari; on the afternoon of Day Twenty-one of a twenty-one day hunt. Darren and I'd enjoyed a challenging hunt for that final species. I've always felt that the more challenging the hunt the greater the value of the trophy. I certainly value my Red Lechwe.

Finally a Red Lechwe trophy, after numerous stalks where the buck would simply disappear, time and again, on an apparently featureless landscape.

NOTES:

An adult male Red Lechwe is about the same height at the shoulder as an adult male Rusa stag, 39–44 inches (.99–1.12m), but the Red Lechwe will be as much as 55lb (23kg) heavier in body weight. As the name suggests the Red Lechwe is a lovely bright chestnut in colour with white underbelly that extends all the way up the neck to the throat.

My buck has a horn length of 24¾ inches a SCI Bronze Medal trophy.

Our Five Star accommodation at Nxakwe Bush Camp in Cape Province. With the familiar thatched roof and mud plastered exterior wall trowelled with intricate pattern, and an exquisitely appointed interior this was a luxury hunting 'camp'.

FOOTNOTE;
Next morning Darren and Thorge delivered Sue and I to the East London Airport in time for us to catch our flight to Johannesburg. Our flight to Victoria Falls departed J'burg at 2.30pm.
A long time friend and safari booking agent, Beverley Wunderlich – J/B Safaris – had strongly recommended we have a few days R&R at Gorge Lodge, close to the Victoria Falls, and we were so grateful for her strong recommendation. Both of us were suffering from insufficient sleep; so a few lazy days at that oasis of green in an otherwise parched desert was just what we needed. Also, Sue had "endured" twenty-one days of hunting safari; it was time for her to have some non-hunting time.
The lodge is located on the very edge of a canyon some 400m above the Zambezi

River below the Victoria Falls. Our host informed us that immediately below the lodge the river was 55m wide and 200m deep. Lots and lots of water! The lodge drew all its water requirements from the river, lifting 800 gallons an hour vertically via two big pumps.
Obviously we visited the Victoria Falls, enthralled to stand where Dr Livingstone and Mr Stanley had stood those many years before. The air temperature was 36°C but by standing in the mist from the falls, whenever the opportunity offered, we endured.

SECTION SEVEN

– Zimbabwe

Zimbabwe

ZIMBABWE

It was just like those "pop-up" target shooting ranges, suddenly, without warning, a target is presented.

As our aircraft began its descent into Zimbabwe's Bulawayo airport both Sue and I were experiencing degrees of apprehension for we'd read much about the unrest in Zimbabwe and Mr Mugabe. We had concerns that we could innocently become embroiled in local issues and unrest, suffer injuries or worst? But, if I wanted a Sable my second priority trophy after a Kudu, I would have to hunt Zimbabwe.

Our worries were groundless for Wayne Williamson, our professional hunters for the Zimbabwe leg of our African safari, met us as we stepped from the aircraft to then personally marshal us smoothly through all entry requirement protocols, staying close at our side throughout. Immediately our gear was aboard his safari car, his two trackers seated on the back, we set off for our hunt destination. Wayne explained that we had a three hour road trip ahead, that we'd be travelling generally south-east; our destination only 90km from the northern border of South Africa. We'd not be far from the famous Limpopo River.

Within an hour or so of departing the Bulawayo airport I realised the terrain in Zimbabwe was very different to areas we'd hunted in South Africa. The trees were much taller and spaced out, creating a more or less parkland landscape, not unlike the landscapes around castles in Britain. The most notable and dramatic difference was the giant volcanic rock upthrusts that regularly appeared in the landscapes. I can only guess these were volcanic cores thrust from deep in the earth. We soon learned that sighting these monoliths would be a daily event. From time to time, we'd sight a giant baobab tree.

Ripple Creek Lodge was the grandest, by far, of the lodges we'd stayed in during our African safari. Whoever had built that complex had spared nothing. Our large bungalow was rectangular with the traditional thatched roof. The facilities were of finest quality. Surrounding the lodge complex were extensive lawns and gardens groomed to perfection, easy winners of "Garden of the Year" anywhere in the world.

Close by our accommodation was an in-ground swimming pool. The whole complex overlooking a very large lake, which we later learned from Wayne was man-made.

Susan was very happy to be "roughing it" in such surroundings.

On Day One we made the usual pre-dawn start. The tactic was to drive to a waterhole, check for spoor of Sable, if fresh spoor was found the trackers would set about following the tracks in the hope of sighting Sable. With the trees being scattered, well apart, it was easy to see far ahead. There was little of the dense thorn brush we'd experienced virtually every day while hunting in South Africa.

At the very first waterhole we checked the trackers discovered fresh Sable spoor, a group including a male. After a brief quiet whispered conversation with Wayne Cornelius, Wayne's number one tracker, set off to follow the tracks. The ground was largely

Close to the lodge in Zimbabwe was a huge man-made lake. Wayne, our PH, dug some worms from the lodge garden and off we went fishing. We caught enough catfish and bream for dinner that evening.

soft sand so not difficult for the tracker to follow. We followed those tracks for fully three hours, not once sighting the group that had made them. The tracks were lost when Cornelius couldn't pick them up again after a large herd of wildebeest had obliterated the Sable tracks. Back to the lodge for a swim, lunch, followed by a siesta.

Same "modus operandi" for the afternoon. Once again we visited a waterhole where tracks of Sable were located, the tracks were followed and lost. Sue and I were finding Zimbabwe to be terribly hot, in fact we both suffered from the heat at 36⁰C and high humidity. At dusk we gratefully soaked away the heat in the swimming pool.

At dinner that evening – in a sumptuous dining room with grand furnishings – Wayne expressed his concern, we were not seeing the numbers of Sable he was used to sighting during a hunt. He gave no explanation, but suggested that the following morning we'd drive and cruise the many roads on the 870,000 acre hunting area in the hope of sighting more Sable. He also explained that Sable is seldom found far from water, so our search would concentrate on locations close to waterholes.

It was a rather dejected hunting party that returned to the lodge about noon that day. We'd seen just five Sable, fleetingly, as they raced across our path. No adult trophy male in the group. We'd also sighted numerous Zebra, Giraffe, (making Sue happy), Waterbuck, Steenbok, and Impala. A swim in the pool, luncheon, the obligatory siesta – all to re-charge batteries, (and

This giant baobab tree in Zimbabwe could be a thousand years old. Below it the author and his wife were shown an ancient native campsite containing everyday simple tools and artefacts.

hope) ready for the late afternoon sortie.

Another change in tactics for the afternoon. Wayne was starting to show his concern for the lack of sightings of Sable, so decided that we'd drive towards the waterhole where spoor had been located the previous morning, then very quietly make our way, on foot, closer to the waterhole, in the hope of an interception.

We were mooching along a meandering four-wheel-drive track when without any warning there on the track ahead of us were a half dozen or more Sable, the male closest to us at about 60 metres. It was just like those "pop-up" target shooting ranges, suddenly, without warning a target is presented. I didn't have Darren beside me for his usual 'quickly' quickly', but could see instantly that the trophy Sable had to take just two steps and he'd be in the thick brush bordering the track.

I remember hastily swinging the sights onto the shoulder, then back onto the ribs, as I triggered a shot. As I recovered from recoil, jacking up another round, I saw that there wasn't a single Sable to be seen. It was one of those sort of ethereal experiences of - "now you see them, now you don't".

Wayne was shouting – "a solid hit, a solid hit" – as he dived into the brush bordering the road. I followed suit. I was lucky we were not in Kudu country at Madikwe for within a second or two we sighted the Sable standing, head down, broadside, let's say 80 metres away. Hastily I sent another couple of 150gr Hornady in the direction of the Sable. At the sound of the shots the Sable began cutting across our front to our left, and that is when Wayne fired his .375, just the once.

In retrospect I probably should have carried my .375 in to

Zimbabwe, instead of leaving it in secure storage at the J'burg airport, for I hadn't realised just how large a fully-grown male Sable was.

After the dejection at lunch our dinner that evening was a jubilant affair. Over dinner Wayne explained that never had he seen so few Sable; he was much puzzled by the lack of?

All the next day we were tourists. Wayne drove us far and wide over the vast hunting area with our continually sighting a wide variety of game. During our safari I had been fortunate to

This was our private accommodation at Ripple Creek Lodge in Zimbabwe. Teams of gardeners kept the grounds in immaculate condition, watering lawns daily.

sight all of the Big Five, whereas Sue had seen Lion, Buffalo and Elephant, but not Rhino or Leopard. So, much of our time that day was spent slowly cruising in the hope of Sue also seeing the famous Big Five. We saw neither Rhino nor Leopard.

After a late afternoon tea Wayne dug some worms from the lodge gardens and equipped with a couple of light spinning rods we went fishing in the lake. Yes, we caught sufficient catfish and bream for our dinner that evening. The pressure was off, I had my last trophy, time for Sue and I to relax and enjoy our last day or two of being on safari in Africa, for we both knew it was unlikely we'd ever return. So, our last day at Ripple Creek was spent being lazy tourists, in and out of the swimming pool whenever we got too hot, packing our gear for the last time, for the long journey home.

So many people who travel in Africa seek to return for they all describe it as a "Magic Place". At the close of our safari we also experienced "African Magic." On our last evening we photographed a dramatic "travel poster" sunset, and on our drive from Ribble Creek Lodge to Bulawayo Sue finally saw leopard and Rhino. The Leopard, a young female, according to Wayne, dashed across the road just forty to fifty metres ahead of the vehicles, and within a few minutes there on a small rise not too distant from the vehicle, stood an old Rhino bull. A wonderful and satisfying finale for Sue. The jacaranda was flowering prolifically.

The author had Sable at #2 on his Trophy Wish List for Africa. Zimbabwe was the recommended destination. Wife Sue was with Gary when the final trophy of their African safari was secured. With 39 inch horns this trophy was SCI Bronze Medal class.

NOTES:

As mentioned earlier in the text I was surprised by the size of my Sable trophy. A full grown adult male will stand about 54 inches (1.38m) at the shoulder and weigh as much as 525lb (240kg). A Sambar stag will weigh anywhere between 500 and 600lb (226-272kg) and stand up to 60 inches (1.54m), so a Sable is about the size of a medium sized Sambar, not a small animal.

The Sable (meaning – black) is a beautifully marked antelope and someone with the funds should consider a full life-size mount. I lacked such funds, but my pedestal mounted Sable draws comment from all who visit my trophy room. Such a mount is an excellent second choice for we who are always working within a budget.

The horns on my Sable measured 39 inches.

Sunset on our very last evening in Africa.

SECTION EIGHT

– 'Bucket List'

Whitetail

M. BAILEY

The Missing Tick On My 'Bucket List'

We were hunting Whitetail. He was crunching through the cactus, smoking, and the wind was cold on the back of my neck. I asked him if he was having me on…?

The biggest Whitetail buck I've ever seen in my life was the very first I sighted. That was away back in 1965. Yes, over forty-five years ago. We were guiding a couple from California, hunting Red stag on Arcadia Station at the head of Lake Wakatipu. After three or four days of the long daily climbs up through the beech forest to the open tussock tops our clients were tired, so we had a day of R&R. But, about mid-afternoon we were all suffering from "cabin fever" (and sandflies) so Bob Hart took the wife for a walk upriver, along the bush edge, I set off for Mt Alfred with the husband.

Nightly we'd heard a goodly number of Red stags roaring from the slopes of Mt Alfred, so figured to go and have a look, for it was close to camp and much less of a climb. The pair of us was ambling along a well-defined farm track when upon cresting a small rise there, not sixty metres ahead, standing broadside on the track, was this outstanding trophy buck. He just stood there sizing us up!

Today, these so many years later, the picture of that wonderful trophy buck is imprinted forever in my mind. Let's say his outside spread was better than 24 inches (60cm), that he carried four or five points aside, each point being closer to ten inches (26cm) than eight inches (20cm). Instantly I knew we were seeing an exceptional buck.

My client had shot no end of good Whitetail in the United States, so we stood discussing the merits and high trophy quality of the antlers; all the time the buck just standing motionless and watching us. Why didn't I have a shot?

We'd been granted permission to hunt only Red stag on Arcadia, Mrs Veitch Senior had looked us squarely in the eye and promised us all manner of purgatory if we so much as scratched one of her Whitetail deer. Yes, she was extremely protective of her "babies" and we accepted that. Whitetail we would not, could not touch. Anyway my client didn't need another Whitetail trophy; he was seeking trophy Red stag. We'd taken only two or three steps towards that wonderful buck when with a couple of bounds he disappeared into the almost head-high pig fern bordering the track, to disappear.

In 1970 we formed a company and took over the pastoral lease of Lilybank Station at the head of Lake Tekapo and for the next decade and a half were busy establishing our guided safari hunting operation and fighting bureaucracy. (Read my third book *Bulls Bucks & Bureaucrats*.) Time off for private recreational hunting trips didn't exist.) It was when our son was fourteen that Sue (my wife) suggested that perhaps a father-and-son hunting trip should be fitted into our busy schedule.

We managed to book the Mason's Bay Block on Stewart Island, and with Niall Coster and Ray Fletcher as members of our party of four we flew direct from Invercargill in a Squirrel.

Stephen had lived his formative years in a hunting lodge; an environment of trophy hunting where nothing was shot until assessed for real trophy quality. So in advance of his excitement-charged prospect of his very first hunt away from home, he determined that he'd shot only the one Whitetail buck; a trophy.

By about the third day of our seven-day hunt Stephen had lowered his sights and announced that the first buck he saw was "going down." As each day passed and we saw few deer and nothing with antlers his standards dropped further and further, to the point where my teenage son was noticeably depressed with Whitetail hunting.

We'd not had the best of weather; wind and rain squalls were with us daily. After lunch on the fifth day we were experiencing strong winds and nasty wetting wind-driven squalls, but, I decided I needed to perk up my son, morale in camp. Wearing all my warm clothes under my Swanndri I set out to find a buck for Stephen. That's how I finally located a large scrape and near it lots of rubbings on trees. Back to camp – an announcement (from father) that this evening Stephen would be shooting his first Whitetail buck, a cuppa, then off and away.

The pair of us was seated, side-by-side, about thirty metres from the scrape, well hidden by thickish scrub. The wind was still lashing the trees above our heads; we could clearly hear the pounding surf, driven by the wind. We didn't hear the buck arrive.

Suddenly, off to our right, across on the far side of the scrape, there was the buck standing. His attention wasn't on us, but something behind us. We dared not turn to look. We did, however, have a whispered conversation and the buck seemingly took no notice of our voices (or he couldn't hear us due to the wind lashing the treetops above our heads.)

Our whispered conversation revolved around who would shoot the buck. Stephen wanted me to have the shot, but he was to my right, so impossible for me to get in position for I'd be forced to make too much movement. I finally told Stephen that it didn't matter who shot the buck, just so long as one of us nailed him. Stephen had a much better chance, for all he had to do was rotate his body through ninety degrees and he'd have a clear line on the buck. Slowly he started to rotate his rear-end, no re-action from the buck. Next Stephen lifted his feet to bring his body around. And that is when he inadvertently snapped a twig… The buck magically disappeared in the blink of an eye…

On that trip we drew a blank on Whitetail buck, but my son and I had shared a wonderful hunting moment.

The years ticked by, we finally sold our company – NZ Trophy Guide Service Ltd – and departed Lilybank, where we'd lived for twenty-two years. But within a month Sue and I had bought a five hundred acre sheep and cattle block north of Fairlie. Developing that block as a deer farm occupied us for the next eight and a half years. Sue shared a few overseas hunting trips with me, but not for Whitetail.

When we sold that deer farm we had time to spare and share, so that's when I really got serious about hunting Whitetail in North America. By now I had no end of reliable "contacts" in the States, so after sifting a mass of information from so many sources we booked to hunt with an outfitter out of Edmonton, Canada.

We humans often experience vibes – sometimes good,

sometimes bad. Sue and I were in the lodge of our Whitetail outfitter, somewhere in a semi-wilderness area nor'west of Edmonton. It was after supper on our first night in camp that our outfitter sat his eight clients down in the lounge to brief us about the week ahead. Each client would have a guide, hunting one-on-one. Each guide would have his own vehicle, we would be departing the lodge an hour before daylight and would hunt until 7pm, the time set by the Game Department for all hunting to stop (to no doubt stop spotlighting). Non-hunters were welcome to accompany their hunting husbands. All good so far.

His next remark was what started unpleasant negative vibes coursing up and down my spine. He looked us all in the eye and announced that few of us would shoot a buck! Due to the fact that winter snows had not yet blanketed the landscape it was going to be very difficult to find trophies!

Sometimes it's very challenging for an experienced professional guide being a client with another outfitter or guide, so although I was very inclined to ask what alternative did he have when there was no snow I said nothing, for as yet we'd not been hunting. My negative vibes really started to vibrate that evening, for next I was introduced to my guide, a lad who was taking the week off high school, a lad who'd never before guided anyone on a hunt!

Here were Sue and I, after travelling halfway across the world, about to be guided by a lad with zero guiding experience, at only sixteen years of age and likely a somewhat limited knowledge of Whitetail. Add to this the "no snow" comment by the outfitter and you know I didn't sleep well that night. The heating in the lodge was excessive.

Negativity compounded the following morning for we set off from the lodge without anyone asking me if I needed to check the sighting of my rifle! I had travelled with the rifle dismantled, to make for easier travel, but after re-assembly only an ignorant idiot would set off on a hunting trip on the other side of the world without first making sure the rifle was on the button. We stopped on the side of the road at a sort of drive-off, a sheet of ply was found, a mark made in the centre. At one hundred paces the rifle appeared to be as I'd sighted it before departing New Zealand.

We hunted for a week with that lad. He was a fine boy, doing his very best for Sue and I, but as the week progressed and we daily failed to see any bucks carrying antlers worth a second glance he started to get stressed, desperate for success. His desperation manifested itself in his wishing to drive back-road after back-road, never seeking to depart the vehicle and stalk a likely location. Yes, and added to this situation was the fact (unbeknown to Sue and I in advance) there were certain farms in the area where the outfitter had permission to hunt his clients, but, also, farms where he was denied access. Our lad-guide was constantly referring to a topo map to ensure where he shouldn't look for a buck for me.

By about the fifth day of the seven-day hunt I told Sue I had a strong negative feeling that I'd not be killing trophy Whitetail buck on the trip. I suggested that she might as well come with me each day, rather than sit it out each day back at the lodge. At

A landscape photo of country typical of where the author hunted White-tail deer (unsuccessfully) in Alberta, Canada. The area was largely grain farms, few fences.

From time to time, while hunting, we would encounter abandoned farms and homesteads. We saw many deer but never a mature trophy buck!

in the negative fifteen to twenty Celsius.

Upon not being able to locate the vehicle Sue had stayed on the farm track and walked back and forth, (to keep warm), knowing that we'd finally return to the vehicle and no doubt locate her on the roadway. Imagine how Sue was feeling, deeply afraid that that night she was going to freeze to death somewhere out on the Canadian prairie.

Luck was with her. A man and wife driving into the general area for an evening hunt encountered Sue on the track. They had a conversation, the couple guaranteeing Sue that in the event of Gary and his guide not finding her they would collect her on their return from hunting and take her home for the night. Upon discovering Sue not at the guide's vehicle Gary and the guide made contact with the hunting couple to discover Sue was walking the track accessing the area. Shortly thereafter there she was in the headlights. There's a twist to the end of this saga. The couple had lived in Gisborne for some years and consoled Sue with the information that if we failed to find her they'd take her home where they had some Watties Baked Beans and a few bottles of DB Lager.

How many Whitetail bucks did clients shoot that week? One. Yes, one buck for eight clients. That one buck was seen by a local farmer hiding in a small copse of trees on his farm. He'd telephoned the outfitter who called the nearest guide.

In summary I feel I am correct in making the statement that most of the eight clients in camp that week were not serious trophy hunters. I had the feeling they were just out for a boy's week away from home. One of them had driven all the way to Edmonton from southern Wyoming. He'd fired five or six shots

least she'd be seeing the landscape of unfenced grain farms and plenty of deer (no trophy bucks.) Meanwhile I had successfully suggested to my boy/guide that a wander along the odd farm track could be productive. So it was that late into the afternoon we were walking yet another farm track, seeing deer constantly (we saw over one hundred that week), when Sue declared that she was getting cold that she'd go back to the vehicle. Neither Sue nor I knew that our boy/guide had moved the vehicle off the track, it was hidden in a thicket near the road, but not on it….!!!

When my guide and I returned to the vehicle, where was Sue? By now it was very close to sunset and the temperature was at a trophy Whitetail buck, missing every shot. When, finally, the outfitter asked if he'd sighted his rifle at home before setting out on the trip, the answer was – "Yes, before I went on a horseback Elk hunt three years ago". Subsequently it was found the rifle was shooting about eight inches low and six inches to the right at 50 yards.

Yes, the outfitter knew me personally, knew I'd travelled a long way to seek success with his outfit. He wasn't guiding any other client so why didn't he guide me when day-after-day he saw my boy/guide wasn't producing results. Ask Sue sometime, she'll tell you that outfitter couldn't make eye contact with me after about the third day, and he never once asked about our day.

As an "insurance" against the Whitetail hunt in Canada failing to produce a result, I had booked a second Whitetail hunt in Texas. Sue and I when on holiday, had previously thoroughly enjoyed San Antonio, so after departing Edmonton our destination was San Antonio, Texas and a few days of R&R before the next hunt.

On the first day of my Texas Whitetail hunt we drove and drove and drove. Not once did my "guide" suggest we leave the vehicle and explore some of the country hidden from the many roads criss-crossing the area. I was fortunate that after supper that evening one of the younger guides asked me about my day, did Jess take me for a walk at all? When I told him that I'd not once left the vehicle I was informed that Jess always drove, never walked.

About two hours into my second day I asked Jess why we didn't take a walk from time to time, to have a close look at the country not visible from the roads. His immediate response was that when I was as old as he was I wouldn't be very keen on walking either. Naturally I asked how old he was, for he had a very weather-beaten face and walked with a definite stoop. He informed me his age, he was close to twenty years my junior. He never did ask how old I was.

I have no idea if Jess knew I'd been a successful professional hunting guide for many years. He sought no information from me about myself, he just seemed to be consumed with his own world. By the end of the second day I was tired of motor-vehicle-hunting. After supper I had a word with the lady owner, who knew my profession, and the next morning she told Jess, in front of me, to take me for some walks into as yet unexplored terrain.

Jess was virtually a chain smoker, so lighting yet another cigarette he climbed from the vehicle and set off across the desert. Yes, we were hunting Whitetail, he was crunching through the cactus, smoking, and the wind was cold on the back of my neck. I asked him if he was having me on?

He stopped, turned, and gave me somewhat of a sullen look. I think he didn't know what "having me on" actually meant. We had somewhat of a discussion. It was clear to me that I had first pricked his ego by having a word with his boss, then further when I drew his attention to his apparent absolute lack of stalking skills. I know I was annoyed, rightly so after the lack of success in Canada, and here it looked like the same was shaping up to happen in Texas. I think Jess had never ever guided with the same knowledge and skill that is so commonplace with our New Zealand professionals.

For the next few days he made no real attempt to lift his game and turn things in my favour. Time after time, walking behind him in his second-hand smoke, I would see quite good Whitetail bucks standing watching Jess walk past, he never having seen them. In retrospect I could have shot a couple of rather nice bucks, but as a professional guide I would have gone out of my tree completely had a client discharged his rifle without my prior permission from behind me. It simply isn't done, ever.

Clearly traditional stalking on foot wasn't Jess's thing so back to driving the roads we went at daylight and dusk. Sue was with us when rather late one evening a smallish buck was sighted well back from the road. He was standing in knee high brush and watching us closely. Jess told me to shoot. I loaded and tried to make up my mind as to the range, I couldn't take a prone or sitting shot for the brush was too high for either. My guess was 275 yards and this I whispered to Jess.

"You're wrong, I've just Rangefinder'd it at 283 yards." (As if the buck would know the difference!)

To this day I am absolutely certain that Jess expected me to miss the shot, so he could go back to camp content in the fact that the lost trophy was my fault, not his. He could also exaggerate the size of the trophy.

But, off-hand, I didn't miss. With the buck in the back of the four-wheel-drive Jess suggested that perhaps he'd better put his tag on the buck, it was very small and not a trophy worthy of the establishment where we were hunting. I declined his offer. I had killed the buck, and despite my strong conviction he'd told me to shoot at the buck certain that I'd miss, I'd made a kill and should stand by my actions.

Interestingly I didn't see Jess again after dark that evening.

One of the many hazards of hunting Whitetail in Texas. Another was a guide who chain smoked and hunted with the wind at his back!

The next morning a very personable young man was assigned to me as my guide. We walked all day, but I couldn't take another Whitetail for I used my one and only tag.

So, here I am today, with the final chapter of this book, a chapter detailing lack of success. We all know, full well that not all hunting trips are successful, that making a kill is not the only criteria for measuring the enjoyment of a hunt. But, we all hope that given that we put in plenty of effort, that we seek help from the right people, that we hunt where there is a real prospect of a fine trophy, eventually success will come our way.

My "Bucket List" still lacks two ticks, a Whitetail buck and

Typical Whitetail hunting country in southern Texas.

a nice big fat kingfish. I'm not doing too badly otherwise for I ticked off "A trout over ten pounds" last year with a thirteen pound fourteen ounce rainbow hen.

Maybe in the next year or so I'll find where the big kingfish swim, and a place where a fine Whitetail buck hangs out…

FOOTNOTE:
I may be being excessively bold, in my old age, but I am bound to state that our New Zealand professional hunting guides are some of the finest in the world. This, no doubt, is due to the fact that they all grew up hunting from a very early age. Being able to hunt fifty-two weeks a year quickly builds up yards of experience that layer after layer creates highly skilful and accomplished guides. Without a doubt the level of skill constantly demonstrated by our New Zealand professionals is superior to the North American counterparts, (in my limited experience), Yes I did say "in my experience" to qualify my comment. The finest guide I've personally hunted with was Darren Baker, employed by Coenraad Vermaak. South Africa has a formal, rigorous training programme that a prospective safari guide must pass before he can be employed as a PH. I do look forward to the day when New Zealand authorities find the courage to provide Government Certification of Hunting Guides as is found in South Africa.

The author's guide told him to take a shot at this small buck, expecting him to miss for the range was 280+ yards…………..!!